BEYOND BORDERS

This groundbreaking work unveils a lesser-known facet of Dr. Martin Luther King Jr.'s legacy: his Pan-African vision and relationships. Through meticulous research and compelling narratives, Jeremy I. Levitt unveils King as a truly international figure. Levitt bridges American and African history, politics, and law to provide a fresh perspective on an iconic global figure, exploring King's often ignored relationship with African leaders and his role in supporting anti-colonial and anti-apartheid movements in Africa. The book offers new insights for scholars, students, and anyone interested in the interconnected history of human rights struggles across the African diaspora. By illuminating King's Pan-African engagements, *Beyond Borders* provides a more complete understanding of his enduring legacy as a champion for global racial equality.

Jeremy I. Levitt, J.D., Ph.D. is Distinguished Professor of International Law, Florida A&M University College of Law. He is one of the world's leading scholars on the international law and politics of Africa. Professor Levitt is the author of eight books, including *Black Women and International Law: Deliberate Interactions, Movements and Actions* (Cambridge University Press, 2015) and *Illegal Peace in Africa: An Inquiry into the Legality of Power Sharing with African Warlords, Rebels, and Junta* (Cambridge University Press, 2010), along with a multitude of articles in academic journals and newspapers.

Beyond Borders

MARTIN LUTHER KING JR., AFRICA,
AND PAN-AFRICANISM

JEREMY I. LEVITT

Florida A&M University College of Law

Shaftesbury Road, Cambridge CB2 8EA, United Kingdom

One Liberty Plaza, 20th Floor, New York, NY 10006, USA

477 Williamstown Road, Port Melbourne, VIC 3207, Australia

314–321, 3rd Floor, Plot 3, Splendor Forum, Jasola District Centre, New Delhi – 110025, India

103 Penang Road, #05–06/07, Visioncrest Commercial, Singapore 238467

Cambridge University Press is part of Cambridge University Press & Assessment, a department of the University of Cambridge.

We share the University's mission to contribute to society through the pursuit of education, learning and research at the highest international levels of excellence.

www.cambridge.org
Information on this title: www.cambridge.org/9781108817998

DOI: 10.1017/9781108862080

© Jeremy I. Levitt 2026

This publication is in copyright. Subject to statutory exception and to the provisions of relevant collective licensing agreements, no reproduction of any part may take place without the written permission of Cambridge University Press & Assessment.

When citing this work, please include a reference to the DOI 10.1017/9781108862080

First published 2026

Cover image: Martin Luther King Jr. and Coretta Scott King are greeted by Ralph J. Bunche, United Nations Under-Secretary, at the United Nations, New York, December 4, 1964. (Photo by Authenticated News/Getty Images.)

A catalogue record for this publication is available from the British Library

A Cataloging-in-Publication data record for this book is available from the Library of Congress

ISBN 978-1-108-49536-3 Hardback
ISBN 978-1-108-81799-8 Paperback

Cambridge University Press & Assessment has no responsibility for the persistence or accuracy of URLs for external or third-party internet websites referred to in this publication and does not guarantee that any content on such websites is, or will remain, accurate or appropriate.

For EU product safety concerns, contact us at Calle de José Abascal, 56, 1°, 28003 Madrid, Spain, or email eugpsr@cambridge.org

Contents

List of Figures		*page* vii
Preface		ix
Acknowledgments		xi
	Introduction	1
1	The Making of Martin Luther King Jr.'s African Consciousness, 1929–1954	7
	1.1 Early Influences	8
	1.2 Morehouse College	16
	1.3 Crozer Theological Seminary	18
	1.4 Boston University School of Theology	25
2	From Montgomery to Accra: Toward a Vision of Black Liberation, 1954–1957	28
	2.1 Globalizing Montgomery	29
	2.2 Radicalizing Inseparable Movements	36
3	Africa Embraces King, 1957–1960	50
	3.1 Africa on My Mind	50
	3.2 Organizing Domestically and Globally	56
	3.3 Birth of New Nationhood: The International Liberation of Black Peoples	60
	3.4 The American Committee on Africa	67
	3.5 Return to Africa	70
4	King Embraces Africa, 1961–1968	75
	4.1 The Continent Calls	75
	4.2 King Responds to Africa	87
	4.3 King and Apartheid	99
	4.4 King Honors Du Bois	103

5	**Beloved Pan-Africanism**	108
	5.1 King, Pan-Africanism, and the Black International Tradition	108
	5.2 What Is Pan-Africanism?	114
	5.3 Pan-Africanism, Black Nationalism, and Black Zionism	122
	5.4 Global Blackness and Reciprocity	141
6	**Conclusion: The Relevance and Impact of Martin Luther King Jr. on Black Liberation**	146
	6.1 My Ancestral Homeland	146
	6.2 Life Achievements, Awards, and Legacy	151
	6.3 Our Heritage Is Africa	160
Bibliography		163
Index		175

Figures

1.1	1935: the Afro-American politician and leader for the civil rights movement Martin Luther King Jr. (1929–1968) when he was six years old.	*page* 7
2.1	February 1958: civil rights leader Martin Luther King Jr. being fingerprinted by police after his arrest during the Montgomery bus boycott.	28
3.1	1957: Martin Luther King Jr. and Rev. Ambrose Reeves, Anglican Bishop of Johannesburg and opponent of segregation in South Africa, hold a press conference.	50
4.1	1960: civil rights leader Martin Luther King Jr. sits next to African nationalist leader (and future first President of Zambia, 1964–1991) Kenneth David Kaunda, who gestures as he speaks with two unidentified men, Atlanta, Georgia.	75
4.2	October 10, 1962: Algerian Premier Ahmed Ben Bella shakes hands with Martin Luther King Jr. in New York.	81
5.1	July 16, 1963: Dr. Martin Luther King Jr., civil rights leader, talks with President Julius Nyerere of Tanganyika at a reception given by Nyerere in honor of President Kennedy, in Washington, DC.	108
6.1	April 15, 1967: Martin Luther King Jr. and anti-Vietnam leaders meet in the office of UN Under-Secretary Ralph J. Bunche in New York.	146
6.2	African stamps showing Dr. Martin Luther King Jr.	153

Preface

In the vast tapestry of history, few figures shine as brightly as Martin Luther King Jr. His unwavering commitment to racial justice and freedom in the United States and Africa, his eloquence in the face of oppression, and his vision of a world free from racial prejudice have cemented his place as a beacon of hope and change. Yet beyond the well-trodden paths of his American civil rights journey lies a profound and often overlooked connection: Dr. King's engagement with Africa and his embrace of Pan-Africanism. In this enlightening volume, I embark on an extraordinary exploration of this crucial aspect of Dr. King's legacy, offering a fresh perspective that is both inspiring and transformative.

As a distinguished legal scholar and political scientist with a deep understanding of international law, African politics, human rights, and African diaspora studies, I bring distinct insights to this exploration. *Beyond Borders* not only sheds light on Dr. King's interactions with African leaders and movements but delves into the broader philosophical and political currents of Pan-Africanism that influenced and were influenced by Dr. King. This book is a vibrant narrative that seamlessly weaves the histories of Africa and America, revealing the powerful synergy between their struggles for freedom and dignity.

As you read this book, you will embark on a journey that uncovers the rich and dynamic relationship between Martin Luther King Jr. and Africa. You will discover how Dr. King's visits to Africa, his dialogues with leaders such as Oliver Tambo, Kwame Nkrumah, Nnamdi Azikiwe, Julius Nyerere, Tom Mboya, and Ben Bella, and his support for anti-colonial movements were integral to his broader vision of justice. I have sought to offer detailed research and engaging prose to bring these stories to life, illustrating the profound impact of Pan-Africanism on Dr. King's thought and activism.

Beyond Borders is more than a historical account; it is a call to action and a source of inspiration. It challenges us to see our struggles' interconnectedness and embrace a global perspective in our fight for racial justice. *Beyond Borders* reminds us that national borders did not confine the dream Dr. King championed but was a universal call for human rights and equality. In these pages, you will find the essence of

Dr. King's dream intertwined with the aspirations of a continent. You will encounter the power of Pan-Africanism as a force for unity and resistance against oppression. I have striven to craft a work that honors the legacy of Martin Luther King Jr. while illuminating the path forward in our collective quest for freedom and justice. With great pride, humble admiration, and deep respect, I present this volume as a testament to the enduring power of Dr. King's vision and legacy and their profound resonance across Africa and the world.

Acknowledgments

I dedicate this book to my beloved daughters, Makayla and Zara. I pray they use their divinely inspired intellects, radical consciousnesses, and natural gifts to empower others. I also humbly offer this research in deep gratitude to the remarkable legacy of Dr. Martin Luther King Jr.'s global ministry.

I began exploring Martin Luther King Jr.'s relationship with Africa and her people in 2002 as a law professor and director of the Center on International Law, Policy, and Africa at DePaul University. My exploration culminated in a generous research grant from DePaul's Office of Diversity, which I used to organize one of the nation's first roundtable discussions on King and Africa, titled "The Relevance of Dr. Martin Luther King Jr. to Africa" (February 25, 2004). The esteemed scholar and lawyer Roger Wilkens (nephew of Roy Wilkens) delivered the keynote address, and the panel included noted legal scholar Dean Linda Sheryl Greene, historian Matthew C. Whitaker, and yours truly. The success of the roundtable led to a panel on King at the 2006 Organization of American Historians Annual Meeting, titled "The Consequences Will Be World Shaking: Martin Luther King, Africa, and Global Justice." Chaired by the eminent historian Quintard Taylor Jr., the event included renowned religious studies scholar Lewis V. Baldwin, as well as Greene, Whitaker, and me. After the meeting, Baldwin, Whitaker, and I considered collaborating on a book project exploring King's Pan-African ministry. The idea was collectively shelved, but it thrived in my imagination and consciousness and eventually led to several published articles in addition to this book.

Beyond Borders, like my earlier works on the subject, has benefited enormously from Baldwin's brilliant scholarship. Not only have his transformative studies of Martin Luther King Jr.'s African ministry profoundly influenced this book, but he provided me with vital archival resources without which this book would not have been possible. I am indebted to his legacy of leading-edge research. I am also indebted to Henry J. Richardson III, Dean of Black International Lawyers, who reconceived King's thoughts, actions, advocacy, and theology through the lens of international human rights law and situated them in the Black International Tradition. Richardson's profound intellect and guidance were vital to this book's completion.

Introduction

Martin Luther King Jr.'s significance as a promising Pan-Africanist – that is, as an advocate and supporter of African liberation, self-determination, and independence, as well as the human rights norms, doctrine, and jurisprudence that inform them – has been largely ignored.[1] While attention has been paid to this aspect of his life and career in the seminal works of James H. Cone, Lewis Baldwin, and Henry J. Richardson III, as well as in my recent essays, no book-length manuscript exists on King's thoughts on and relationship to the African continent and its peoples beyond Louis Baldwin's *Toward the Beloved Community: Martin Luther King, Jr. and South Africa* (1995).[2] Moreover, King's ideals, ministry, advocacy, activities, initiatives, and influence on Africa, African leaders, and US foreign policy on Africa are largely unknown, though they form a critical part of the Black International Tradition (BIT), Pan-Africanism, and King's global legacy.

This oversight is quite peculiar and indeed indefensible, as King spoke vigorously, consistently, and comparatively about the harmful effects of colonialism, imperialism, racism, and Apartheid on the peoples and nations of Africa and African

---

[1] Pan-Africanism may be broadly defined as a movement for the internationalization of African liberation and unity aimed at empowering people of African descent all over the world to maximize their human potential by obtaining freedom, equality, and justice from the domestic and global forces of white domination and supremacy. Jeremy I. Levitt, *Pan-Africanism*, ENCYCLOPEDIA OF GLOBALIZATION, VOLUME THREE, N to T, Routledge (2007), 935–936, available at SSRN: https://ssrn.com/abstract=2221627.

[2] See generally, Jeremy I. Levitt, *Beloved Pan-Africanism: Martin Luther King's Stride toward Africa, International Human Rights, and the Black International Tradition*, Z. Yihdego et al. (eds.), ETHIOPIAN YEARBOOK OF INTERNATIONAL LAW 2019, https://doi.org/10.1007/978-3-030-55912-0_8. See also: James Cone, *Martin Luther King Jr., and the Third World*, JOURNAL OF AMERICAN HISTORY, Vol. 74, No. 2 (1987), 455–467; Lewis V. Baldwin, TOWARD THE BELOVED COMMUNITY: MARTIN LUTHER KING JR. AND SOUTH AFRICA (Cleveland, OH: Pilgrim Press, 1995); Henry J. Richardson III, *From Birmingham's Jail to beyond the Riverside Church: Martin Luther King's Global Authority*, 59 HOWARD L.J. 169, 169–172 (2015); Henry J. Richardson III, *Dr. Martin Luther King, Jr. as an International Human Rights Leader*, 52 VILL. L. REV., 471, 472 (2007); Jeremy I. Levitt, *Beyond Borders: Martin Luther King, Jr., Africa and Pan-Africanism*, TEMPLE JOURNAL OF INTERNATIONAL AND COMPARATIVE LAW, Vol. 31, No. 1 (Spring 2017).

Americans. Building on my published articles, which are among the first to foray into the subject matter, *Beyond Borders* is an effort to correct this glaring omission.[3] It offers a multidisciplinary expedition canvassing the various King archives to forthrightly explore the intersections between King's contributions to fighting anti-Black racism in the US and supporting anticolonial and anti-Apartheid struggles in Africa – what I refer to as King's global ministry, or "Beloved Pan-Africanism." Beloved Pan-Africanism is normatively rooted in theological and human rights-based suppositions. Elsewhere, I have argued that King's Beloved Pan-Africanism was naturally conceived alongside his Beloved Community thesis, which reflected his global vision that all people "can share the wealth of the earth" and where "poverty, hunger and homelessness" would not be "tolerated because international standards of human decency" would not allow it.[4] King's Beloved Community, I have asserted, "seems to universalize and cross-fertilize Beloved Pan-Africanism with experiential insights from the Montgomery Bus Boycott and his sojourn to Ghana."[5]

The "Kingsian" notion of Pan-Africanism is derived from vertical and horizontal conflict and normative friction birthed in the vertical conflict of global racial oppression and the horizontal inequalities spawned by it in the United States. The normative friction is generated by the various claims to internal and external law by Black people oppressed by colonial, imperial, and racist regimes in Africa, the Caribbean, and the United States.[6] Indeed, the confluence of these evils anchors Beloved Pan-Africanism, which I define as follows:

> *Beloved Pan-Africanism* is governed by King's opposition to what he concluded were the three evils of racism, poverty, and militarism, which manifest through various forms of systematic oppression, including racial segregation, Apartheid, colonialism, imperialism, and unjust war. King viewed racial and colonial oppression as evil. Hence, his *Beloved Pan-Africanism* rested on five pillars: love [global Blackness], radical nonviolent resistance, empathy, grave personal sacrifice, and divine justice. King's *Beloved Pan-Africanism* was inherently antiracist, anticolonial, and antiwar with all their tragic civil, political, economic, social, and cultural antecedents.[7]

Understanding King's global ministry is essential to understanding him in the context of the American civil rights movement, the international human rights crusade

---

[3] Jeremy I. Levitt, *Beyond Borders: Martin Luther King, Jr., Africa and Pan-Africanism*, supra note 2. See also Jeremy I. Levitt, *Beloved Pan-Africanism: Martin Luther King's Stride toward Africa, International Human Rights, and the Black International Tradition*, supra note 2.

[4] Jeremy I. Levitt, *Beyond Borders: Martin Luther King, Jr., Africa and Pan-Africanism*, supra note 2 at 304. See also, *The King Philosophy*, in Martin Luther King, Jr. Papers from 1950 to 1968, The Center for Nonviolent Social Change, The King Center, Atlanta, GA, available at www.thekingcenter.org/king-philosophy.

[5] *Id.* 305.

[6] The words Black American, Black people, and African American are used interchangeably in this text.

[7] Jeremy I. Levitt, *Beyond Borders: Martin Luther King, Jr., Africa and Pan-Africanism*, supra note 2 at 305.

against European colonization, and white supremacy.[8] *Beyond Borders* will thus illuminate, frame, and solidify what King termed "the widest liberation struggle" of oppressed peoples "in history."[9] Along the way, it will explore his credentials as a Pan-Africanist, a human rights activist, and an iconic symbol of freedom and justice, fortifying his significance as a world leader.

Beyond Borders seeks to locate Martin Luther King Jr.'s relationship with, and contribution to, Africa and African liberation, as well as to assess the extent to which he conjoined the Black American civil rights movement with Africa's decolonization and liberation struggles. I have argued elsewhere that "King's Pan-African advocacy helped reshape and internationalize Black American distinctiveness, oppression, and claims to outside law, namely by refashioning American civil rights law and international human rights law through the prism of Pan-Africanism."[10] The book further examines several related questions: What was the relationship, if any, between Martin Luther King Jr. and African leaders? What impact did King have on African liberation in Africa? What intersections – ideological, political, material, spiritual, or otherwise – did King fashion between the antiracist, antipoverty, and antiwar struggles in the US and Africa? Was King a Pan-Africanist? If so, what circumstances, experiences, and phenomena influenced his Pan-African outlook? To what extent did King invoke the binding authority of domestic and international law to advocate for Black Americans, Blacks in the African Diaspora, Africa, and Africans? How, if at all, might Beloved Pan-Africanism be employed to edify Kingsian scholarship? These questions raise and perhaps build on others that inform the analysis, such as: How valid is the claim that "King's vision included national and international topics even in high school" or in undergraduate collegiate training?[11] At what point in his career as a civil rights leader did King begin to address international and African issues? What significance did this hold for his developing consciousness of, and views on, Africa? What impact did King's family, church ties, and training at Morehouse College, Crozer Theological Seminary, and Boston University (BU) have on his emerging racial consciousness and perspectives on Africa and her people?

The text consists of six chapters. Chapter 1 covers the period between 1929 and 1954. It traces the development of King's Black transnational consciousness from his childhood up to his doctoral studies at BU. It gives special attention to familial and church influences, particularly King's father and his early exposure to Benjamin E. Mays, Mordecai Johnson, the writings of Mohandas K. Gandhi, and

---

[8] *Id.* at 304–305.
[9] Martin Luther King Jr., WHERE DO WE GO FROM HERE: Chaos or Community? (Boston: Beacon Press, 1968), 169–170.
[10] See generally, Jeremy I. Levitt, *Beyond Borders: Martin Luther King, Jr., Africa and Pan-Africanism*, supra note 2 at 303.
[11] Michael G. Long, AGAINST US, BUT FOR US: MARTIN LUTHER KING, JR. AND THE STATE (Macon, GA: Mercer University Press, 2002), 6 n.17.

other experiential and intellectual sources. King grew up in a home and church environment that encouraged concern for racial justice and world affairs, especially African affairs, as will be demonstrated. Chapter 1 of this study is particularly interested in those political, economic, legal, cultural, religious, social, and intellectual influences that shaped and informed King's Beloved Pan-Africanism, or what I have elsewhere referred to as "King's nascent internationalist and Pan-Africanist leanings."[12]

Chapter 2 examines the period between 1954 and 1957. It assesses King's attitude toward Africa and African liberation as it unfolded from the time of the Montgomery Bus Boycott up to his trip to Ghana in 1957. During this period, King fought wars of freedom on two major fronts: the US and Africa. America's lawfare against African American freedom and equality was total and complete, as was the utilization of federal resources such as the Federal Bureau of Investigation (FBI) to disrupt, dismantle, and destroy civil rights organizations and leaders, including King. Chapter 2 addresses King's development as a stalwart racial justice activist, budding Africanist and Pan-African thinker, minister, and advocate, focusing on his insistence on relating the Black freedom crusade in America to the struggles of African peoples abroad as well as his assessment of the bonds and obligations that existed between peoples of African ancestry across the globe. King was convinced that African Americans should form the vanguard in a struggle for universal African liberation and independence, while also claiming that African freedom struggles had a significant impact on Black Americans.

King's interest in and efforts for the international liberation of peoples of African descent from March 1957 until early 1961 are treated in Chapter 3. "The Birth of a New Nation," a sermon that King preached on African independence after returning from Ghana, is referenced heavily, along with various communications concerning Ghana, Nigeria, and South Africa. Invited to attend Ghana's independence celebration by Prime Minister Kwame Nkrumah in that year, King was exposed to African politicians and activists from various parts of the continent. His evolution as an "Africanist" continued during his trip to Nigeria at independence, a journey taken at the behest of Governor-General Nnamdi Azikiwe in 1960. These trips had a significant impact on his developing perspective on Africa and her problems. In 1957, for example, he joined the national committee of the American Committee on Africa (ACOA), a New York-based interracial group devoted to the financial and moral support of defiance campaigns inside South Africa and in other anticolonial movements throughout Africa. He remained on the national committee until his death, serving alongside other notables such as George Houser, Bayard Rustin, and Bill Sutherland of the Congress of Racial Equality. It was during the years of 1957

---

[12] Matthew C. Whitaker, *Africa on My Mind: The Making of Martin Luther King, Jr.'s Transnational Consciousness*, an unpublished paper, delivered at the Annual Meeting of the Organization of American Historians, Washington, DC (April 23, 2006), 1–12. (on file with author).

through 1961 that Africa embraced King and the period in which the Pan-African ingredients in his vision found their greatest clarity and expression – both in his ability to organize domestically and internationally through ACOA and emergence of his Beloved Pan-Africanism.

Chapter 4 explores the period between mid-1961 and King's death in 1968. During these years, Africa called on King to engage her more practically and prophetically, and he embraced her with open arms. His embrace included tripling his efforts to support anticolonial movements, stop intrastate armed conflicts, lobby for US development assistance, and fund scholarships for African students to attend American universities. His leadership in and support of the American Negro Leadership Conference on Africa (ANCLA) provided a strong vehicle for him to sustain and amplify these activities. Chapter 4 analyzes King's embrace of Africa and sets the stage for a discussion of King's Pan-African legacy. The timelessness of King's specific concerns about the Black World and Africa becomes apparent, as does his ideological proximity to W. E. B. Du Bois and the meaningfulness of King for our own time.

Chapter 5 contemplates how King's thinking and global ministry personified and exemplified Pan-African currents into Beloved Pan-Africanism. While George M. Houser contended that King "was not essentially a Pan-Africanist, although his and Du Bois's position had a great deal in common," I suggest that this perspective is not supported by the weight of the evidence.[13] Chapter 5 similarly revisits Lewis Baldwin's observation in *Toward the Beloved Community* (1995) that "King was too much of an integrationist and a believer in a common culture shared by blacks and whites in America to fit neatly into the traditions of Pan-Africanism."[14] Baldwin's thinking was not set in stone; rather, he encouraged me to research and resolve the issue. I contend King was essentially a Pan-Africanist despite any inconsistencies.[15] This contention is based on a careful reading of King's speeches, sermons, interviews, letters, and other sources and leadership activities in Africa. Indeed, my focus on his activities and works on behalf of Africa and African independence will undoubtedly stir debate and discussion in the scholarly literature. Some sense of how King fits into the entire history of Pan-African theory and praxis will be evident from a close reading of this chapter. It explores definitional variations in the meaning of Pan-Africanism and identifies King's unique brand, which may have reflected many Black Americans' views during his time.

---

[13] George M. Houser, *Freedom's Struggle Crosses Oceans and Mountains: Martin Luther King, Jr., and the Liberation Struggles in Africa and America*, in Peter J. Albert & Ronald Hoffman eds., WE SHALL OVERCOME: MARTIN LUTHER KING, JR., AND THE BLACK FREEDOM STRUGGLE, 183 (1993).

[14] Baldwin, TOWARD THE BELOVED COMMUNITY, supra note 2, 189 n.18.

[15] See generally, Jeremy I. Levitt, *Beyond Borders: Martin Luther King, Jr., Africa and Pan-Africanism*, supra note 2. See also Jeremy I. Levitt, *Was Martin Luther King, Jr. a Pan-Africanist?*, an unpublished paper, delivered at the Annual Meeting of the Organization of American Historians, Washington, DC (April 23, 2006), 1–12.

The concluding chapter of *Beyond Borders*, Chapter 6, examines the complexity and grandeur of King's advocacy domestically and internationally, as well as his thinking on Africa. Examining his influence in Africa and beyond, particularly how African leaders and the Black Diaspora honored him, this final chapter intimates a way forward focusing on King's Beloved Pan-Africanism.

Beyond Borders fills a part of the longstanding gap in the academic discourse and literature about King's political and spiritual philosophy and his involvement in human rights and racial justice issues outside the United States. It challenges the tendency, even among King scholars, to limit the civil rights leader to a pioneering American integrationist, by properly locating him in a more universal and revolutionary context. This study is poised to influence the direction of the literature on King, the civil rights movement, and Black American relations with Africa well into the future.

1

The Making of Martin Luther King Jr.'s African Consciousness, 1929–1954

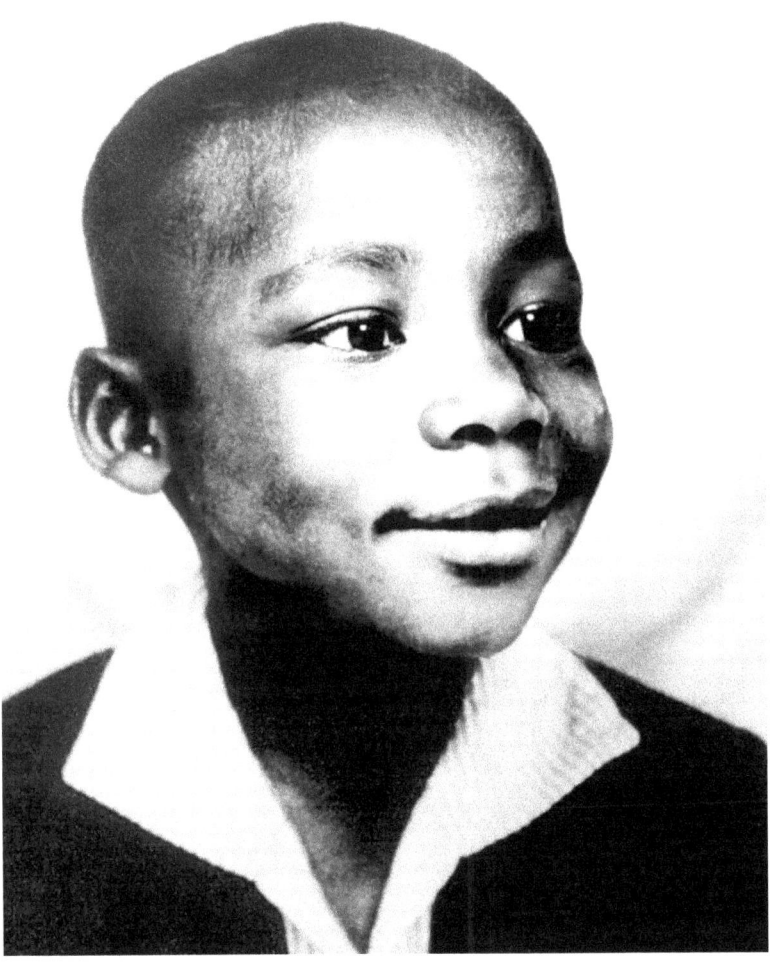

FIGURE 1.1 1935: the Afro-American politician and leader for the civil rights movement Martin Luther King Jr. (1929–1968) when he was six years old.

1.1 EARLY INFLUENCES

King's radical and transnational consciousnesses intersected with and were framed early in his life by three significant influences: his fundamentalist Christian identity; his father, Martin Luther King Sr. (Daddy King); and American racism and poverty. One might argue that King's upbringing was unremarkable for an upper-middle-class, Black, Baptist child in a racially stratified Atlanta, Georgia. Still, his socio-economic class in and of itself may in fact be remarkable when considering the economic conditions of most Black Atlantans in the early twentieth century. In the 1920s and 1930s, most Black people in Georgia and throughout the United States were poor.[1] King was privileged. He grew up in what he referred to as a deeply religious community of "average income" and "ordinary in terms of social status."[2] Perhaps King's definition of ordinary was modest, as he was raised in a largely middle-class, upwardly mobile area called Sweet Auburn. King's father was a "prosperous young pastor" who "never lived in a rented home."[3] Indeed, King enjoyed the privilege and comforts Daddy King provided.[4]

Comprising only about two square miles in size, Sweet Auburn was not just a Black middle-class and upper-middle-class Christian community; it was the gathering place of a generation of men and women who rose above Georgia's legacy of enslavement and Black codes and were devoted to defeating Jim Crowism. In 1956, *Fortune* magazine described Sweet Auburn and Auburn Avenue, specifically, as the "richest Negro Street in the world."[5] It was the political, cultural, social, spiritual, and commercial center of Black life in Atlanta; it was also the home of Ebenezer Baptist Church, where three generations of Kings served as pastors. Sweet Auburn was a national beacon of light for African American business, entrepreneurship, and civic engagement. Auburn Avenue hosted offices for the National Association for the Advancement of Colored People (NAACP), the Odd Fellows, the Prince Hall Masons, the National Urban League, Big Bethel African Methodist Episcopal Church, the *Atlanta Daily World* (one of the nation's oldest Black-owned newspapers), and a host of restaurants and clubs. Racial segregation forced Sweet Auburn to birth its own values-based culture. It was an amalgam of diverse types of Black folk – inclusive of experienced business owners, radical preachers, civil rights activists, and artisans – along with the struggles they endured atop a harsh brand of Jim Crowism.

---

[1] Martin Luther King Jr., THE AUTOBIOGRAPHY OF MARTIN LUTHER KING JR. (Clayborne Carson (ed.), Boston: Beacon Press, 1998), 1–2.
[2] *Id.* at 2.
[3] Reverand Martin Luther King Sr., DADDY KING: AN AUTOBIOGRAPHY (Boston: Beacon Press, 2017), 89.
[4] Martin Luther King Jr., *Autobiography*, supra note 1 at 5.
[5] Emmet John Hughes, *The Negro's New Economic Life*, FORTUNE 54 (September 1956), 248.

1.1 Early Influences

Sweet Auburn had a sense of its own history and values. King flourished in it. Though surrounded by the brutalities of Jim Crow America, the community provided King with a racial safety net – physically and intellectually – like most segregated communities. Professor Samuel Livingston argues that, in this context, "it is not possible to overstate the influential role of location, in King's case, Sweet Auburn as a site of cultural memory and identity formation."[6] Livingston notes:

> Sweet Auburn and Black Atlanta throbbed with the ideas and energy of its local activists, including the leading Pan-Africanist and African Methodist Episcopal Bishop, Henry McNeal Turner, the intellectual force that was Du Bois and, interestingly, the world's most successful Pan-Africanist proselytizer, the Honorable Marcus Mosiah Garvey. Rev. A. D. Williams and Bishop Turner both shared a childhood shadowed by the harsh reality of enslavement and its vestiges, which fostered a radical commitment to Africans in America born of resistance.[7]

This was the environment that cultivated King. His early consciousness can be traced to his upbringing in Sweet Auburn.

King's intellectual and cultural environment inside the home was, arguably, even more profound than that outside of it. According to King, his family dressed and ate well, and enjoyed considerable respect in the greater Atlanta community. He was a physically healthy and psychologically strong child, which he credited to his hereditary line (Figure 1.1). King believed that his home life was idyllic; he asserts that his parents did not argue or have significant conflicts.[8] For King, life was comfortable because his parents provided him with love, stability, and security from the cradle into adulthood. He later remarked that his life "had been wrapped up for me in a Christmas package."[9] King noted that it was "quite easy for me to think of a God of love mainly because I grew up in a family where love was central and lovely relationships were ever present."[10] Because of his fortunate "childhood experiences," King was an eternal optimist who viewed the universe and the world as sociable and innocent.[11]

By all accounts, King inherited his "strong determination for justice" from his father and his gentleness, sense of self-worth, and ethics from his mother.[12]

---

[6] Samuel T. Livingston, *An Unbroken Bond: The Role of Africa in Martin Luther King's, Jr's Liberation, Thought and Praxis*, unpublished essay submitted to the Editorial Review Board of THE COMPASS: JOURNAL OF THE ASSOCIATION FOR THE STUDY OF CLASSICAL AFRICAN CIVILIZATIONS (July 21, 2016), 8 (on file with author).

[7] Id.

[8] Martin Luther King Jr., *Autobiography*, supra note 1 at 2.

[9] Id. at 5.

[10] Id. at 2.

[11] Id. at 3.

[12] Martin Luther King Jr., *Autobiography*, supra note 1 at 3–4.

His inclination for racial justice, Black pride, and self-respect was rooted in his psychology. This may explain why, in part, King's conscience was so extraordinary and deeply rooted in what Cedric Robinson referred to as the Black Radical Tradition long before it was an idiom.[13] King's mother, Alberta Williams King (Mother King), was his first teacher, educating him in the art of confidence, dignity, and bravery. She imprinted him early with an authentic historical education about slavery, the Civil War, and racial segregation, with all of its limitless normative inequalities.[14] King's radical consciousness was seeded by his mother's early historical, social, and political teachings, which aimed to protect his innocence from inferior thinking by bolstering his self-esteem, motivation, and pride before Jim Crowism emblazoned itself upon him. Mother King was formidable. Her pioneering father (King's maternal grandfather), Reverend A. D. Williams, had fortified her profound awareness of racial inequities. Williams was a stalwart antiracist, a human rights activist, and perhaps one the most courageous men of his time in the King family sphere. He served as the first President of the NAACP in 1910, which was a perilous position to hold due to the prevalence of the Ku Klux Klan (KKK) and white citizenry violence against Blacks. This dangerous reality was institutionalized by the KKK's marriage with local and state law enforcement as well as municipal governments across the South. Williams's daughter, Mother King, equipped King with the confidence and the will to fight. Meanwhile, Daddy King, who was by far the most influential force in shaping King's activist consciousness, taught him who, where, and how to fight.

Daddy King was one of Atlanta's most prominent preachers, ensuring the King family's economic, social, and political mobility inside and outside Atlanta's segregated places and spaces. As a result of his father's prominence, King was certainly more upwardly mobile than the Black masses he would eventually lead. In fact, King was a fourth-generation preacher; all the men on his father's side were preachers, starting with his great-grandfather and including his brother and uncle. As a Black man raised in the late 1920s and 1930s during the Great Depression and the height of Jim Crowism, it was King's God-centered and ancestral epistemological foundation that laid the brick and mortar for what would evolve into an uncompromising African and transnational consciousness. His father's influence in this respect was paramount.

While King ultimately found his spiritual favor and anointing fighting American brokenness in the form of racism, poverty, and war, little about his early life in the segregated South predicted his development into a prophetic, Black, militant, global leader who would reshape the racial and sociopolitical landscape of the US,

---

[13] See Cedric J. Robinson, BLACK MARXISM: THE MAKING OF THE BLACK RADICAL TRADITION (University of North Carolina Press, 1983), Chapter 6.
[14] Martin Luther King Jr., *Autobiography*, supra note 1 at 3–4.

influence freedom movements in Africa, and continue to inspire civil rights campaigns around the world. Yet the enormous contradictions between God's law and the evils of racial caste in America stirred King's soul at an early age. He first articulated his understanding of this contradiction in relation to the issue of poverty when, at the age of five, in the midst of the Great Depression, he asked his parents about the massive breadlines. He later attributed his "anticapitalistic feelings" to first-hand knowledge of American poverty during the Great Depression, with all its racialized suppositions and disparities.[15]

King's African consciousness was influenced by his development in the Black church tradition – encompassing Judeo-Christian theology interpreted through Black fundamentalist tradition – from birth through adulthood. One can only assume that King's early empathy and compassion toward persons in poverty were inspired by his father's liberation-orientated preaching and the benevolent mission of the Black church. Daddy King's sermons and activities lit a slow-burning fire in King's consciousness. King's early training and introduction to Ebenezer's emphasis on social justice – "to feed the poor, liberate the oppressed, and welcome the stranger"[16] – profoundly impacted his thinking and theological development. The racial justice education he received from Ebenezer influenced his human rights cosmogony and, arguably, rooted his notion of the three evils of racism, poverty, and war.[17] When taken together, these focal nodes created nesting dualities with Ebenezer's core tenets: to liberate the oppressed *from racism*; feed the poor *to end poverty*; and welcome the stranger *to mitigate war*. The symmetry between King's three evils and Ebenezer's social justice principles is thought-provoking; Ebenezer defined its three-pronged social justice mission, and King demarcated the three evils that sought to undermine it.

Daddy King pastored at Ebenezer Baptist Church for forty-four years (1931–1975), seeding King's racial justice and transnationally oriented theology. Daddy King was far more than an Atlantan preacher. By 1934, when King was only five years old, Daddy King had already traveled to Europe (France, Italy, and Germany), Africa (Tunisia, Libya, and Egypt), and the British Mandate for Palestine. On his return, he attended the 1934 World Baptist Conference in Berlin, Germany, and heard the explosive "discourses" of Adolf Hitler on the radio. He witnessed first-hand the militarization of Germany, with the "march of jackboots" and the "unfurling flags with swastikas emblazoned on them."[18] Motivated by the Holy Land and nourished

---

[15] Martin Luther King Jr., *Autobiography*, supra note 1 at 2.
[16] Ebenezer Baptist Church, *Social Transformation*, available at www.ebenezeratl.org/our-vision/.
[17] Martin Luther King Jr., *America's Chief Moral Dilemma*, PACIFICA RADIO ARCHIVES, AMERICAN ARCHIVE OF PUBLIC BROADCASTING, Boston, and Washington, DC (May 17, 1967), available at http://americanarchive.org/catalog/cpb-aacip-28-fn1opox51h_. See also, Martin Luther King, *The Three Evils of Society*, Address Delivered at the National Conference on New Politics (August 31, 1967).
[18] Daddy King, *Autobiography*, supra note 1 at 88.

spiritually by the "new worlds" he visited, Daddy King continued the fight against racial inequality, inequity, and injustice in the United States.[19] With this background, one can only surmise that these transnational experiences, combined with his understanding of racial tyranny in the US, awakened new insights that Daddy King shared with his son, emboldening his knowledge, understanding, and interconnectedness with the world outside the US. In fact, in 1935, less than a year after Daddy King's sojourn in the Global South and Europe with ten other ministers, he claimed to have uncovered the "mysteries of the South's racial arrangement," which he described as a dehumanizing system.[20] One can only wonder what mysteries he shared with King and the impact such understandings had on his son's development.

In the foreword to *Daddy King: An Autobiography of the Reverend Martin Luther King, Sr.*, the Honorable Andrew Young opined that Daddy King "laid a firm foundation from which his son could build the civil rights movement in the Sixties" because the younger King "grew up hearing his father preach against the injustices of a segregated society."[21] King's racial awareness and global consciousness were thus birthed at home and in church. As Young put it, "speaking out against injustice was a way of life in Martin's family."[22] Daddy King was a serious person, an "upright Black man" and "change leader" long before such phrases were commonplace. In his confrontations with institutionalized racism and white power structures, Daddy King harkened back to the nightmarish experiences that his own father, James Albert King, had under the tyranny of Jim Crow. He believed that white people did not view Black people as human beings and thus were shameless in their cruelty and savagery toward them.[23] From Reverend A. D. Williams and Daddy King to Alberta Williams King, Martin Luther King Jr. was thus nurtured into the theology of the Black radical tradition and naturally viewed the plight of Black people, from Atlanta to Addis Ababa, as one people struggling to combat and transform the evils of white domination worldwide.

Daddy King's truth-telling clearly influenced King. Like father, son, and grandson, their legacy reveals a shared racial history of confrontation and resistance. Daddy King's penchant for negotiating with the "top man" in charge would also be adopted by King himself, a get-it-done Servant Leader not interested in wasting time dealing with whites who held no real power or authority. Andrew Young argues that King's bravery was fortified by witnessing Daddy King's "own determination to fight fearlessly for freedom and justice."[24] King witnessed his father fight for racial justice and human equality on the front lines of Jim Crowism in Georgia, firmly believing that there would be "great combat" wherever the Negro lived. Indeed, Daddy King

---

[19] *Id.*
[20] *Id.* at 89.
[21] *Id.* at 1.
[22] *Id.* at 2.
[23] *Id.* at 16.
[24] *Id.* at 3.

thought that the racialized nature of the American Civil War had never really ended and that, by the 1940s, it would be need to be "fought on several fronts: moral, legal, social, and political."[25] He believed that his sons, including King, would "be needed in an ongoing, ever-difficult battle" to free America from its racist past and present.[26] For Daddy King, Blacks had to struggle because there was "no place to surrender to, no place where people could be spiritually alive. If anything were to give, it would have to be on the white side, where there was room to budge or space to change."[27]

In his autobiography, Daddy King recollected a painful memory from when, at the age of six, the father of Jay, one of his white friends, referred to him as "just one of my niggers" after being asked who was playing with his son. Being called a nigger by Jay's father, "reached inside and twisted" young Daddy King up.[28] He felt dehumanized, not unlike his son King felt when, at the impressionable age of six, the father of two white playmates whose family owned the community store in front of King's house ordered their sons not to play with him anymore. Like Daddy King, the younger King had been shocked and saddened. For both father and son, the cruel realities of American racism conveyed through the multi-generational impacts of anti-Black racism outraged them and vandalized a vital part of their innocence. In fact, from that moment forward and for years to come, King "was determined to hate every white person" until redirected by his parents not to "hate the white man."[29] It was a struggle with an age-old question: "How could I love a race of people who hated me and who had been responsible for breaking me up with one of my best childhood friends?"[30] The duality of father and son, wrestling with the same indignities of racism as children of distinct generations, nurtured a shared resentment for America's system of racial segregation and its dangerous impacts on Black life and liberty.

Unfortunately, Daddy King and his son also witnessed other grave injustices. Daddy King witnessed the robbery, beating, and torturous lynching of an innocent Black man for allegedly grinning – a crime perpetrated by jealous white men who worked at a local mill.[31] This tragedy caused Daddy King to vehemently hate whites, not unlike the sentiments expressed by King decades later after witnessing the "Klan actually beat a Negro" and seeing "spots where Negroes had been savagely lynched."[32] King recounted another grim, soul-breaking act of discrimination that he described as one of his angriest moments: At the age of eight, a white woman slapped him in the face and called him a nigger for allegedly stepping on her foot.[33]

---

[25] *Id.* at 112.
[26] *Id.* at 112.
[27] *Id.* at 112.
[28] *Id.* at 7.
[29] Martin Luther King Jr., *Autobiography*, supra note 1 at 7.
[30] *Id.*
[31] Daddy King, *Autobiography*, supra note 3 at 21–22.
[32] Martin Luther King Jr., *Autobiography*, supra note 1 at 10.
[33] *Id.* at 9.

White-on-black violence sorely molded father and son when they were children and shaped their perceptions of America, whites, racism, violence, and justice more generally.

The multi-generational impacts of discrimination would inevitably ensnare father and son together when a white clerk tried to force Daddy and a young King to move from sitting in the front of a shoe store to the rear to receive service. The ensuing struggle profoundly affected King and underscored his disdain for racial segregation. He claimed that his conscience was framed during this encounter, as Daddy King refused to sit in the rear and walked out of the store rather than buy Jim Crow shoes.[34] It was a nonviolent, financial protest of sorts from a man who would not submit to institutionalized racism. One can only infer that at the ages of six and eight, King's resentment of white supremacy and racial injustice hardened because of these experiences.

Daddy King's courage did not end with contesting racial segregation in public spaces; he also contested racism by law enforcement. King recounts when his father was pulled over in his vehicle and was pejoratively referred to as "Boy" by a police officer. In response, Daddy King boldly admonished the officer with a stern gaze. He told him that he was "not a boy" before driving away, instilling in King the will and courage to fight structural and interpersonal racism as a social evil.[35] Needless to say, Daddy King's actions were taboo and risky in the American South in the 1920s, constituting dangers that King would also challenge head-on in the future.

These childhood experiences prepared King to endure racial segregation with great resilience. From Atlanta's segregated public parks and YMCAs to its segregated restaurants and theaters, King's contempt for Jim Crowism was growing, and his willingness to confront it was ripening. For example, when King was fourteen, he traveled from Atlanta to Dublin, Georgia, to compete in an oratory or debate competition, which he won. His speech, "The Negro and the Constitution," was a sophisticated indictment of Jim Crow and American democracy – realities that he vividly experienced during his bus ride home to Atlanta.[36] King and his teacher, Mrs. Sarah Grace Bradley, were ordered to move to the back of the bus and stand to accommodate white passengers.[37] After being cursed at by the bus driver, King was resolved not to move until his teacher persuaded him to do so in obedience to segregationist law.[38] They stood in the aisle for ninety miles until reaching Atlanta. King felt dehumanized and stated that the experience, which was the "angriest" he had ever been, would never leave his memory.[39]

[34] *Id.* at 8
[35] *Id.*
[36] *Id.* at 10.
[37] *Id.*
[38] *Id.*
[39] *Id.*

Daddy King's example and a raw set of childhood experiences shaped King's sense of racial justice long before the civil rights movement. Having personally experienced and endured racialized violence, verbal abuse, and dehumanizing bus rides, as well as witnessing KKK violence, economic injustice, police brutality, and racial injustice in the courts, King abhorred racial segregation and its battery of repressive and savage performances. In his autobiography, he wrote, "I had grown up abhorring not only segregation but also the oppressive and barbarous acts that grew out of it."[40] This burning desire for equity, equality, and justice inspired him. In a 1967 speech to the American Psychological Association, he argued:

> If the Negro needs social sciences for direction and self-understanding, the white society is in even more urgent need. White America needs to understand that it is poisoned to its soul by racism, and the understanding needs to be carefully documented and consequently more difficult to reject. The present crisis arises because although it is historically imperative that our society take the next step to equality, we find ourselves psychologically and socially imprisoned. All too many white Americans are horrified not with the conditions of Negro life but with the product of these conditions – the Negro himself.[41]

These thoughts and hardships were consistent in his consciousness for most of his life, providing King with an uncanny ability to empathize with human suffering in his late teens. This ability deepened during two summers of work in a racially integrated plant, where he "saw economic injustice firsthand, and realized that the poor white was exploited just as much as the Negro."[42] This experience made him aware of the interracial complexities of economic inequality and injustice in American society.[43]

His new understanding appears to have broadened his unitary conceptions of racism, which greatly expanded after spending his post-high school summer working on racially integrated tobacco farms in Simsbury, Connecticut.[44] It was here that he attended his first multiracial church, led an integrated Sunday school class of 107 boys, and socialized in racially mixed restaurants without Jim Crow's architecture dictating social relations. King's freedom from openly hostile racism in Simsbury permitted him to socialize with whites in ways unforeseen in the segregated South.[45] When he

---

[40] Id.
[41] Martin Luther King Jr., *The Role of the Behavioral Scientist in the Civil Rights Movement*, September 1967 (speech on file with author). Reprinted in the JOURNAL OF SOCIAL ISSUES, Vol. 24, No. 1 (1968).
[42] Martin Luther King Jr., *My Pilgrimage to Nonviolence*, September 1, 1958 (on file with The Martin Luther King, Jr. Research and Education Institute, Stanford University), available at https://kinginstitute.stanford.edu/king-papers/documents/my-pilgrimage-nonviolence.
[43] Martin Luther King Jr., *Autobiography*, supra note 1 at 10–11.
[44] Id. at 11.
[45] Martin Luther King Jr., *Letter to Martin Luther King, Sr.*, June 15, 1944, Simsbury, CT (on file with The Martin Luther King, Jr. Research and Education Institute, Stanford University, CKFC, INP, Christine King Farris Collection, in private hands), available at https://kinginstitute.stanford.edu/king-papers/documents/martin-luther-king-sr-1.

returned home after his "freedom summer," King recounts his bitterness about the incomprehensible and dehumanizing feeling of riding the train from New York to Washington as a freeman and being forced to travel in a segregated "Jim Crow car" from the nation's capital to Atlanta.[46] That summer of 1944 proved to be a watershed moment in King's social consciousness and development. The evils of racial segregation adversely affected his "growing personality" and cemented his dedication to fighting racial injustice to preserve his young sense of "dignity and self-respect."[47]

1.2 MOREHOUSE COLLEGE

At the age of fifteen, King entered Morehouse College, which had a dual enrollment program that accepted 11th graders in the wake of the negative impact of the wartime draft on college enrollment among Black people during World War II. He was a legacy student, as his father and maternal grandfather had also attended Morehouse, one of America's finest historically Black universities and only all-Black men's college. It is worth noting that, in 1944, King was a third-generation university student, which is remarkable given that only 29 percent of Black Americans hold bachelor's degrees today. The physical and intellectual safety of Morehouse College allowed King to discuss racialized topics, among others, without retribution. Morehouse professors nurtured a transparent and politically incorrect learning environment where students could imagine "solutions to racial ills."[48] This approach was consistent with its motto: "And there was light," or the Latin *Et Facta Est Lux*.

Morehouse offered the ideal learning environment for King, who had already developed a "substantial" concern for racial justice issues.[49] At Morehouse, he was introduced to many scholarly works, such as Henry David Thoreau's classic essay "On Civil Disobedience."[50] King found Thoreau's willingness to be imprisoned rather than pay taxes that would be used to support war and slavery liberating. The notion that nonviolent resistance could be employed against evil and racist systems fit King's moral epicenter and eventually rooted his belief in nonviolent resistance. Notably, as King studied the theory of nonviolence in collaboration with whites as a racial justice worker with the Intercollegiate Council,[51] his resentment of the white race softened. A new spirit of cooperation sprouted in his heart as more whites demonstrated their interest in being allies in the fight against racial segregation.

It was at this stage that King envisioned himself "playing a part in breaking down the legal barriers to Negro rights."[52] This urge to fight racial injustice was reflected

---

[46] Martin Luther King Jr., *Autobiography*, supra note 1 at 11–12.
[47] *Id.* at 12.
[48] *Id.* at 13.
[49] *Id.* at 14.
[50] *Id.* at 12. See generally, Henry David Thoreau, CIVIL DISOBEDIENCE (Empire Books, 2011).
[51] Martin Luther King Jr., *Autobiography*, supra note 1 at 12.
[52] *Id.* at 14.

in a letter to the editor titled "Kick Up Dust," published in the *Atlanta Constitution* newspaper,[53] which he penned during his sophomore year. In challenging the contradictions of white men on the issue of racial integration, King noted that the various advocates of separation and racial purity were also the leaders of "the total mixture in America," harkening back to the forced rape and subjugation of Blacks during enslavement, particularly of women.[54] In a tone reminiscent of Marcus Garvey, King's essay reminded readers that Black men were not "eager to marry white girls, and we would like to have our own girls left alone by both white toughs and white aristocrats."[55] He then turned his attention to challenging the innumerable racial injustices plaguing African-Americans. That same year, King also wrote an article titled "The Purpose of Education" in Morehouse's literary journal, the *Maroon Tiger*. He argued that one of the aims of education was to give people "unbiased truths," not "half-truths," prejudices, and propaganda. He advocated for the importance of critical thinking and suggested that the "goal of true education" should be "intelligence plus character."[56]

As King's social consciousness widened, he began to question his faith-calling in ministry, as his studies stirred doubts in his mind about his faith, Negro emotionalism in the church, and religious fundamentalism. He opined that his studies demonstrated that science and religion were often at odds, making him more skeptical about Christianity. He began questioning whether traditional religious predilections "could serve as a vehicle to modern thinking," commenting that "if we, as a people, had as much religion in our hearts and souls as we have in our legs and feet, we could change the world."[57] Such youthful contemplations were not unusual for a sixteen-year-old developing himself as a man and thinker. During this time, King was intellectually curious and a critical Christian thinker but did not initially distinguish himself at Morehouse despite excelling in oratory and debate.[58] And, after immersing himself in a Bible course likely taught by Dr. George Kelsey, who instructed him in philosophy and religion, King discovered profound truths that caused him to snap back into the greater ecclesiastical understanding of the world.

---

[53] Martin Luther King Jr. (Morehouse College), *Kick Up Dust*, Letter to the Editor, ATLANTA CONSTITUTION (August 6, 1946), in Clayborne Carson et al. (eds.), *King Papers, Volume I: Called to Serve* (January 1929–June 1951), 121.

[54] Martin Luther King Jr., *Kick Up Dust*, supra note 53.

[55] Martin Luther King Jr., *Autobiography*, supra note 1 at 15.

[56] Martin Luther King Jr., *The Purpose of Education* (January 1, 1947–February 28, 1957), in Clayborne Carson, et al. (eds.), *King Papers, Volume I: Called to Serve* (January 1929–June 1951), 124. See also Chapter 2: *Morehouse College* (on file with The Martin Luther King, Jr., Research and Education Institute, Stanford University), available at https://kinginstitute.stanford.edu/king-papers/publications/autobiography-martin-luther-king-jr-contents/chapter-2-morehouse-college.

[57] Martin Luther King Jr., *Autobiography*, supra note 1 at 13.

[58] Morehouse College, January 1, 1867, to December 31, 1867 (on file with The Martin Luther King, Jr. Research and Education Institute, Stanford University), available at https://kinginstitute.stanford.edu/morehouse-college. He was "president of the sociology club ... student council, glee club, and minister's union." He served as a member of "Morehouse chapter of the National Association for the Advancement of Colored People and played on the Butler Street YMCA basketball team." Id.

This growth was also profoundly influenced by Dr. Benjamin Mays, president of Morehouse College from 1940 to 1967, whom King referred to as a family friend, spiritual and intellectual mentor, and "one of the great influences in my life."[59] Mays understood the value and power of historically black colleges and universities (HBCUs) and challenged King and other "Morehouse students to struggle against segregation rather than accommodate themselves to it."[60] Like many Black leaders, Mays was influenced by Mahatma Gandhi, whom he befriended. Mays studied Gandhi's philosophy of nonviolence and activism years before King became familiar with him. Mays likely first introduced King to Indian freedom movements, including Gandhi's nonviolent living philosophy of *Satya* (truth) and *ahimsa* (nonviolence). When taken together, King's radical consciousness paralleled Mays's pro-Black, antiracist, and nonviolent social psychology.

The intellectual giants who influenced King during his time at Morehouse were ministers, scholars, leaders, and learned men "of all of the trends in modern thinking."[61] Within this balance between traditional and modern, King sought guidance and, in many ways, deliverance. His years at Morehouse were also the first time he was taught and mentored by men of significant stature and intellectual standing other than his father. His hunger for ministry grew during his senior year at Morehouse College, as did his interest in seminary school.

1.3 CROZER THEOLOGICAL SEMINARY

In September 1948, at nineteen years old, King entered Crozer Theological Seminary in Chester, Pennsylvania, to identify a theological basis to "eliminate social evil."[62] He immersed himself in the social, ethical, and philosophical literature of Europe's preeminent ancient and modern philosophers, including Plato (Greek), Aristotle (Greek), Jean-Jacques Rousseau (Genevan), Thomas Hobbes (English), Jeremy Bentham (English), John Stuart Mill (English), and John Locke (English). He also studied and was influenced by the writings of Walter Rauschenbusch (American), whom he credits for ingraining in him a "theological basis for the social concern" at an early age.[63] One might argue that King's early philosophical education and mindfulness were framed, in part, by the scholarly works of these renowned intellectuals, who offered a smorgasbord of social

---

[59] Martin Luther King Jr., STRIDE TOWARD FREEDOM (New York: Harper and Row, 1958), 145. Mays's influence on King is also discussed by Robert E. Johnson, William G. Pickens, and Charles V. Willie in Renee D. Turner, "Remembering the Young King," EBONY 43 (January 1988), 42–46; and Oliver "Sack" Jones in an interview by Herbert Holmes (April 8, 1970), MLKP/OH-GAMK.

[60] Benjamin E. Mays, *The Color Line around the World*, JOURNAL OF NEGRO EDUCATION, Vol. 6, No. 2 (April 6, 1937), 141.

[61] Martin Luther King Jr., *Autobiography*, supra note 1 at 16.

[62] *Id.* at 17.

[63] *Id.* at 18.

ethics rooted in ancient Africa (Egypt) and purloined and acculturated by leading Greek intellectuals and their progeny in Europe and the United States. For example, Aristotle credits Egypt for providing him with advanced knowledge and wisdom, declaring that "Egyptians are reputed to be the oldest of nations, but they have always had laws and a political system."[64] Similarly, Plato spent thirteen years in Egypt studying with the African Horite priest Sechnuphis, as did other leading Greek scholars, including Pythagoras, who studied with the Kemetian arch-Prophet Sonches. Thales, Hippocrates, and Socrates also studied in Egypt. All learned Kemetic (Egyptian) knowledge and spirituality at the temple universities of *Waset* and *Ipet Isut* (The Most Select of Places) in ancient Egypt. Hence, King reappropriated what the Greeks misappropriated and mistook – African knowledge and philosophy, particularly the MA'AT concept from ancient Egypt – and applied it to help liberate persons of African descent in the United States.[65]

King's transcendental or global thinking quickly evolved at Crozer, and his convictions grew even more quickly. His human rights-centered perspectives were derived from lived experiences – a pregnant combination of Black Baptist doctrine, pastoral inheritance, academic training, and imprint, on the one hand, and American racism, poverty, and war on the other. King's societal critiques were domestic and global; not even the church escaped criticism. For example, he argued that "any religion that professes concern for the souls of men and is not equally concerned about the slums that damn them, the economic conditions that strangle them, and the social conditions that cripple them is a spiritually moribund religion only waiting for the day to be buried."[66] King's human rights sensibilities were thus fortified at Crozer, where he employed the Gospel of Jesus as his guiding framework and charter. In the same way that human rights and civil rights attorneys employ the United Nations Charter and the US Constitution, respectively, to advance the more significant moral imperatives of civilized society, King's foundational doctrine was rooted in the biblical New Testament teachings of Jesus Christ.

---

[64] Aristotle, ARISTOTLE'S POLITICS (Oxford: Clarendon Press, 1905), Section 1329b.

[65] The goddess MA'AT was the ultimate arbiter of justice – soul justice – on earth and beyond and was simultaneously an abstract metaphysical construct predicated on natural justice precepts intended to order and regulate individual and collective behavior. MA'AT is the oldest known psychocultural and legal philosophy and served as the moral epicenter or conscience of Egyptian society, a naturalist identity that transcended Pharaoh and the state. In ancient Egypt, Pharaoh's primary purpose was to "make MA'AT, to make harmony, balance, reciprocity, justice, truth, and righteousness." Asa G. Hilliard, III, *The African Origins of Law*, Lecture presented to the Georgetown University College of Law (Spring 1993) (on file with the Author). See John A. Wilson, *Authority and Law in Ancient Egypt*, Supplement to 74:3 J. AM. ORIENTAL SOC'Y (1954). *See also*, IAN BROWNLIE, PRINCIPLES OF PUBLIC INTERNATIONAL LAW 515 (5th ed. 1998). MA'AT was the "force" that ensured "an ideal state of the universe" and accordingly guided human and institutional behavior and informed the intellectual template from which morality, justice and rule construction, including treaties, emanated. Jeremy I. Levitt, *The African Origins of International Law: Myth or Reality?*, UCLA JOURNAL OF INTERNATIONAL LAW AND FOREIGN AFFAIRS, Spring 2015, 115.

[66] Martin Luther King Jr., *Autobiography*, supra note 1 at 18.

Indeed, King's foundational training at home and in Sweet Auburn's greater community, as well as at Morehouse College, evolved into liberation fruit during seminary school at Crozer, where he authored a research paper titled *"Light on the Old Testament from the Ancient Near East."*[67] The 1948 paper, which is indicative of King's "Afro-centric" thinking at the early age of nineteen, was written for Professor James Bennett Pritchard's class on the Old Testament. It provides insight into King's thinking about Africa's role in biblical history through the Hebrew Prophets and in relation to Near East or Ancient Egyptian literature and wisdom. King's understanding of the connection between Black Egyptian literature and biblical psalms and the spiritual ethos of the modern world was remarkable. For example, he argued that the "composing of proverbs were begun in Egypt" and credited their emergence to Ptah-Hotep, whom he regards as one of the "greatest proverb writers to appear on the Egyptian scene: during the 5th Dynasty (2675 BCE)."[68] Ptah-Hotep was vizier (chief adviser and administrator) to Pharaoh Djedkare Isesi and is known as one of ancient Egypt's leading literary figures. He noted elements that were "strikingly" similar to the "Biblical book of Proverbs."[69] In the paper, King further examines the influences of King Amenemope III's (1390–1354 BCE) thinking about "honesty, integrity, self-control and kindness" to the Hebrews, particularly in "Jeremiah, Psalms, and Proverbs."[70] These *Ma'at*-like principles would later serve as the cornerstone of King's African ministry.

The reclamation and return of biblical history to its African roots was not unique among Pan-African thinking clergy during this period. King followed suit. For example, quoting J. H. Breasted, King also examined the impact of Amenhotep IV, also known as King Akhenaton (1570–1150 BCE), for being "the first individual of history" because he offered a "new idea of God" and birthed monotheism while his empire was predominated by polytheism.[71] King accurately opines that Akhenaton composed the two hymns of Aton, which he argues are like the 104th Psalm of Hebrews "in thought and sequence" and thus tremendously influenced biblical writers. Referring to the Old Testament and its Black Egyptian roots, King argues that, if accepted as truth, the hymns of Aton are "one of the most logical vehicles of mankind's deepest devotional thoughts and aspirations, couched in language which retains its original vigor and moral intensity."[72] King's awareness of Africa's significant influences on biblical history was inimitable and reflective of

---

[67] Martin Luther King Jr., *Light on the Old Testament from the Ancient Near East* (on file with The Martin Luther King, Jr. Research and Education Institute, Stanford University, [September 14, 1948]), available at https://kinginstitute.stanford.edu/king-papers/documents/light-old-testament-ancient-near-east.
[68] *Id.*
[69] *Id.*
[70] *Id.*
[71] *Id.*
[72] *Id.*

his African consciousness. One might argue that his research on Africa's determinative influences on biblical history radicalized him. Egypt's authoritative role in biblical antiquity emboldened King's African awareness and the historical and spiritual ethos that cultivated and nurtured it long before he emerged as a national and global human rights leader and icon. King remained a prolific student of ancient and modern Black history and theology in Africa, the Near East, and North America, eventually amassing a personal library of over 1000 books by his early thirties.

From an early age, his access to prominent African American literary works framed his consciousness. In the first part of the twentieth century, only a few mainstream publishers distributed scholarly books by Black scholars. In the segregated South, access to such works was even more difficult; some were even banned. Poor Blacks had virtually no way to obtain the pioneering works of Black scholars; however, King was a fourth-generation pastor and civil rights activist from an upper-middle-class background. There was a library in Daddy and Mother King's home. Coretta and Martin built a formidable collection of books in the 1950s that included groundbreaking works incorporating various topics, including enslavement, slavery, racism, Africa, poverty, and Christianity. King appeared to have been significantly influenced by *David Walker's Appeal*, Howard Thurman's *Jesus and the Disinherited*, Kwame Nkrumah's *Ghana: Autobiography*, and the teachings and writings of Benjamin Mays. In addition, several classical works on Africa, Pan-Africanism, religion in Africa, and Black reparations informed his library and seemingly his thinking, such as Louis E. Lomax's 1960 classic, *Reluctant African*; Mahatma Gandhi's 1928 *Satyagraha in South Africa*; Ralph Korngold's 1945 biography *Citizen Toussaint*; Ralph Ellison's 1945 masterpiece *Invisible Man*; George Padmore's 1956 masterpiece, *Pan-Africanism, or Communism? The Coming Struggle for Africa*; and the Civil Rights Congress's bold 1951 *We Charge Genocide: The Historic Petition to the United Nations for Relief from a Crime of the United States Government against the Negro People*. King likely read most of these texts before the age of twenty-five and developed notable expertise on the intersections of racism, colonialism, and Apartheid on Africa and Black Americans.

Likewise, King's study and reflections on the predominant global economic theories and systems, such as capitalism and communism, was bold. He patently rejected the works of Karl Marx and other communist theorists despite being accused of having socialist leanings, a typical smear levied by the Federal Bureau of Investigation's Counter-Intelligence Program (COINTELPRO). He shunned communism's "secularistic and materialistic" orientation, unethical means-to-an-end relativism, proclivity for political totalitarianism, and deprivation of individual freedoms. King argued, "Man is not made for the state; the state is made for man," and, "Man must never be treated as a means to an end of the state, but always as an end within himself."[73] In his

---

[73] Martin Luther King Jr., *Autobiography*, supra note 1 at 20–21.

view, communism had "no place for God," and, thus, he could never accept it. King considered communism "basically evil," a system comprised of "false assumptions and evil methods."[74] He also prophetically opined that capitalism raised vital concerns "about the gulf between superfluous wealth and abject poverty" and too often inspired people to "be more concerned about making a living than making a life."[75] King questioned the moral foundations of capitalism, God, and profit. He valued people above profit, human development over economic development, and "service and relationship to humanity" over the profit motive matrix.[76] He argued that capitalism might evolve into a practical materialism that would be as "pernicious as the materialism taught by communism."[77]

King's ability to grasp the theoretical and practical aspects of Cold War politics, economics, and theatrics in the late 1940s was extraordinary, as was his ability to use Black Christian values to critique them. To King, "The Kingdom of God is neither the thesis of individual enterprise nor the antithesis of collective enterprise, but a synthesis which reconciles the truths of both."[78] He embraced the biblical belief that the life and death of Jesus Christ were intended to give people peace with God and themselves, which is why King taught his disciples and followers to turn the other cheek when assaulted by evil, to resolve conflicts peacefully, to be peacemakers in society, and that all happenings in the world occur when God chooses. He appears to have grasped onto the sacred biblical principle reflected in the Book of Matthew: "Blessed are the peacemakers, for they shall be called children of God."[79] King understood that Jesus sends his disciples into an ugly, violent, and hateful world to make peace between God and men, among nations, and among the people themselves.

Crozer Theological Seminary greatly influenced King's thinking and approach to American racism. And while his philosophical approach was derived from the Gospel of Yehoshua, his thinking received fortification while attending a lecture by Dr. A. J. Muste, executive director of the Fellowship of Reconciliation (FOR). FOR was "an international pacifist organization that drew on Gandhi's philosophy of peaceful resistance," as Jonathan Eig notes.[80] He continues, "FOR's leading voice was A. J. Muste, a minister who called for the conscious violation of unjust government laws and actions and encouraged his followers to go to jail for their beliefs."[81] Muste believed that incarceration and aggression were necessary to awaken the public's conscience, a tactical position that became the cornerstone of King's philosophy of nonviolence.

---

[74] *Id.*
[75] *Id.* at 21.
[76] *Id.*
[77] *Id.*
[78] *Id.* at 22.
[79] Matthew 5:9, New International Version, BibleGateway, www.biblegateway.com/passage/?search=Matthew%205%3A9&version=NIV.
[80] Jonathan Eig, KING: A LIFE (Farrar, Straus, and Giroux, New York, 2023), 165–166.
[81] *Id.*

King sought to expose the violence and brutality of those opposing racial equality, using his enemies' violence as a negative good. While King was acutely aware that war couldn't serve a "positive or absolute good," he opined that "it could serve as a negative good" by halting an "evil force" such as regimes predicated on Apartheid and other forms of totalitarianism such as Racism, Nazism, Fascism, or Communism.[82] Interestingly, this "negative good" logic underscored the rationale for the creation of the UN's first large-scale and heavily armed peacekeeping operation in the Congo in 1960, where it used defensive violence for an adverse good. King supported this UN action. At this juncture, though vacillating on the "power of love to solve social problems," King provisionally believed that the "only way" to defeat segregation was through "armed revolt,"[83] a theoretical position akin to many Pan-Africanist and Black Nationalist thinkers and activists at the time. He believed that the "Christian ethic of love was confined to individual relationships" and not applicable to social evils; he did not yet know how love could be employed to combat social conflict.[84] However, his thinking shifted after attending a sermon by Dr. Mordecai Johnson, president of Howard University. Johnson, a mentor to King, preached about the life, teachings, and legacy of Mahatma Gandhi, leaving an enduring impression on King.[85] From this point forward, King immersed himself into the Gandhian philosophy of nonviolent resistance, which influenced his approach to fighting social evil for the rest of his life.

Gandhi's transcendental philosophy of nonviolence was not simply theoretical but a way of life. It was and is aggressive, used as a "moral weapon" that relies on "soul force over physical force."[86] It seeks to win the "enemy through love and patient suffering."[87] Derived from the Satyagraha philosophy, which means "soul force," not "brute force," Gandhi originated his philosophy of nonviolent resistance to combat white South African repression in South Africa and British domination in India.[88] Satyagraha is predicated on three concepts: *Satya* (truth), *Ahimsa* (nonviolence, or refusing to injure others), and *Tapasya* (self-sacrifice). Although the cosmogony of *Satyagraha* had Indian roots, its birthplace was in Johannesburg, South Africa,

---

[82] Martin Luther King Jr., *Autobiography*, supra note 1 at 22–23.
[83] Martin Luther King Jr., *His Influence Speaks to World Conscience*, HINDUSTAN TIMES (January 30, 1958), available at https://kinginstitute.stanford.edu/king-papers/documents/his-influence-speaks-world-conscience.
[84] *Id.*
[85] Martin Luther King Jr., *Autobiography*, supra note 1 at 23.
[86] Martin Luther King, Jr., To Chester Bowles (on file with The Martin Luther King, Jr. Research and Education Institute, Stanford University [October 28, 1957]), available at https://kinginstitute.stanford.edu/king-papers/documents/chester-bowles.
[87] Gandhi's Philosophy of Nonviolence, https://www.mkgandhi.org/africaneedsgandhi/gandhis_philosophy_of_nonviolence.php.
[88] M. K. Gandhi. *Satyagraha in South Africa* in Shriman Narayan (ed.), Valji Govindji (trans.), The Selected Works of Mahatma Gandhi Volume Two (Rupees One Hundred Fifty for set of five volumes, Navajivan Trust, 1968), 107. See also Gandhi Book Centre, Mahatma Gandhi, *Gandhi's Philosophy of Nonviolence* (Bombay Sarvodaya Mandal), available at www.mkgandhi.org/africaneedsgandhi/gandhis_philosophy_of_nonviolence.php.

where Gandhi fought for the civil rights of Indians. Gandhi later employed it in India to engage in massive civil disobedience, leading to the renowned 1930 Salt March against British colonial domination. Ironically, King's adoption of Satyagraha philosophy and tactics as a strategy and approach to combat racial segregation in the US reflected the reclamation of strategies that originated in his ancestral homeland, Africa. King commented, "It was in this Gandhian emphasis on love and nonviolence that I discovered the method for social reform that I had been seeking."[89]

Initially, King struggled with the power of love as a vehicle for social change outside of the context of interpersonal conflict, and he questioned Christianity's "turn the other cheek" and "love your enemies" philosophies.[90] Initially, he did not believe that love was a potent weapon against racial conflict or interstate disputes; however, through Gandhism, his skepticism diminished when he discovered love's power in the "area of social reform."[91] King remarked, "Gandhi was probably the first person in history to lift the love ethic of Jesus above mere interaction between individuals to a powerful and effective social force on a large scale."[92] Indeed, Satyagraha's effectiveness against racism in South Africa and Jim Crowism in the US validated its bona fides as a potent antiracist Indo-African philosophy and methodology. Despite being sixty years apart in age and advocating in different eras and regions of the world, Gandhi and King employed nonviolent resistance for the same reasons: racial segregation in public transportation, including buses and trains, as well as equal voting rights with whites.

Simply put, King's eyes opened at Crozer. He enjoyed his spiritual pilgrimage there and sharpened his critical thinking and analytical skills. Ultimately, he fully embraced Gandhism not only to upend racism but to address theological liberalism. He was especially drawn to "its devotion to the search for truth, its insistence on an open and analytical mind, and its refusal to abandon the best light of reason."[93] King went so far as to suggest that the "Gandhian approach" may "bring about a solution to the race problem in America."[94] This enormous intellectual pronouncement steered King's approach to America's race dilemma until his untimely death. Ultimately, Crozer helped fortify and influence King's intellectual and spiritual awareness through its diverse intellectual voices and its introduction to transnational philosophical criticisms and interpretations of biblical literature and social change. While at Crozer, the works of luminaries such as A. J. Muste, Gandhi, and Karl Paul Reinhold Niebuhr (American), nourished King's growing consciousness and spiritual solutions to America's entrenched race problem.

---

[89] Martin Luther King Jr., *Autobiography*, supra note 1 at 23–24.
[90] *Id.*
[91] *Id.* at 23.
[92] *Id.* at 24.
[93] Martin Luther King Jr., *Pilgrimage to Nonviolence*, published article, CHRISTIAN CENTURY (April 13, 1960), available at www.christiancentury.org/article/pilgrimage-nonviolence. See also, Martin Luther King Jr., *Autobiography*, supra note 1 at 25.
[94] Martin Luther King Jr., *His Influence Speaks to World Conscience*, supra note 83.

1.4 BOSTON UNIVERSITY SCHOOL OF THEOLOGY

In September 1951, King began his doctoral studies at Boston University's School of Theology (BU). He was interested in attending BU because of the scholarly writings and pursuits of faculty members like Edgar S. Brightman (an American philosopher), with whom he desired to study, and because George W. Davis, one of his choice professors at Crozer, had studied there and supported his admission.[95] King's intellectual sojourn evolved to the next level at BU, particularly his thinking about nonviolent movements. BU provided King with access to various scholars, practitioners, and domestic and international student practitioners of nonviolent resistance, pacifism, and social justice. King seemed particularly fond of Dean Walter Muelder and Professor Allen Knight Chalmers because of their profound concern for the human condition. Their teachings encouraged him to deepen his understanding of the philosophy and theory of nonviolence as it related to the challenges of liberalism as a cure for social evils and the relevance of neoorthodoxy to racial justice.[96] Overall, BU allowed him to build and expand on his interests in the ecclesiastical intersections between racial justice and nonviolence.

King's heightened interests in the symbiotic relationship between social justice and pacifism expanded under professors Brightman and Lotan Harold DeWolf (an American Minister and Theologian).[97] King credits Brightman for giving him "the metaphysical and philosophical grounding for the idea of a personal God."[98] This meant that an individual's personal experience centered their faith because, in Brightman's view, "all religion is of, by, and for persons. Religion ascribes a unique value to persons and has a unique interest in their welfare and their salvation."[99] Brightman heavily influenced King's philosophy, particularly his belief in Personalistic philosophy – the notion that reality was, in the long run, found in personality. This approach reinforced King's belief in a personal God with whom one could be in a vertical relationship. It was, in King's words, "a metaphysical basis

---

[95] Martin Luther King Jr., *Autobiography*, supra note 1 at 28. See also Edgar Sheffield Brightman, *Biography*, September 20, 1884, to February 25, 1953 (on file with The Martin Luther King, Jr. Research and Education Institute, Stanford University), available at https://kinginstitute.stanford.edu/encyclopedia/brightman-edgar-sheffield.

[96] Martin Luther King Jr., *Autobiography*, supra note 1 at 30–31.

[97] DeWolf was also a former student of Brightman.

[98] Martin Luther King Jr., *Facing the Challenge of a New Age*, Address Delivered at NAACP Emancipation Rally, January 1, 1957, in *King Papers, Volume IV: Symbol of the Movement* (January 1957–December 1958), 75; Also, Edgar Sheffield Brightman, *Biography*, supra note 95.

[99] Edgar S. Brightman, *Religion as Truth*, in CONTEMPORARY AMERICAN THEOLOGY, ed. Vergilius Ferm, 1932, p. 73. See also Edgar Sheffield Brightman, September 20, 1884 to February 25, 1953 (on file with The Martin Luther King, Jr. Research and Education Institute, Stanford University), available at https://kinginstitute.stanford.edu/brightman-edgarsheffield#:~:text=Brightman%20believed%20that%20personal%20experience,as%20Truth%2C%E2%80%9D%2073.

for the dignity and worth of all human personality,"[100] which itself is a core human rights principle enshrined in the United Nations Charter (1945) and the Universal Declaration on Human Rights (1948).[101] For example, the Preamble of the United Nations Charter reaffirms "faith in fundamental human rights, in the dignity and worth of the human person, in the equal rights of men and women and of nations large and small."[102] Furthermore, Article 1 of the United Nations Charter states, "All human beings are born free and equal in dignity and rights. They are endowed with reason and conscience and should act towards one another in a spirit of brotherhood."[103] Articles 2 and 3 build on this foundation by prohibiting racial segregation and other forms of discrimination and by codifying the right to life, liberty, and security for every living being.[104] King was aware of the UN's human rights doctrine, and, intuitively, his belief in one's upright relationship with God and the natural dignity of every human being became the cornerstone of Kingsian thinking. These beliefs specifically influenced the direction of his doctoral dissertation. Titled "*A Comparison of the Conception of God in the Thinking of Paul Tillich and Henry Nelson Wieman*," it provides a sojourn into the "central place" God "occupies in any religion" as well as the need for people to "interpret and clarify the God-concept."[105]

Interestingly, when King prepared his dissertation, "America's" most prominent and recognized theologians and philosophers of mainstream religion were white Americans and Europeans, as were the theoretical constructs of God that influenced King. It is remarkable, therefore, that in *Stride Toward Freedom*, King did not refer to Howard Thurman, the Black theological luminary who was a friend and former classmate of Daddy King at Morehouse College and who served as the first Black Dean of Boston University's Marsh Chapel for at least one year during King's tenure as a doctoral student.[106] Unlike King, Thurman met with and developed a relationship with Mahatma Gandhi (1936), who, despite having a questionable history of supporting Black liberation in South Africa, demonstrated a keen interest in the African-American freedom struggle. He even prophetically opined to Thurman that "it may be through the Negroes that the unadulterated message of nonviolence will be delivered to the world."[107] King's failure to reference Thurman is puzzling

---

[100] Martin Luther King Jr., STRIDE TOWARD FREEDOM, supra note 59 at 100. See also *Personalism* (on file with The Martin Luther King, Jr. Research and Education Institute, Stanford University), available at https://kinginstitute.stanford.edu/personalism.
[101] Martin Luther King Jr., *Autobiography*, supra note 1 at 32.
[102] Preamble, Charter of the United Nations and Statute of the International Court of Justice. 1945. New York: United Nations, Office of Public Information.
[103] Article 1, Charter of the United Nations, supra note 102.
[104] Articles 2 and 3, Charter of the United Nations, supra note 102.
[105] Martin Luther King Jr., *Autobiography*, supra note 1 at 32.
[106] Kyle Desrosiers, Beacons of Hope: Our Interreligious S/Heroes – Rev. Howard Thurman | Hebrew College (June 7, 2023), https://hebrewcollege.edu/blog/beacons-of-hope-our-interreligious-s-heroes-rev-howard-thurman/.
[107] Quinton Dixie and Peter Eisenstadt, VISIONS OF A BETTER WORLD: HOWARD THURMAN'S PILGRIMAGE TO INDIA AND THE ORIGINS OF AFRICAN AMERICAN NONVIOLENCE (Boston:

given that Thurman deepened King's understanding of Gandhi, served as his spiritual mentor, and laid the groundwork for King thirty years before his ascendency as a global leader. Thurman was among the first African Americans to study and adopt Gandhi's Satyagraha approach to nonviolent resistance, and he had extensive experience traveling and working in Africa, particularly in Egypt (1935), Djibouti (French Somaliland, 1935), and Nigeria (1960), where he taught at the University of Ibadan. Despite not appropriately recognizing him in his works, King clearly embraced Thurman's teachings and was undoubtedly influenced by his transnational theology, as evidenced by his strong embrace of Thurman's seminal work, *Jesus and the Disinherited*, during his doctoral studies. Significantly, King carried Thurman's book with him during the Montgomery Bus Boycott.

Still, King's omission of Thurman and others in his biographical works is disconcerting because it deprives the reader of learning more about the diverse and even radical intellectual influences on King's thinking and theology. On this point, Clayborn Carson notes that "[rather] than citing these African American influences, King presented himself in *Stride* as a black leader familiar with European America [and European] intellectual trends."[108] One can surmise that he did not reference any towering Black figures as influences because he maintained personal relationships with them, particularly Mays, Johnson, and Thurman, whom he corresponded with for several years after graduating from Boston University. Nevertheless, the Anglicized and Europeanized concepts King gravitated toward were built upon the Black radical tradition of interpretive preaching that originally rooted his thinking and racial justice analytics. King's mother, father, and the world that was Sweet Auburn and Ebenezer Baptist Church seeded his "conviction that nonviolent resistance was one of the most potent weapons available to oppressed people in their quest for social justice."[109] King embraced Daddy King's liberating theology and philosophy before being baptized by the thinking of white theologians and scholars, but he employed knowledge from both quarters to inject moral ethics and liberation theology into his fight against white supremacy or the dominant culture. He was committed to uprooting social evil in society even without, at this stage, knowing how "to organize it in a socially effective situation."[110]

Beacon Press, 2011). See also, Sudarshan Kapur, Raising up a Prophet. The African-American Encounter with Gandhi, Boston: Beacon Press (1992), 81–93 (India trip), 87–90 (discussion with Gandhi), 89 (singing of Spiritual while Gandhi prayed), 88 & 89–90 (quotes). Mahadev Desai Notes, "With Our negro Guests," Harijan 4 (4 March 1936), 38–40. Harijan was an English-language weekly published from 1933 to 1956 (published in Poona 1935–36) by the Harijan Sevak Sangh, a society founded by Gandhi to help untouchables.

[108] Carson indicates that there were others King ignored in his writing as well, including George Kelsey, his religion professor at Morehouse College, prominent Atlanta activist William Holmes Borders, J. Pius Barbour, and his mentor at Crozer Theological Seminary. Clayborne Carson, *Introduction*, in Martin Luther King Jr., Stride toward Freedom: The Montgomery Story (Boston: Beacon Press, 1958), xv.

[109] Martin Luther King Jr., *My Pilgrimage to Nonviolence*, supra note 42.

[110] Martin Luther King Jr., *Autobiography*, supra note 1 at 32.

2

From Montgomery to Accra

Toward a Vision of Black Liberation, 1954–1957

FIGURE 2.1 February 1958: civil rights leader Martin Luther King Jr. being fingerprinted by police after his arrest during the Montgomery bus boycott. (Photo by Don Cravens/Getty Images.)

2.1 GLOBALIZING MONTGOMERY

This chapter examines King's mindset toward Africa and African liberation from the 1954 Montgomery Bus Boycott to his attendance at Ghana's independence celebration in March 1957. During this period, King's standing and prophetic human rights leadership flourished. The Montgomery Boycott began when Rosa Parks, an African American woman activist and leader, was accosted, arrested, and fined for refusing to give her bus seat to a white man in Montgomery, Alabama, at the height of Jim Crow segregation.[1] At the age of twenty-six, King's leadership of the ensuing boycott through the auspices of the Montgomery Improvement Association (MIA) catapulted him from a relatively unknown pastor of the Dexter Avenue Baptist Church and newly minted Doctor of Systematic Theology to a global icon (Figure 2.1).

No one predicted that, on December 5, 1955, the supposed one-day boycott of segregated city buses in Montgomery, Alabama, would evolve into a formidable year-long movement (381 days) that ended on December 20, 1956.[2] The Montgomery Bus Boycott was among the largest sustained demonstrations against racism in world history. Approximately 40,000 Black bus riders actively participated, bringing the City of Montgomery to a standstill. Buoyed by the masterful litigation skills of Fred D. Gray, the MIA's chief counsel; civil rights attorneys Thurgood Marshall and Robert L. Carter of the National Association for the Advancement of Colored People (NAACP); and attorneys Clifford Durr and Charles D. Langford, among others, the boycott succeeded in challenging segregated busing laws locally and nationally. The practice was found to violate the 14th Amendment to the US Constitution in *Browder v. Gayle* (1956),[3] which guarantees all citizens equal protection under the law, irrespective of race.[4]

Browder v. Gayle is one of American history's most significant yet unknown civil rights cases. Four Black women from Montgomery (Aurelia S. Browder, Susie McDonald, Claudette Colvin, and Mary Louise Smith) sued for being forced to give up their seats to white people on Montgomery buses. Browder was arrested on April 19, 1955, nearly eight months before Rosa Parks's arrest, for violating Montgomery's segregated bus policy. On February 1, 1956, Fred D. Gray filed a federal civil rights lawsuit against William A. Gayle, the mayor of Montgomery, challenging the constitutionality of racial segregation in busing.[5] Notably, the legal case challenging Montgomery's system of racial segregation was filed two days after King's home was bombed, which appears to have been an impetus for the filing. King's home was bombed on January 30, 1956, while he was delivering an address to 2,000 congregants at the First Baptist Church in Montgomery, shortly after his ascension to the presidency of the MIA.

---

[1] King, Martin Luther Jr. STRIDE TOWARD FREEDOM (Boston: Harper and Row, 1958), chapters 3–5.
[2] Id.
[3] Browder v. Gayle, 142 F. Supp. 707 (M.D. Ala. 1956).
[4] Id.
[5] Other defendants included Montgomery's police chief, Montgomery City Lines, Inc., two bus drivers, and representatives from Montgomery's Board of Commissioners and the Alabama Public Service Commission.

The lengthy litigation process overlapped with King's developing leadership in the national and international fields. Though the NAACP Legal Defense Fund offered political and financial support, the MIA, which largely funded the litigation, suffered a significant setback in February 1956 when King and eighty-eight other boycott leaders were indicted for violating Alabama's 1921 anti-boycott law. King was prosecuted in March 1956 and convicted of violating the law (*State of Alabama v. M.L. King, Jr.*).[6] He was sentenced to 386 days in jail and fined $500.[7] None of the other boycott leaders were prosecuted.

Despite this setback, *Browder v. Gayle* was heard by a three-judge panel on June 5, 1956, which ruled that enforced racial segregation in busing violated the US Constitution, specifically the Equal Protection Clause of the 14th Amendment. The City of Montgomery and the State of Alabama appealed the ruling to the US Supreme Court, which affirmed the lower court's ruling on November 13, 1956. The ruling put the proverbial death nail into racial segregation in public transportation in Alabama. The victory in the *Browder* case led to a cessation of the Montgomery Bus Boycott nearly a month later when the ruling was officially served to the City of Montgomery.

King learned about the *Browder* ruling in the Montgomery courthouse while being prosecuted locally over the legality of the boycott's carpools. At the time, King had not anticipated that the boycott would endure, nor had he predicted that its aim would shift from improving the treatment of Black passengers through a non-racialized first-come, first-served seating arrangement to the grandiose idea of fair and equitable treatment. Yet Black people wanted full enfranchisement – racial equity, equality, and justice – consistent with the norms and standards of global human rights. The success of the Montgomery Bus Boycott thus provided King with a worldwide platform to advocate for Black civil rights in the US and beyond. King sought to enumerate those fundamental rights in the American Constitution and the 1945 UN Charter for Black Americans. These included equal rights, self-determination, and "respect for human rights and for fundamental freedoms for all without distinction as to race, sex, language, or religion."[8]

The development of outside law and the codification of core international human rights norms in the UN Charter was not missed by Black American leaders, activists, and common folk. It can reasonably be argued that King's evolution and

---

[6] Judgment and Sentence, State of Alabama v. M. L. King, Jr., No. 7399 (Cir. Ct. Montgomery Cnty., Ala. Mar. 22, 1956) (on file with CMCR-AMC, Montgomery Cnty. Records, Montgomery Cnty. Courthouse, Montgomery, Ala.).

[7] The booking picture of King was taken by the Montgomery County Sheriff's Department on February 22, 1956. The word "Dean" was written on it with the date April 4, 1968, after King was assassinated in Memphis, Tennessee.

[8] Article (1)(2)(3), *Charter of the United Nations and Statute of the International Court of Justice*. 1945 (New York: United Nations, Office of Public Information).

effectiveness as a human rights activist were influenced by the international advocacy of Black human rights groups such as the National Negro Congress (NNC),[9] NAACP,[10] and, most prominently, the Civil Rights Congress (CRC). African Americans have consistently appealed to "outside law," whether it be the "Law of God," international human rights law, or moral cultural codes to contest American social evils in the form of slavery, Black codes, racial segregation, and the other vestiges of institutionalized racism. On December 17, 1951, for example, years before King emerged as a national leader, the CRC submitted a petition to the General Assembly of the United Nations "on behalf of the Negro people in the interest of peace and democracy."[11] Titled "We Charge Genocide: The Historic Petition to the United Nations for Relief From a Crime of The United States Government Against the Negro People," the petition charged the Government of the United States of America with genocide and human rights violations for enslavement, racial discrimination, white extremist vigilantism, and government inaction and complicity.[12] Notably, this 237-page indictment included or incorporated all of the issues that would eventually form the basis of King's agenda, including state-sanctioned anti-Black violence (e.g., murder, lynchings, beatings, and police brutality), deadly police violence, violent white extremism, voter suppression including poll taxes, and systemic inequalities in health, wealth, and employment.

The establishment of the UN and the adoption of the 1948 Universal Declaration of Human Rights occurred concurrently with global anticolonial movements – mainly in Africa and the Caribbean – and the emergence of America's civil rights movement in the 1950s.[13] King was acutely aware of the inherent contradictions to headquartering the United Nations, an international organization dedicated to protecting the human rights and dignity of people around the world, in the US, given the latter's racist treatment of Blacks and its proclivity for militarism. On this point, quoting former Russian Premier Nikita Khrushchev, King stated:

> Just this week, the most eloquent spokesman of the Communist bloc, Nikita Khruschev, suggested in his speech to the U.N., among other things, that the

---

[9] In 1946, the NNC delivered a statement on racial segregation and discrimination to the UN Secretary-General.

[10] In 1947, the NAACP led by W.E.B. DuBois, delivered a scathing 100-page complaint to the United Nations against the United States for its treatment of Black Americans.

[11] Civil Rights Congress (U.S.), WE CHARGE GENOCIDE: The Historic Petition to the United Nations for Relief from a Crime of the United States Government against the Negro People (New York, [publisher not identified]), 1951.

[12] The petition was submitted to a UN official in Paris by Executive Director William L. Patterson and activist and singer Paul Robeson, who delivered a copy to a UN official in New York. The US government attempted to prevent the submission of the petition to the UN, and the Justice Department and State Department sought to detain and limit the travel of W. E. B. Du Bois, Robeson, and Patterson.

[13] In 1945, the UN was established and headquartered in New York City in the wake of the Harlem Renaissance and the Harlem Race Riot of 1935, which set the stage for Harry S. Truman to issue Executive Order 9981 (July 1948) ending racial segregation in the US military (but nowhere else).

headquarters of this great organization be moved from the United States. The American press generally was very careful to conceal one of the reasons Mr. Khruschev gave for suggesting this move. His direct words were: "Facts are known … of representatives of young African and Asian states being subjected to racial discrimination in the United States."[14]

Speaking to the intersectionality between American racism, militarism, and international law, King elaborated further, stating:

> Nothing more clearly demonstrates our nation's abuse of military power than our tragic adventure in Vietnam. This war has played havoc with the destiny of the entire world. It has torn up the Geneva Agreement, it has seriously impaired the United Nations, it has exacerbated the hatred between continents and worse still between races. It has frustrated our development at home, telling our own underprivileged citizens that we place insatiable military demands above their critical needs. It has greatly contributed to the forces of reaction in America and strengthened the military industrial complex.[15]

King openly and candidly contested the Vietnam War primarily because he abhorred war and the role of Western powers in perpetrating violence in poor, colored nations.

King's astute appeal to Geneva Conventional Law (also known as humanitarian law), a body of rules governing hostilities during armed conflict, was extraordinary in the context of his broader international law and human rights argumentation and advocacy. What's more, his comparative invocation of race, human rights, and international law to indict America's involvement in the Vietnam War was remarkable. He argued that "[w]e arm Negro soldiers to kill on foreign battlefields but offer little protection for their relatives from beatings and killings in our own South. We are willing to make a Negro 100% of a citizen in Warfare but reduce him to 50% of a citizen on American soil."[16] King was frustrated by the contradictions of white America and white Americans,

---

[14] Martin Luther King Jr., *The Negro and the American Dream*, September 25, 1960, Excerpt from Address at the Annual Freedom Mass Meeting of the North Carolina State Conference of Branches of the NAACP in Clayborne Carson, et al. (eds.), *King Papers, Volume V: Threshold of a New Decade* (January 1959–December 1960). Speech by Mr. Khrushchev, Chairman of the Council of Ministers of the Union of Soviet Socialist Republics, at the 869th Plenary Meeting of the 15th Session of the United Nations General Assembly, Friday, September 23, 1960 (New York) (on file with Wilson Center Digital Archive, Washington, DC), available at: https://digitalarchive.wilsoncenter.org/document/speech-mr-khrushchev-chairman-council-ministers-union-soviet-socialist-republics-869th. See also, Nikita Khrushchev, *Address to the United Nations General Assembly on (September 23, 1960)* (Internet Modern History Sourcebook, Fordham University), available at: https://sourcebooks.fordham.edu/mod/1960khrushchev-un1.asp.

[15] Martin Luther King Jr., *The Three Evils of Society*, Address Delivered at the National Conference on New Politics, August 31, 1967, Audio Transcript (on file with The Martin Luther King, Jr, Research and Education Institute, Stanford University), available at https://okra.stanford.edu/link/document670831-004.

[16] *Id.*

especially members of the US Congress that voted "joyously to appropriate billions of dollars for the War in Vietnam" but "loudly against" fair housing that would allow "Negro veteran[s] to purchase a decent home."[17]

The founding of the UN, the adoption of the Universal Declaration of Human Rights, the launch of the American civil rights movement, and the sustained activism of the Montgomery Bus Boycott all occurred within one decade of one another – a collection of human rights conflations that would underwrite and magnify King's leadership at the national and international levels. Perhaps these advances encouraged and were encouraged by the US Supreme Court's 1954 *Brown v. Board of Education*[18] decision ending *de jure* racial segregation in public schools, essentially dealing a deathblow to its 1896 *Plessy v. Ferguson*[19] ruling that institutionalized racial segregation and the doctrine of "separate but equal" throughout the nation.

The year 1954 had been a noteworthy year for King. He had been invigorated by the various legal, political, and transnational assaults on systemic racism and racial segregation in the US and beyond. He and his new wife, Coretta, decided that he would complete his doctoral work in Montgomery, Alabama because they wanted to witness and partake in the "remarkable" change they believed was afoot in the South.

King's *raison d'être* was well known. In his application to Crozer years earlier, he indicated a strong "urge to serve society,"[20] and his early sermons conveyed a commitment to fighting social evil using the social Gospel of Jesus to minister to the sick, dying, poor, battered, broken-hearted, and disenfranchised. King's installation as pastor of the Dexter Avenue Baptist Church in Montgomery in May 1954 was the spark that empowered him to contribute mightily to the already established Montgomery Movement. When King was formally installed, local civil rights leaders in Montgomery – including Jo Anne Robinson of Montgomery's Women's Political Council and other NAACP principal figures – were poised for a major clash with Jim Crowism.

The March 1955 arrest of fifteen-year-old Claudette Colvin for refusing to move to the back of the bus (the inciting incident of *Browder v. Gayle*) incensed local community leaders. As a new social and political actor in Montgomery, King appeared anxious to make a mark and joined local leaders to "meet with city and bus company officials" about the inhumanity of Montgomery's bus segregation ordinance.[21] They met with little success. However, as previously noted, when Rosa Parks was arrested in December 1955, nine months after Colvin's detention, Black Montgomery was prepared to challenge Jim Crowism in public transportation through a potent combination of non-violent direct action and litigation. During

---

[17] Id.
[18] Brown v. Board of Education of Topeka, 347 U.S. 483 (1954).
[19] Plessy v. Ferguson, 163 U.S. 537 (1896).
[20] David Garrow, *The Intellectual Development of Martin Luther King, Jr.: Influences and Commentaries* UNION SEMINARY QUARTERLY REVIEW 40 (January 1986), 7. See also "Young King Inspired by Time on Conn. Farm," CBS News, January 17, 2011.
[21] Martin Luther King Jr. STRIDE TOWARD FREEDOM, supra note 1 at xi.

the nine months between Colvin and Parks's arrest, King distinguished himself as a dedicated trailblazer within Montgomery's progressive leadership, which included Robinson, E.D. Nixon, and NAACP leaders such as Parks. Consequently, he was asked to lead the Montgomery Improvement Association, which served as the organizing arm for the Montgomery Bus Boycott; he was elected president of the MIA on December 5, 1955 – the very same day the boycott challenging racial segregation on Montgomery City Lines Inc. was launched.

Montgomery City Line Inc. relied on Black passengers for 70 percent of its business. Thus, white Montgomery sought to continue the legacy of exploiting Black bodies for profit while simultaneously relegating them to second-class citizenship. The boycott aimed to ensure that seating would be available on a first-come, first-served basis while maintaining segregated entrances, that white bus drivers would treat Black passengers courteously, and that Black drivers would be used for busing in predominantly Black areas. Nearly 5,000 "Negroes" agreed to this agenda at an impromptu meeting.

Little did King know that the boycott would serve as the fault line that would fracture Jim Crow segregation in the American South by evolving into a 381-day racial justice sojourn. Nor could he have predicted that it would morph into a nationally and internationally recognized human rights movement against anti-Black racism and violence in America and beyond. According to *Time Magazine*, Montgomery was the "cradle of the Confederacy."[22] It served as the battlefront that rapidly propelled King into the national and international spotlight and concurrently solidified his position as one of Black America's most feared and respected leaders. Black leaders in the US fighting similar desegregation battles in Atlanta, Birmingham, Los Angeles, Miami, New Orleans, and Tallahassee all sought "advice and counsel" from the 28-year-old King.[23] Leaders in Africa and beyond also paid close attention to him and the "Montgomery Story" as they battled Europe's violent, oppressive, and extractive colonial states and enterprises – many seeking non-violent means to shed the yolks of white colonization.

King's approach was psychological, pastoral, physical, and metaphysical. He led Montgomery's Blacks into a divinely inspired racial justice pilgrimage. Despite a constant barrage of beatings, arrests, bombings, and death threats, he demonstrated dynamic courage, believing that God was by his side. In Montgomery, common Black folk physically removed their bodies from public transportation to confront the immoral character of racial inequality in public transit. The spiritual gravitas of the boycott cannot be overstated. King's moral authority and leadership inspired already radically minded Blacks, primarily Christians, to wage spiritual warfare – through prayer, fasting, and boycotting – against southern racism in the heart of the

---

[22] *The South: Attack on the Conscience*, TIME MAGAZINE (Monday, February 18, 1957). *Time Magazine* featured King on the cover in this edition.
[23] *Id.*

old Confederacy. King also pursued a higher virtue in the unaccomplished goal of "ending prejudice in man's mind," believing that there "[was] an element of God in every man,"[24] despite the white man's deployment of personal, communal, and state violence against Blacks to maintain a monopoly on power through racial segregation. White violence in the face of Black nonviolence stirred the conscience – even "tortured the souls" – of many white southerners, particularly prominent white clergy.[25] The boycott also galvanized support in the form of donations "from across the U.S. and from as far away as Tokyo,"[26] leading white leaders to undermine, defame, threaten, harass, abuse, and criminalize the boycott's leaders. These efforts included targeting King and countless other carpool drivers who were arrested for "speeding" and for participating in the boycott.

Threats of violence against King and his family were relentless during this period. As previously noted, King's in January 1956, just two weeks after his twenty-seventh birthday, assassins bombed his home with dynamite, nearly killing Coretta Scott King, his daughter Yolanda King, and a neighbor. After that, King and Ralph Abernathy, King's closest friend and a central figure in the Montgomery Bus Boycott, purchased handguns, though they were denied gun permits by the local sheriff and James E. Folsom, governor of Alabama.[27] King also requested gun permits for his bodyguards, to no avail. This did not dissuade him from taking armed self-defensive measures in his personal life despite loathing any form of violence or violent confrontation during organized protests or civil disobedience activities. According to Rev. Glen Smiley, national field secretary for the Fellowship of Reconciliation (FOR), King's place was an "arsenal," as was the "whole movement" around him.[28] Still, before long, King's position on gun ownership and armed violence shifted to a more "Gandhi-like view."[29] In February 1956, Bayard Rustin persuaded King to adopt a form of non-violent purism in all aspects of his life, leading him to dispose of his guns and those of his bodyguards. King referred to this evolved conception of fundamental nonviolence as the "regulating ideal" of Christian love, which combined Gandhian principles with the African American social gospel.[30] Indeed, his experiences in Montgomery informed his worldview about how non-violent disobedience might be used to defeat colonial rule in Africa, Asia, and America in the same way that Gandhi originated and implemented it in India.

---

[24] Id.
[25] Id.
[26] Id.
[27] Jonathan Eig, KING: A LIFE (Farrar, Straus and Giroux, 2023), 162.
[28] Smiley to John M. Swomley and Alfred Hassler, February 29, 1956, *Fellowship of Reconciliation Records, 1943–1973* (Swarthmore College Peace Collection, Swarthmore, Pa.), in Clayborne Carson, et al. (eds.), KING PAPERS, VOLUME III: BIRTH OF A NEW AGE (DECEMBER 1955–DECEMBER 1956), 2020 reprint.
[29] Id. at 20.
[30] Id. at 21.

2.2 RADICALIZING INSEPARABLE MOVEMENTS

In March 1956, while addressing a multiracial audience in Brooklyn, King argued that "Christ showed us the way, and Gandhi in India showed it could work," revealing his thinking and his philosophy's transnational and transcendental elements. This was, in fact, a manifestation of his Beloved Pan-Africanism.[31] In May 1956, King's Pan-African inclinations defied the divisive realities of Cold War politics. They were typified in an address to the NAACP Legal Defense and Education Fund in New York, where he noted, "The great struggle of the Twentieth Century has been between these exploited masses questing for freedom and the colonial powers seeking to maintain their domination."[32] King's opposition to colonialism, imperialism, neocolonialism, and their vestiges was unmistakable; he despised them because of their total repression and exploitation of the darker peoples of the world.

King often spoke on behalf of the "colored people" of the world, arguing that colonialism and imperialism projected social evil through racism or second-class citizenship. He further warned that if a more just and equitable distribution of wealth and opportunity did not occur, even America "[would] discover that the uncommitted peoples of the world [were] in the hands of a communist ideology."[33] Ultimately, his antiracism, antiwar, and antipoverty social philosophy birthed a forceful anticolonial consciousness anchored in Black American cultural distinctiveness. King believed that the Black American freedom struggle was the same as Africa and Africans seeking to free themselves from colonial rule and Apartheid. His connection between the African American, African, and Asian freedom and anticolonial struggles became more forceful and pronounced after the boycott. In *Stride Toward Freedom*, King noted:

> This determination of Negro Americans to win freedom from all forms of oppression springs from the same deep longing that motivates oppressed peoples all over the world. The rumblings of discontent in Asia and Africa are expressions of a quest for freedom and human dignity by people who have long been the victims of colonialism and imperialism. So, in a real sense, the racial crisis in America is a part of the larger world crisis.[34]

---

[31] Levitt, Jeremy I. *Beloved Pan-Africanism: Martin Luther King's Stride toward Africa, International Human Rights, and the Black International Tradition*. In: Yihdego, Z., Desta, M. G., Hailu, M. B. (eds.), ETHIOPIAN YEARBOOK OF INTERNATIONAL LAW 2019 (Springer, Cham.) https://doi.org/10.1007/978-3-030-55912-0_8. See also Smiley to John M. Swomley and Alfred Hassler, February 29, 1956, *Fellowship of Reconciliation Records, 1943–1973*, supra note 28 at 21.

[32] Martin Luther King Jr., *The Death of Evil upon the Seashore*, in Clayborne Carson, et al. (eds.), *King Papers, Volume III: Birth of a New Age* (December 1955–December 1956), 283, 286.

[33] Martin Luther King Jr. *The Montgomery Story*, Address Delivered at the Forty-seventh Annual NAACP Convention, June 27, 1956 (on file with The Martin Luther King, Jr. Research and Education Institute, Stanford University), available at https://kinginstitute.stanford.edu/king-papers/documents/montgomery-story-address-delivered-forty-seventh-annual-naacp-convention.

[34] Martin Luther King Jr., STRIDE TOWARD FREEDOM, supra note 1 at 184.

His recognition of the interwoven struggle of African Americans and oppressed people of color globally was revolutionary. As early as 1956, King openly embraced the global brotherhood espoused by the Pan-Africanism of W. E. B. Du Bois and C. L. R. James. Through his racial justice lens, he fully understood that "[p]rivileged groups never give up their privileges without strong resistance."[35] He further understood that "when oppressed people rise up against oppression, there is no stopping point short of full freedom. Realism compels us to admit that the struggle will continue until freedom is a reality for all the oppressed peoples of the world."[36]

In June 1956, King's global ministry was organically launched by applying the social gospel of Jesus "against principalities, against powers, against the rulers of the darkness of this world, against spiritual wickedness in high places."[37] This spiritual wickedness included colonialism, imperialism, violent repression, racism, and Apartheid. King began this work by providing historical context:

> They [Africans] were brought here from the soils of Africa, and unlike the Pilgrim fathers who landed at Plymouth a year later, they were brought against their [will]. For more than two hundred years Africa was raped and plundered, her native kingdoms disorganized, her people and rulers demoralized, and the whole continent inflicted with pains and burdens unparalleled by any other race in the history of the civilized world.[38]

This quotation demonstrates King's firm embrace of his African roots and kinship with continental Africans, whom he routinely referred to and considered brothers. King further developed his transnational, antiwhite supremacist gospel by challenging American foreign policy in Africa and Asia. He felt a strong sense of racial kinship with Africa and considered Asia a continent of colored people suffering from racial and economic exploitation. King saw that Africans were contesting violent and genocidal colonial regimes, including those instituted by Britain, France, Belgium, Spain, Portugal, Italy, Holland, Germany, and Denmark. These regimes had "dominated politically, exploited economically, segregated and humiliated" Africa and her people.[39] King opined that a new world order was being born, and the "old world was passing away."[40] The "rhythmic beat of the deep rumblings of discontent

---

[35] Martin Luther King Jr., *Nonviolence and Racial Justice*, CHRISTIAN CENTURY, February 6, 1957, in *King Papers, Volume IV: Symbol of the Movement* (January 1957–December 1958), 118–112. King initially submitted this article on November 26, 1956,.

[36] Id.

[37] Bible Gateway, *Ephesians* 6:12, *King James Version*, available at www.biblegateway.com/verse/en/Ephesians%206%3A12.

[38] Martin Luther King Jr., *The "New Negro" of the South: Behind the Montgomery Story*, in *King Papers Volume III: Birth of a New Age* (December 1955–December 1956), 281.

[39] Martin Luther King Jr., *Facing the Challenge of a New Age*, Address Delivered at NAACP Emancipation Rally, January 1, 1957, Atlanta, Georgia, in in Clayborne Carson, et al. (eds.), *King Papers, Volume IV: Symbol of the Movement* (January 1957–December 1958), 75.

[40] Id.

from Asia, the uprisings in Africa, the nationalistic longings of Egypt, the roaring cannons from Hungary, and the racial tensions of America," he extolled, "are all indicative of the deep and tragic midnight which encompasses our civilization."[41]

King exhibited an uncanny ability to internationalize the Black American freedom struggle and connect it with freedom movements in Africa, Asia, and beyond. For instance, in January 1957, in "A Statement to the South and the Nation" issued by the Southern Negro Leaders Conference on Transportation and Nonviolent Integration, King's authorship is unmistakable:

> Asia's successive revolts against European imperialism, Africa's present ferment for independence, Hungary's death struggle against Communism, and the determined drive of Negro Americans to become first-class citizens are inextricably bound together. They are all vital factors in determining whether twentieth-century mankind will crown its vast material gains with the achievement of liberty and justice for all or whether it will commit suicide through lack of moral fiber.[42]

King utilized intersectional analysis to create symmetry between oppressed people globally while linking the Black American freedom struggle to freedom movements abroad, but he went further. He attacked colonial and imperial systems for having "international dimensions" that fortified enslavement, racial segregation, and discrimination in the US.[43] He often reminded his audiences that the "vast majority" of the people in the world were persons of color, with the majority living in Africa and Asia, noting that, in the 1940s, nearly all of the colored people and nations of the world were being exploited by Western foreign powers.

By 1957, King firmly believed and spread the word that the yolks of colonialism and imperialism were cracking, as the colored world was "tired of being trampled over by the iron feet of oppression."[44] In his speeches and commentary, King strongly critiqued colonial powers and commended the people of Africa and Asia for breaking the chains of colonialism.[45] These sentiments and observations are consistent with the suppositions of the leading Pan-Africanists of his time. However, King's anticolonial and antiracist fervor was unique in that he employed "Black nativist" argumentation, using moral equivalency to indict America's cognitive dissonance with respect to Black Americans. For example, by challenging the administration of President Dwight D. Eisenhower to pay as much attention to Mississippi, Alabama,

---

[41] Martin Luther King Jr., *Facing the Challenge of a New Age*, Address Delivered at the First Annual Institute on Nonnviolence and Social Change, December 3, 1956, Montgomery, Alabama, in Clayborne Carson, et al. (eds.), *King Papers, Volume III: Birth of a New Age* (December 1955–December 1956), 453.

[42] *A Statement to the South and the Nation*, Issued by the Southern Negro Leaders Conference on Transportation and Nonviolent Integration (January 10–11 January 1957), Atlanta, Georgia, in *King Papers Volume IV: Symbol of the Movement* (January 1957–December 1958), 103.

[43] Martin Luther King Jr., *Facing the Challenge of a New Age*, supra note 41 at 75.

[44] Id.

[45] Id.

and Georgia as it did to communists in Hungary, King juxtaposed Eisenhower's defense of Hungarians in Austria with his bold apathy toward the violent oppression of American Negroes. King even wrote to Vice President Richard Nixon to encourage him to make a "fact-finding trip to the troubled areas of the South" to witness firsthand the racial oppression, violence, and bombings "directed against the persons and homes of Negroes" – just as Nixon demonstrated deep concern for the Hungarian people during a trip to Austria.[46] The contradictions between openly racist domestic policies, law, and human rights-oriented foreign policies troubled King. He wanted the US Government to take a "course of action that might be as effective as [its] efforts on behalf of the Hungarian refugees."[47] While one might counter King's Hungary critique with strategic, geopolitical, and national security imperatives, the truth remains that his assessment raised ethical incongruities between America's domestic and foreign policies, showcasing how the US government disadvantaged African Americans at home and privileged white people abroad.

King's belief that the colored world was "tired of being trampled over by the iron feet of oppression" was prophetic;[48] Africa today is free from physical colonization, and most nations are progressively developing. Given the elevated standing of China, India, South Korea, and Indonesia in world politics, Asia is developing at unprecedented rates. As the renowned scholar James Cone observes:

> When Martin Luther King Jr. achieved international fame as the leader of the Montgomery bus boycott in 1955–1956, no African country below the Sahara had achieved political independence from the colonial regimes in Europe. When he was assassinated in Memphis, Tennessee, twelve years later, in 1968, the great majority of African countries had gained their independence.[49]

Additionally, within twenty-five years after King's assassination, Apartheid fell, Black South Africans and Namibians ended white colonial rule, Eritreans gained independence, and all three nations became enfranchised under new democratic constitutions. Since 1968, South Africa, Nigeria, Ghana, and Egypt, among others, have become critical players in global governance.

King's prophetic analyses and activism caught the attention of various global progressives, including the radical Black Trinidadian historian and pioneering Pan-Africanist C. L. R. James, whom King met in London in March 1957 during

---

[46] King, *To Richard Nixon*, January 11, 1957 Atlanta, Georgia, in in Clayborne Carson, et al. (eds.), *King Papers, Volume IV: Symbol of the Movement* (January 1957–December 1958), 101.
[47] Id.
[48] Martin Luther King Jr., *Address to MIA Mass Meeting at Holt Street Baptist Church*, Montgomery, Alabama, November 14, 1956 (on file with The Martin Luther King, Jr. Research and Education Institute, Stanford University), available at https://kinginstitute.stanford.edu/king-papers/documents/address-mia-mass-meeting-holt-street-baptist-church.
[49] James Cone, *Martin Luther King, Jr., and the Third World*, JOURNAL OF AMERICAN HISTORY, Vol. 74 (1987), 455–467.

his sojourn to Ghana's Independence ceremony. James was impressed with the effectiveness of the Montgomery boycott and its ability to dismantle Jim Crowism nonviolently, succeeding where so many "movements led by Marxist ideologues had failed."[50] James referred to the Montgomery boycott as "one of the most astonishing events of endurance by a whole population that I have never heard of" and encouraged Black radicals and revolutionaries to embrace its historical significance.[51] It was, he believed, an example of "tremendous boldness" showcasing "the strategic grasp and the tactical inventiveness" of a movement that began before and arose concurrently with African liberation movements.[52] James directed Pan-Africanists and other progressives to study King closely and see the power of non-violent direct action as a revolutionary vehicle for change.[53] From this background, perhaps, the genius of King's non-violent approach was that radical and militant Black power movements could easily incorporate non-violent tactics, making them more flexible, and debatably, more durable than forceful activities.

When King was invited to Ghana's independence celebration by Prime Minister Kwame Nkrumah, it was not his first invitation to meet with leaders abroad. He had already been exposed to African politicians and activists from various parts of Africa, the African diaspora, and Asia. For example, Indian Prime Minister Jawaharlal Nehru and several associates and family members of Mahatma Gandhi had invited the King's to visit India in January 1956.[54] Dorothy M. Steere, a well-known Quaker and member of the American Friends Service Committee (AFSC), had delivered Nehru's invitation and many others to King.[55] Yet King prioritized his invitation from Nkrumah over all other travel, indicating his connectedness to Africa and Black liberation.[56] In King's invitation letter, Nkrumah states, "it would give me great personal pleasure if you should be able to attend …" as "a guest of the Government."[57]

Nkrumah invited many Black American leaders to Ghana, including Malcolm X, King's public rival. In the mid-1950s, while King was fraternizing with world leaders and Africa's revolutionary class, Malcolm X (El Hajj Malik el-Shabazz) was also seeking to curry favor with them. Both men understood the interrelatedness between

---

[50] *CLR James to Martin and Jessie Glaberman*, March 25, 1957 (on file with Walter P. Reuther Library of Labor and Urban Affairs, Wayne State University, Detroit, MI, Martin and Jessie Glaberman Papers [1942–1965]).
[51] *Id.*
[52] *Id.*
[53] *Id.*
[54] *To Dorothy M. Steere*, January 31, 1957, Montgomery, Alabama (on file with Douglas Steere and Dorothy Steere Papers, Haverford College, Haverford, PA, Box 65).
[55] *Id.*
[56] Bayard Rustin and Bill Sutherland organized his invitation. Sutherland was an "African American pacifist then working for Nkrumah's finance minister, K.A. Gbedemah." *Kwame Nkrumah*, in *King Papers, Volume IV, Symbol of the Movement* (January 1957–December 1958), 115.
[57] *Id.* at 112.

African decolonization and independence movements, and the Black American civil rights movement. They embraced their African identity and heritage and believed in the broader Pan-African project of connecting the diaspora to the continent. Indeed, it was Africa that would eventually bring them closer together. King's intellectual and pragmatic understanding of Africa and her relationship with the West eclipsed Malcolm X's, who did not genuinely mature in his knowledge until his spring and summer 1959 sojourn in Egypt, Lebanon, Saudi Arabia, Nigeria, Ghana, Morocco, and Algeria. Even though King rejected Malcolm X's arguably violent messaging, and Malcolm X rejected King's debatably nonforceful approach, they seemed to respect one another's dedication to racial justice and pro-Africa agendas.

Nevertheless, the organizations they represented, the Southern Christian Leadership Conference (SCLC) and the Nation of Islam, were too religiously, philosophically, and politically divided to work together. Malcolm X's anti-white, Black nationalist, and anti-Christian/pro-Islam thinking, as well as his platform of forceful self-defense, directly contradicted King's theology of Black liberation through racial unity, racial integration, and nonviolence. Moreover, King and Malcolm X engaged in stinging critiques of one another, making unity difficult. Philosophical differences predominated in their relationship between 1957 and 1960, and sporadic insults continued through 1964. During these periods, Malcolm X publicly made King out to be an Uncle Tom who sought to appease white folk and convert radical Negroes into passive ones.[58] King labeled Malcolm X and the Nation of Islam a violent hate group. However, once Malcolm X began to break away from the Nation of Islam, his outreach to King intensified. As Lewis Baldwin eloquently notes:

> Despite their many differences – religiously, philosophically, politically, and organizationally – Malcolm [X] and King, both ministers, were drawn together in a dialectic of social activism by the nourishment they shared in the Black folk tradition, by their common devotion to the liberation of the oppressed, by the ideas and convictions they shared, by the personal admiration and respect that they had for each other, and by the impelling moral, spiritual, and intellectual power they received from one another.[59]

Malcolm X began referring to King as a "spokesman and fellow leader of our people" and, from 1957 onward, regularly sent him correspondence in the form of invitations, articles, and papers.[60] Malcolm X's rationale and motivations were

---

[58] Malcolm X, MALCOLM X SPEAKS: SELECTED SPEECHES AND STATEMENTS, George Breitman eds. (New York: Merit Publishers, 1965), 4. See also Charles E. Lincoln, THE BLACK MUSLIMS IN AMERICA (WM. Beerdmans Publishing, 1994), 153–175.

[59] Lewis Baldwin, A Reassessment of the Relationship between Malcolm X and Martin Luther King, Jr., THE WESTERN JOURNAL OF BLACK STUDIES, Vol. 2, No. 2 (1989), 103.

[60] Malcolm X to King, Vol. 5 (July 21, 1960), MLKP-MBU, in King Papers (1954–1968), Howard Gotlieb Archival Research Center, Boston University, 491; Ballou to Malcolm X, Vol. 4 (February 1, 1957), MLKP-MBU, in King Papers (1954–1968), 117 (on file with Howard Gotlieb Archival Research Center, Boston University).

mixed – righteous yet provocative. He sought to introduce King to the teachings of Elijah Muhammad, provoke creative tension between them and organize Black leaders, including King, to confront American racism. Nonetheless, Malcolm X's harsh attacks on King caused the latter to rebuff his efforts, "leaving communication with [Malcolm X] to his secretary, Maude Ballou."[61]

Despite King's misgivings about Malcolm X, they had an impromptu meeting in March 1964 in Washington, D.C., during the US Senate debate on the Civil Rights Act of 1964. The meeting happened by chance in the hallway of the Senate and was brief. In an April 1964 letter to Abram Eisenman of *The Savannah Sun* in Georgia, King noted that Malcolm X "came and spoke to me, and I readily shook his hand" because "my position is that of kindness and reconciliation."[62] Given their philosophical and political differences, it was an uncomfortable embrace for both men.[63] Nonetheless, it created an open space for the two leaders to connect in person and recognize each other's humanity and dedication to Black freedom.

As Malcolm X's spiritual and philosophical position evolved, King's rejection of him foreclosed the opportunity for relational redemption. As noted, Malcolm X's Africa and Middle East trips in 1964 changed him, especially his trips to Ghana and Nigeria and his pilgrimage to Mecca, where he bonded with Muslims of every race and background. Nevertheless, as with King, racial justice in the US preoccupied his thinking, advocacy, and concerns. For example, Ku Klux Klan threats and physical assaults against King infuriated Malcolm X. On June 30, 1964, when King was facing violent threats, drive-by shootings of his cottage, and other attacks while spearheading the St. Augustine movement in Florida, Malcolm X sent him a telegram stating:

> We have been witnessing with great concern the vicious attacks of the white racists against our poor defenseless people there in St. Augustine. If the Federal Government will not send troops to your aid, just say the word and we will immediately dispatch some of our brothers there to organize self-defense units among our people, and the Ku Klux Klan will then receive a taste of its own medicine. The day of turning the other cheek to those brute beasts is over.[64]

---

[61] *Malcom X, King Encyclopedia, Biography*, May 19, 1925 to February 21, 1965 (on file with The Martin Luther King, Jr. Research and Education Institute, Stanford University), available at https://kinginstitute.stanford.edu/encyclopedia/malcolm-x.

[62] *King to Abram Eisenman*, April 3, 1964, in *Martin Luther King, Jr. Papers* (1950–1968), Martin Luther King, Jr., Center for Nonviolent Social Change, Inc., Atlanta, GA.

[63] Chapter 25: *Malcolm X* (on file with The Martin Luther King, Jr. Research and Education Institute, Stanford University), available at https://kinginstitute.stanford.edu/king-papers/publications/autobiography-martin-luther-king-jrcontents/chapter-25-malcom-x.

[64] *A Telegram from Malcom X to Dr. Martin Luther King, Jr., St. Augustine, Florida*, June 30, 1964, in *Martin Luther King Jr. Papers from 1950–1968* (on file with The Martin Luther King, Jr. Center for Nonviolent Social Change, Atlanta, GA, The King Center Archives). See also, Phil Edwards; This is the telegram MLK sent Malcolm X's wife after her husband's assassination, Vox, available at www.vox.com/2015/2/21/8078739/mlk-malcolm-x-telegrams.

2.2 Radicalizing Inseparable Movements 43

This was one of two telegrams that Malcolm X sent King expressing grave concern for the safety and security of King and other civil rights activists.[65] Malcolm X went so far as to threaten George Lincoln Rockwell, leader of the American Nazi Party, with violent retaliation if he did not refrain from harming King and other Black activists. Should they persist, he warned, they "will be met with maximum physical retaliation from those of us who are not handcuffed by the disarming philosophy of nonviolence, and who believe in asserting our right of self-defense by any means necessary."[66] While King had no interest in Malcolm X's overtures for violent assistance, the latter was genuinely shaken by white violence against King, remarking that the brutalization that King experienced in St. Augustine "hurt" him and that he wished he were there to come to King's assistance.[67]

On February 4, 1965, Malcolm X traveled to Selma, Alabama, to "witness firsthand the movement there" and offer his assistance after King was arrested and jailed.[68] However, King was displeased that Malcolm X was invited to Selma by the Student Nonviolent Coordinating Committee (SNCC) and considered his arrival an affront to his own political territory.[69] King argued:

> I couldn't block his coming, but my philosophy was so antithetical to the philosophy of Malcolm X, so diametrically opposed, that I would never have invited Malcolm X to come to Selma when we were in the midst of a nonviolent demonstration, and this says nothing about the personal respect I had for him. I disagreed with his philosophy and methods.[70]

Nonetheless, while in Selma, Malcolm X met with Coretta Scott King on February 21, 1965. He shared with her his concern for King, believing he could provide some assistance, and expressed a desire to work with him. His overtures impressed Coretta, who thought Malcolm X was sincere.[71] Malcolm X claimed that we went to Selma to help King because "if the white people realize what the alternative is, perhaps they will be more willing to hear Dr. King."[72] Irrespective of their philosophical

---

[65] Lewis Baldwin, A *Reassessment of the Relationship between Malcolm X and Martin Luther King, Jr.*, supra note 59 at 108.
[66] *Rockwell Gets Warning from Malcolm X*, THE MILITANT (February 1, 1965), 8. See also Malcolm X, MALCOLM X ON AFRO-AMERICAN HISTORY (New York, NY: Pathfinders Press, 1970), 43–44.
[67] *Id.*
[68] Lewis Baldwin, A *Reassessment of the Relationship between Malcolm X and Martin Luther King, Jr.*, supra note 59 at 109.
[69] Alvin Adams, *Malcolm X "Seemed Sincere" about Helping Cause: Mrs. King*, JET MAGAZINE (March 11, 1965), 28ff.
[70] A Transcript of Testimony in Williams vs. Wallace, unpublished document (March, 1965), 74–75 (on file with author); and David Garrow, PROTEST AT SELMA: MARTIN LUTHER KING, JR. AND THE VOTING RIGHTS ACT OF 1965 (New Haven, CT: Yale University Press, 1978), 111–112, 272 n5, and 278 n43.
[71] Coretta Scott King, MY LIFE WITH MARTIN LUTHER KING, JR. (New York, NY: Holt, Rinehart and Winston, 1969), 259–260.
[72] *Id.* at 256.

differences, King became increasingly open to meeting with Malcolm X as the latter evolved his thinking. In the fall of 1964, King shared that he looked forward to meeting with Malcolm X after the Selma movement, given the latter's commitment to transforming ghettos in the American North, which fit squarely into the SCLC's advocacy agenda.[73]

To King's great dismay, Malcolm X was assassinated in Harlem by members of the Nation of Islam just weeks after King expressed his interest in working with him. King had witnessed Malcolm X's evolution: his break from the Nation of Islam, his outreach to African leaders to unify the anticolonial and Civil Rights movements in Africa and the US, respectively, and his attempts to build a platform for all Black leaders to work together. Although King had some concerns about working with Malcolm X, he was deeply saddened by his assassination, especially given that it happened "when Malcolm X was reevaluating his own philosophical presuppositions and moving toward a greater understanding of the nonviolent movement and toward more tolerance of white people generally."[74]

But it had not simply been philosophical differences, insults, or political rivalry for the hearts and minds of Negroes that kept the two apart. It was instead a nasty cocktail of sorts. First, King believed that Malcolm X's severe and public criticism of him as an Uncle Tom and enemy of Black freedom led to several assaults against King by Blacks and others. He was stabbed, shot at, egged, defamed, threatened, and bombed. Second, Malcolm X's unwillingness to denounce violence as a liberating force, as well as his antiwhite rhetoric and antisemitic attacks on Jews, made it unwise for King to develop a relationship with him despite King's misgivings about white moderates.[75] Third, Malcolm X wanted King to recognize him as a legitimate Black leader and may have harbored some jealousy given King's exalted status among many Black Americans.[76] And finally, between 1956 and 1971 the forces of white liberal divisionism and the FBI's Counterintelligence Program (COINTELPRO) worked to discredit, divide, and neutralize Black civil rights organizations and leaders.

Yet COINTELPRO did not weaken King's resolve, and in February 1957 his tone shifted, and his public sentiments became more direct and radical. It's fair to say that

---

[73] David J. Garrow, BEARING THE CROSS: MARTIN LUTHER KING, JR., AND THE SOUTHERN CHRISTIAN LEADERSHIP CONFERENCE (New York, NY: William Morrow), 392. See also Peter Goldman, THE DEATH AND LIFE OF MALCOLM X (Champaign, IL: University of Illinois Press, 2013), 391.

[74] King, Press conference on Malcolm X's assassination, February 24, 1965, in *Martin Luther King Jr. Papers from 1950–1968* (on file with The Martin Luther King, Jr. Center for Nonviolent Social Change, Atlanta, GA, The King Center Archives).

[75] King was disillusioned by the failure of white moderates to support the civil rights movement. He argued that white moderates served as a greater "stumbling block" to racial justice than white citizens councils and the Ku Klux Klan. He believed that the former was "more devoted to order than justice and sought to delay and dictate Black freedom." Letter from Birmingham Jail (ext) by Rev. Martin Luther King, Jr., April 16, 1963.

[76] Lewis Baldwin, *A Reassessment of the Relationship Between Malcolm X and Martin Luther King, Jr.*, supra note 59 at 105.

the absurdity of Jim Crow and King's growing stature as a national leader emboldened him. In an edition published by the left-leaning weekly magazine *Christian Century* on February 6, 1957, King authored a seminal article titled "Nonviolence and Racial Justice," which exposed his radical thinking and impatience with the racial status quo. In it, he challenged "southern legislative halls" that sought to undermine, through "interposition" and "nullification," the US Supreme Court's desegregation orders in *Brown v. Board of Education* (1954),[77] and he highlighted the "radical change in the Negro's evaluation of himself."[78] He attacked what he referred to as the "modern version of the Ku Klux Klan," which wore the cloak of "respectable white citizens' councils", today's far right. He also praised the "revolutionary change" in the "Negro's conception of his own nature and destiny."[79] The article thus refers to the psycho-spiritual and cultural awakening of the masses of Blacks who refused to accept a societal position of inferiority, inequality, inequity, and injustice. It furthermore demonstrated King's keen understanding of the historical forces responsible for the enslavement, oppression, and disenfranchisement of Blacks in the US.

Notably, the article also identified Africa as the homeland of "Negroes." King addressed the inhumane way in which they were treated by whites as a "depersonalized cog in a vast plantation machine" – namely, a "thing to be used, not a person to be respected."[80] To embolden his point, he specifically referenced the US Supreme Court's wicked decision in the Dred Scott case of 1857, which, in King's words, determined that the "Negro is not a citizen of the United States; he is merely property subject to the dictates of his owner."[81] King's interpretation was spot on, as Chief Justice Roger Taney had opined that the Negroes of the African race,

> had for more than a century before been regarded as beings of an inferior order, and altogether unfit to associate with the white race, either in social or political relations; and so far inferior, that they had no rights which the white man was bound to respect; and that the negro might justly and lawfully be reduced to slavery for his benefit. He was bought and sold, and treated as an ordinary article of merchandise and traffic, whenever a profit could be made by it.[82]

In many ways, King's ministry struggled to answer the roguishly powerful question authored by Justice Taney in the *Dred Scott* decision: "The question is simply this: Can a negro whose ancestors were imported into this country, and sold as slaves, become a member of the political community formed and brought into existence by the Constitution of the United States"?[83] If there were ever a question about

---

[77] Martin Luther King Jr., *Nonviolence and Racial Justice*, supra note 35 at 188, 165–167.
[78] Id.
[79] Id.
[80] Id.
[81] Id.
[82] Dred Scott v. Sandford, 60 U.S. (19 How.) 393 (1857), available at www.loc.gov/item/usrep060393a/.
[83] Id.

the incorporation of Blacks into the American political community, the battle over slavery and racial segregation was a case in point. The *Dred Scott* decision fortified, legitimized, and normalized institutional racism nationally. *Dred Scott* was further reinforced by the Supreme Court's opinion in *Plessy v. Ferguson*, where, as King notes, "a new kind of slavery came into being" called "separate but equal" that became the "law of the land."[84]

King was acutely aware that the denial of Black citizenship under *Dred Scott* and the normalization of separate but equal throughout the land "without the slightest intention to abide by the equal" essentially plunged the "Negro into the abyss of exploitation where he experienced the bleakness of nagging injustice."[85] These are not the words of a romantic dreamer or accommodationist but rather of a racial justice leader comfortable with toppling a negative peace premised on Jim Crowism. King sought to overthrow the "uneasy peace" that forced Blacks to "wait patiently" and "submit to insult, injustice, and exploitation." He believed that true peace necessitated positive force, that is, "justice, goodwill, and brotherhood."[86] The self-respect brought about by Black exposure to urban sprawl, gainful employment, increases in literacy, and empowering religious doctrine ushered in a new era of self-esteem, motivation, and pride, undermining the "south's negative peace," which King believed the "white man refused to accept."[87] Prophetically, as if he were addressing Americans in the early twenty-first century rather than the mid-twentieth century, King posited that "race relations today can be explained in part by this revolutionary change in the Negro's evaluation of himself and his determination to struggle and sacrifice."[88] To use an aphorism incorrectly credited to Mark Twain, "history doesn't repeat itself but it often rhymes." With Trumpism, far-right politics, and white supremacy dominating the US, we might be at another inflection point.

King celebrated Black optimism and was prepared to fight against "every form of oppression," not unlike the peoples of Africa and Asia seeking to shed the yolk of colonial rule.[89] King's ability to examine the race problem in America through a transnational, geopolitical lens was profound, and he firmly believed that when oppressed people rose change was inevitable. He also maintained that the goal was to free all oppressed people from the jaws of white supremacy, a core tenet of Pan-Africanism and point on which he and Malcolm X had aligned. The liberation and unification of persons of African descent globally and the liberation of oppressed persons in Asia and Latin America fit well within the epistemological world in which King lived. His fervent activism opposing the Vietnam War is a case in point. King's human rights-oriented ministry was not rooted in race or politics *per se* but

---

[84] Martin Luther King Jr., *Nonviolence and Racial Justice*, supra note 35 at 119.
[85] *Id.*
[86] *Id.*
[87] *Id.*
[88] *Id.*
[89] *Id.*

2.2 Radicalizing Inseparable Movements

instead entrenched in the idea of racial justice: defeating racism, tyranny, and the allied systems they produce.

Unlike most Pan-Africanists who converted to various forms of political or religious atheism, King directly challenged those in power – mainly white Christians – to "obey the eternal demands of the Almighty God" or "capitulate to the transitory demands of the defenders of segregation."[90] To do the latter, he argued, would be to abort the "fashioning [of] a truly Christian nation."[91] In King's orbit, America couldn't be a Christian nation and simultaneously accept systemic and institutional racial tyranny as the norm. His message was clear, and his appeals to outside law unmistakable: Obey the human rights-oriented social Gospel of Jesus by normalizing racial equity, equality, and justice for all Americans or continue to embrace the social evil that undermines Christian values and any pretense of American democracy. He encouraged Black Americans to assert their rights rather than submit to incremental freedoms. King thus noted that Blacks needed to be forceful and, referring to white people, concluded:

> It is both historically and sociologically true that privileged classes do not give up their privileges voluntarily. And they do not give them up without strong resistance. And all of the gains that have been made, that we have received in the area of civil rights, have come about because the Negro stood up courageously for these rights, and he was willing to aggressively press on.[92]

Looking within and beyond the US, King saw an interconnected system of oppression: white supremacy masquerading as colonialism, imperialism, Jim Crowism, and Apartheid. To King, white on Black oppression was the same anywhere and everywhere. Montgomery had radicalized and globalized King. As Chapter 3 will show, his calls for assertive action against Jim Crowism, together with his radically developing perspective on Africa and her problems, were so strong that, by the end of 1957, he had joined ACOA, a New York-based interracial group devoted to the financial and moral support of defiance campaigns inside South Africa and anticolonial crusades throughout Africa.

The US government feared King's growing popularity and influence domestically and internationally and increased its surveillance of him and other Black leaders beginning in the mid-1950s. King's radical consciousness and growing influence after the Montgomery Bus Boycott alarmed the administrations of Dwight D. Eisenhower (1953–1961), John F. Kennedy (1961–1963), and Lydon B. Johnson (1963–1969), which collectively sanctioned US government covert action intended to disrupt, dismantle, and destroy him and other Black leaders and organizations.

---

[90] Martin Luther King Jr., *For All…A Non-Segregated Society, A Message for Race Relations Sunday*, February 10, 1957, in Clayborne Carson, et al. (eds.), *King Papers, Volume IV: Symbol of the Movement* (January 1957–December 1958), 125.

[91] *Id.*

[92] *Interview by Richard D. Heffner for "The Open Mind,"* in Clayborne Carson, et al. (eds.), *King Papers, Volume IV: Symbol of the Movement* (January 1957–December 1958), 126.

The Federal Bureau of Investigation (FBI) began monitoring King in 1955 and engaged in robust covert operations against him after the Montgomery movement until he died in 1968.[93] Said actions were authorized at the highest levels of government, including, for example, by Attorney General Robert Kennedy, a so-called liberal progressive and friend to the Negro. Kennedy authorized the FBI to surveil and disrupt King's ability to unify with other civil rights and human rights workers and organizations by discrediting him with false allegations and injecting misinformation and dissention, essentially seeking to dismantle the civil rights movement in the US and, thus, its ability to support freedom movements in Africa and elsewhere.

The FBI, under director J. Edgar Hoover, particularly feared King's growing radical consciousness and his influence on radical elements domestically and internationally. This was precisely why Hoover established the "Racial Matters Program," which targeted "individuals and organizations involved with racial politics,"[94] as well as the COINTELPRO to target King and other supposed "Black Nationalist-Hate Groups" that allegedly threatened national security. The FBI's monitoring of King during the Montgomery Bus Boycott – wiretapping his home and workplace – continued until his assassination.

On February 18, 1957, King's prominence reached a zenith after *Time* magazine, one of America's most respected and learned magazines, published an article about him and his efforts to dismantle Jim Crow. The article was appropriately titled "The South: Attack on the Conscience" and referred to King as a "scholarly, 28-year-old Negro Baptist minister … who in little more than a year has risen from nowhere to become one of the nation's remarkable leaders of men."[95] The article acknowledged King's appeal to "influential white clergy" and highlighted, in King's words, his evolving social psychology on race: "I was ready to resent all the white race," he shared.[96] But, he continued, "as I got to see more of white people, my resentment was softened, and a spirit of cooperation took its place. But I never felt like a spectator in the racial problem. I wanted to be involved in the very heart of it."[97]

King's passion and willingness to put himself in harm's way and combat Jim Crowism distinguished him from most activists whose "freedom ministries" procrastinated. In many ways, King's desire to serve people and communities derived from his youthful desires to be a firefighter, a doctor, and a lawyer. Such yearnings

---

[93] See generally, Kenneth O'Reilly, *Racial Matters: The FBI's Secret File on Black American, 1960–1972*, FREE PRESS, COLLIER MACMILAN, NEW YORK, LONDON (1989). See also *Federal Bureau of Investigation (FBI), Biography*, March 16, 1909 (on file with The Martin Luther King, Jr. Research and Education Institute, Stanford University), available at https://kinginstitute.stanford.edu/encyclopedia/federal-bureau-investigation-fbi.

[94] *Federal Bureau of Investigation (FBI), Biography*, March 16, 1909 (on file with The Martin Luther King, Jr. Research and Education Institute, Stanford University), available at https://kinginstitute.stanford.edu/encyclopedia/federal-bureau-investigation-fbi.

[95] TIME MAGAZINE, *The South: Attack on the Conscience*, February 18, 1957, supra note 22.

[96] *Id.*

[97] *Id.*

gave King a public service core that blossomed into a human rights-oriented social consciousness that coalesced into concrete activism to uproot anti-Black racism and its social, cultural, and legal norms and doctrine in the US and abroad. Ultimately, King sought to break down the legal and social barriers that oppressed Black people by advancing a new way of thinking about liberty. He continued to apply pressure for equal rights in the US even as he pledged his support for Africa's freedom movements. King did not believe that other peoples and nations under domination, such as the Congo, could be free if America's race problem was not addressed. As Chapter 3 shows in detail, he could not see the fight against colonists in Africa and segregationists in the US as separable.

3

Africa Embraces King, 1957–1960

FIGURE 3.1 1957: Martin Luther King Jr. and Rev. Ambrose Reeves, Anglican Bishop of Johannesburg and opponent of segregation in South Africa, hold a press conference. (Photo by Nick Peterson/NY Daily News Archive via Getty Images.)

3.1 AFRICA ON MY MIND

Immediately following the Montgomery Bus Boycott (December 20, 1956), King's popularity grew considerably. He became a global icon, particularly to leaders in new and emerging African, Asian, Caribbean, and Latin American states (Figure 3.1). This is evidenced by the numerous requests, communications, and invitations that he received to speak, attend national independence celebrations and other observances as well as pleas for financial and political assistance. For example, as noted in Chapter 2, Kwame Nkrumah, Ghana's Prime Minister, invited King to attend the country's Independence Day celebrations, signaling its transition from Britain's Gold Coast to a newly minted nation. Nkrumah's January 22, 1957, invitation to King confirmed his legitimacy as an institutional leader.¹ King's March 1957 trip to Ghana was his first visit to the continent. King and Coretta Scott King were accompanied by, among others, many of the Black diaspora's most progressive leadership, including Prime Minister Norman W. Manley of Jamaica; Ralph Bunche, African American political scientist, civil rights leader, diplomat, UN official, and Nobel Peace Prize winner; Adam Clayton Powell, famous African American Baptist pastor, and US Congressman; Lester B Grange, executive secretary of the National Urban League; A. Philip Randolph, famed African American labor unionist and organizer of the Brotherhood of Sleeping Car Porters; and Roy Wilkins, executive director of the National Association for the Advancement of Colored People (NAACP) (1955–1977) and one of the American civil rights movement's senior statesmen.

King was elated to receive Nkrumah's invitation and equated it to a "fraternal greeting to the Negro people of Montgomery whose tenacious struggle and sacrifices had won the admiration of all freedom-loving people."² King was mindful of Ghana's struggle against British colonization and the close ancestral bonds between Blacks in America and the Gold Coast, given that "a very large number of us trace our ancestry to that part of Africa" (referring to West Africa and Ghana specifically).³ He was also acutely aware that, while Ghanaians were realizing their freedom and independence as a people and nation, Black American rights were being violently repressed by the evils of de jure racial segregation with its disenfranchising effects in all areas of life and well-being. Hence, King took great "interest and pride" in Ghana's independence and viewed it as a victory for the "world-wide movement of colonial peoples toward the dawn of our freedom."⁴ Inspired by Ghana's liberation, King considered the fight for equal rights and justice in the US as part of the "great democratic upsurge" across the Black world, and he was confident that Black Americans would defeat Jim Crowism in his lifetime.⁵

The Kings were impressed with Ghana's public infrastructure. They observed that its streets were beautiful and its hotels "modern and luxurious," and that the racist propaganda about Africa being "primitive and dirty" was false – a genuine white lie.⁶ Notwithstanding, as Lewis Baldwin noted, the Kings were "deeply disturbed" and even heartbroken by what they perceived as Ghana's servant-based culture, or

---

¹ To King, *From Kwame Nkrumah* (January 22, 1957), in Clayborne Carson et al. (eds.), *King Papers, Volume IV: Symbol of the Movement* (January 1957–December 1958), 112–113.
² Martin Luther King Jr., *A Statement Regarding the Invitation from Prime Minister Kwame Nkrumah* (unpublished document) (March 1957) MLKP-MBU, in *Martin Luther King, Jr. Papers, 1954–1968* (on file with Howard Gotlieb Archival Research Center, Boston University), 1.
³ Id.
⁴ Id.
⁵ Id.
⁶ Coretta Scott King, MY LIFE WITH MARTIN LUTHER KING, JR. (New York, NY: Henry Holy & Company, 1992), 164.

"servile attitude."[7] However, they attributed the attitude to colonialism rather than assuming that it was informed by any obsequiousness inherent in the culture.[8]

During this period, Nkrumah was arguably Africa's foremost Pan-African statesman, and Ghana was Africa's beacon of liberation and freedom. Except for Ethiopia and Liberia, which have dissimilar colonial episodes Ghana was Africa's first state to achieve independence during the modern era of decolonization. Hence, Nkrumah's recognition of and invitation to King legitimates the view that King was, at a minimum, recognized as a kindred soul among principal Pan-African leaders and debatably a member of the "Pan-African club." Nkrumah's invitation also shed light on his understanding of the critical role that Black Americans could play in Africa's development. As a graduate of Lincoln University, one of America's preeminent historically Black universities, Nkrumah was trained and mentored by African American professors along with a cohort of the young Black intelligentsia, including former Nigerian President Nnamdi Azikiwe and the Black literary giant Langston Hughes.

King was famous among Africa's radical leaders, and his admirers reached out to him for the same reason that Hoover's FBI sought to destroy him: They believed that "he could become a 'messiah' who could unify black nationalists [and Pan-Africanists]" and influence US foreign policy.[9] From the mid-1950s onward, African leaders acknowledged King's Pan-African consciousness, supported the Black struggle in the US, and appealed to him for backing. For example, Nkrumah respected King and believed he was well-informed about Africa's challenges. Tom Mboya, a founding father of Kenya and one of Africa's most prominent educators, politicians, and Pan-African thinkers, shared with King that "the Negro struggle is universal and to us indivisible" from Africa's anticolonial and antiracist movements.[10] His words attested to the Pan-African spirit and legitimacy that King enjoyed with the continent's most forward-thinking leadership.[11] Similarly, in November 1957, Oliver Tambo, South Africa's revered freedom fighter and Secretary-General of the African National Congress (ANC), wrote to King requesting his support for the "upcoming international day of protest against apartheid" given "South Africa's continuous

---

[7] Lewis V. Baldwin. TOWARD THE BELOVED COMMUNITY: MARTIN LUTHER KING, JR., AND SOUTH AFRICA (Cleveland, OH: Pilgrim Press, 1995), 168–169.

[8] Coretta Scott King, MY LIFE WITH MARTIN LUTHER KING, JR., supra note 6 at 164. See also, Lewis V. Baldwin, TOWARD THE BELOVED COMMUNITY, supra note 7 at 168–169.

[9] Id. Referring to the SCLC, Hoover instructed FBI filed agents to "prevent the rise of the 'messiah' who could unify, and electrify, the militant black nationalist group." See also, *The National Security Agency and the Fourth Amendment Rights: Hearing before the Select Committee to Study Governmental Operations with Respect to Intelligence Activities of the United States*, 94th Congress (October 29 and November 6, 1975), 24–25. See also, *Alleged Assassination Plots Involving Foreign Leaders: An Interim Report of the Select Committee to Study Governmental Operations with Respect to Intelligence Activities* (November 18 and 20, 1975).

[10] *A telegram from Tom Mboya to Martin Luther King, Jr., care of A.G. Gaston Auditorium*, Birmingham, Ala. (September 24, 1962), MLKP, MBU (on file with Howard Gotlieb Archival Research Center, Boston University, Martin Luther King, Jr., Papers, 1954–1968), 54–68.

[11] Id.

violation of the Declaration of Human Rights."[12] King was also communicating with Adelaide Tambo, Oliver Tambo's wife, who hosted him in London in May 1962 and sought his support to help alleviate the institutional and physical violence against women who were "opposed to social discrimination."[13] Adelaide Tambo specifically requested that King "give material help" to the African Woman's League and use his influence to raise other funds to help her organization support "deported and banned Mothers" and "also to look after the children" of persecuted mothers and fleeing families being targeted by the South African government.[14]

In March 1960, King was even invited to be a delegate to a conference in Accra, Ghana, to develop nonviolent strategies to combat European atomic bomb testing in Africa, particularly in the Sahara.[15] King openly opposed the development, testing, and use of nuclear weapons, stating:

> I definitely feel that the development and use of nuclear weapons of war should be banned. It cannot be disputed that a full-scale nuclear war would be utterly catastrophic. Hundreds and millions of people would be killed outright by the blast and heat, and by the ionizing radiation produced at the instant of the explosion.[16]

A month earlier, in a sermon titled "Loving Your Enemies," King had also addressed what he referred to as our "atomic civilization," referring to atomic energy, nuclear energy, and racism, calling for listeners to embrace a "great fellowship of love and bow down at the feet of Jesus."[17]

These events and communications join many others and evidence King's global *bona fides* among Africa's revolutionary class.[18] King was a stalwart anti-Apartheid activist who combined and synthesized his antiracism, anticolonial, and antiwar philosophy with African liberation.[19] He recognized the importance, dynamic synergy and interdependent destiny of African Americans and continental Africans, opining, "I have no doubt that the question of the relationship of the American

---

[12] *Letter from Oliver Tambo to Rev. Martin Luther King* (Nov. 18, 1957), in Clayborne Carson et al. (eds.), *King Papers, Volume IV: Symbol of the Movement* (January 1957–December 1958), 325.

[13] *Letter from Adelaide Tambo to Dr. Martin Luther King, Jr., African National Congress of South Africa Women's League* (May 5, 1962) (loose document on file with author).

[14] *Id.*

[15] *Western Union Telegram from Government of Ghana to Martin Luther King, Jr. Southern Leadership Conference*, March 14, 1960 (loose document on file with author).

[16] Martin Luther King Jr., *Advice for Living*, EBONY, 120, December 1957 (on file with The Martin Luther King, Jr. Research and Education Institute, Stanford University), available at https://kinginstitute.stanford.edu/king-papers/documents/advice-living.

[17] Martin Luther King Jr., *Loving Your Enemies*, Sermon delivered at the Dexter Avenue Baptist Church, Montgomery, Alabama (November 17, 1957) (on file with The Martin Luther King, Jr. Research and Education Institute, Stanford University), available at https://kinginstitute.stanford.edu/king-papers/documents/loving-your-enemies-sermon-delivered-dexter-avenue-baptist-church.

[18] *Letter from Oliver Tambo to Rev. Martin Luther King*, supra note 12.

[19] See generally Lewis V. Baldwin, TO MAKE THE WOUNDED WHOLE: THE CULTURAL LEGACY OF MARTIN LUTHER KING JR. (Minneapolis: Fortress Press, 1992).

Negro to Africa is one of great importance. I am convinced that we have a moral as well as a practical responsibility to keep the civil rights movement in America close to our African brothers."[20] His Pan-African leanings were apparent. King understood that Africans and Black Americans were fighting against the same social and global forces.

King was in great demand because he was far more than a dreamer. Africa's revolutionary leadership admired and respected King because his love for and commitment to Africa was profound and radical, not circumspect. Perhaps the best description of him in this context involves his defense of Jesus: King argued that Jesus was not merely a "utopian dreamer" and "impractical idealist"; rather, his command to "love thine enemy" was "an absolute necessity for the survival of our civilization."[21] King embraced Jesus's command and reasoned how difficult it was to love one's enemies – especially in the domestic struggle for racial justice and the international struggle between the US and the Soviet Union during the Cold War – contending that the first step in loving thine enemy was internal reflection.[22]

King received and responded to hundreds of letters weekly from every part of the US, Africa, Europe, and the Caribbean. Writing for *Sepia Magazine*, Alfred Duckett perhaps best captured this demand:

> All over the nation Martin Luther King is in demand for personal appearances before NAACP chapters, Urban League locals, church meetings, civic mass rallies, seminars, national conventions of services groups, Greek letter societies and award-proffering luncheons and dinners. The Prime Minster of India and the leader of the new black Republic of Ghana extended him invitations to visit their countries. Former U.S. ambassador to India Chester Bowles, Mrs. Eleanor Roosevelt and labor chieftain A. Phillip Randolph have organized a fund to send him to visit foreign countries where he will be on display as a symbol of the true restlessness and health of American democracy – for Martin King has come to represent the very essence of American democracy – the meaning of the spirit of democracy – that it is a perfect ideal, imperfectly practiced but capable of growth.[23]

Requests from African students seeking financial assistance to study in the US accounted for a large percentage of the requests. They asked for everything from college tuition and books to American pen pals. Moreover, students, activists, scholars,

---

[20] A Letter from Martin Luther King, Jr. to Theodore E. Brown (April 1, 1963) (on file with Center for Non-Violent Social Change, The King Center, The Archives of the Martin Luther King, Jr., loose document on file with author).
[21] Id.
[22] Id.
[23] Alfred Duckett, article for Sepia Magazine, *New Negro in the South: The Martin Luther King Story* (on file with Howard Gotlieb Archival Research Center, Boston University, Martin Luther King, Jr. Collection, SPE-127, bulk: Box 25 Folder 1, March 22, 1957).

and politicians regularly sent him information about their organizations and the world at large and dedicated drawings and poems to him. For instance, in July 1956, Mabel Dove Danquah, a leading women's rights activist, journalist, creative writer, and politician of the "Gold Coast,"[24] dedicated the following poem, titled *Golden As Our Land*, to the freedom-loving "noble band" of "warriors" of the Montgomery Bus Boycott:

> It's wonderous strange
> That this our Race
> Which bore the brunt
> Of man's brutality to man
> Has come unscathed to be a light
> To generations yet unborn.
>
> Its wonderous strange
> That scars and wounds
> From alien hands
> Have left no stains
> To soil our hands
> In hatred of our brother man
>
> Its wonderous strange
> In spite of great vicissitudes
> And sojourn into foreign lands
> We still remain the child of cheer
> The hope of the depressed and joyless million on the earth
>
> Its wonderous strange
> That in this arm of ebony
> This darkened form of night
> There lurks a heart
> As golden as on land
> And full of love,
> Embracing all humanity.[25]

King inspired Danquah's poem (and many others) and, in turn, was inspired by her. One cannot overestimate the enthusiasm for freedom that King engendered in people around the world. Admirers sent him works of fiction and nonfiction, inspiring notes, and suggestions for solving America's race problem. Remarkably, King could rouse people at the national and global levels and establish connectivity between streams of consciousness that unified activists in Africa and the US.

---

[24] Mabel Dove Danquah was the first female member of the Legislative Assembly of the Gold Coast (1954).

[25] *Mabel Dove to Martin Luther King, Jr.* (on file with Howard Gotlieb Archival Research Center, Boston University, Martin Luther King, Jr. Collection, SPE-127, bulk: Box 25 Folder 1, March 22, 1957).

Indeed, King's granular appeal to America through storytelling was an influential part of his appeal. In his "Letter from a Birmingham Jail," for example, King captured the profound sense of urgency facing Black people, writing:

> When you take a cross county drive and find it necessary to sleep night after night in the uncomfortable corners of your automobile because no motel will accept you; when you are humiliated day in and day out by nagging signs reading "white" and "colored"; when your first name becomes "nigger," your middle name becomes "boy" (however old you are) and your last name becomes "John," and your wife and mother are never given the respected title "Mrs."; when you are harried by day and haunted by night by the fact that you are a Negro, living constantly at tiptoe stance, never quite knowing what to expect next, and are plagued with inner fears and outer resentments; when you are forever fighting a denigrating sense of "nobodiness" – then you will understand why we find it difficult to wait. There comes a time when the cup of endurance runs over, and men are no longer willing to be plunged into the abyss of despair. I hope, sirs, you can understand our legitimate and unavoidable impatience.[26]

His authentic description of Negro life was soul-piercing and undeniable, and it was this emphasis on collective humanity that made him so influential among his African contemporaries.

3.2 ORGANIZING DOMESTICALLY AND GLOBALLY

On December 23, 1956, King's home was attacked by shotgun fire.[27] Two days later, on December 25, 1956, Fred Shuttlesworth of Birmingham's church house was bombed.[28] And only a few days into the New Year, on January 3, 1957, a cross was found burning at the church and home of C. K. Steele of Tallahassee.[29] Shortly after, on January 10–11, 1957, King, Shuttlesworth, and Steele called an emergency conference of Negro leaders around the country. The conference, titled the Southern Negro Leaders Conference on Transportation and Non-Violent Integration, aimed to dismantle racial segregation in the American South, specifically targeting transportation systems. They also sought to develop a "unified strategy" to confront the dreaded willful minority of white Southerners "dedicated to violence" in the form of

---

[26] Martin Luther King Jr., LETTER FROM BIRMINGHAM JAIL (London: Penguin Classics, 2018).
[27] *Shotgun Fired into King Home* (December 23, 1956) (on file with The Martin Luther King, Jr. Research and Education Institute, Stanford University), available at https://kinginstitute.stanford.edu/shotgun-fired-king-home.
[28] *Bombing of Fred Shuttlesworth's House beside Bethel Baptist Church on 29th Avenue North in Birmingham, Alabama*, Birmingham News (December 25, 1956) (on file with the Alabama Department of Archives and History, Alabama Media Group Collection, available at https://digital.archives.alabama.gov/digital/collection/amg/id/195666.
[29] Byron Dobson, *Tallahassee Civil Rights Icon Rev. C.K. Steele Gets Section of Orange Avenue Renamed in His Honor*, TALLAHASSEE DEMOCRAT, January 18, 2019, available at www.tallahassee.com/story/news/2019/01/18/late-civil-rights-hero-rev-c-k-steele-gets-roadway-named-his-honor/2600413002/.

3.2 Organizing Domestically and Globally

"threats, shootings, cross burning and bombing."[30] Bayard Rustin provided the intellectual template for the conference structure, based on seven papers he produced with the help of New York City-based activists Ella Baker and Stanley Levison. The seven papers revolved around the following themes: (1) Dealing with violence directed toward the Negro communities; (2) The role of law in the struggle; (3) A unified strategy in the campaign for integrated buses; (4) Economic sharing; (5) Dedication to nonviolence; (6) The relation of registration and voting to all efforts for justice. The conference manifesto was bold in that it asserted that "the treatment of Negroes is a basic spiritual problem ... and that far too many white Southerners have stood silently by."[31] The proposal simultaneously called on Black Americans "to seek justice and reject all injustice" through nonviolent means.[32] The meeting occurred at Ebenezer Baptist Church in Atlanta, Georgia, and laid the political foundation for establishing the Southern Christian Leadership Conference (SCLC).

On January 11, 1957, in a letter to US President Dwight D. Eisenhower, the conference requested federal intervention to stop deadly violence against Blacks seeking to vote. On behalf of the sixty leaders that attended, King and reverends C. K. Steele, F. L. Shuttlesworth, and T. J. Jemison appealed to Eisenhower to stop the violent displacement of Blacks from their land and homes, as well as the constant threats, violent attacks, stoning, cross burnings, and bombings of Black homes and churches. Though unsuccessful, they appealed to Eisenhower to visit the South and make a significant speech encouraging Southerners to abide by the Supreme Court's desegregation decisions. King and the other leaders wanted Eisenhower to help end the "state of terror" and "anarchy" in the South by showing white Southerners the "moral nature of the problem faced at home and abroad by the unsolved civil rights issues and the violent disorder that will arise again and again until these issues are resolved."[33]

Then, on February 10, 1957, King gave an interview with Richard Heffner, producer of the NBC Sunday television program "The Open Mind," in which he highlighted the connections he saw between Black migration, self-respect, civil disobedience, the Supreme Court's 1954 *Brown v. Board of Education*, and transnational Black freedom:

> I think [*Brown*] had tremendous impact and influence on the Negro and bringing about this new self-respect. I think it certainly is one of the major factors, not the

---

[30] *Montgomery Improvement Association Press Release, Bus Protesters Call Southern Negro Leaders Conference on Transportation and Nonviolent Integration* (January 7, 1957) (on file with The Martin Luther King, Jr. Research and Education Institute, Stanford University), available at https://kinginstitute.stanford.edu/king-papers/documents/montgomery-improvement-association-press-release-bus-protesters-call-southern.

[31] Id.

[32] Id.

[33] To Richard Nixon (January 11, 1957), in Clayborne Carson et al. (eds.), *King Papers, Volume IV: Symbol of the Movement* (January 1957–December 1958), 126.

only – I think several other forces, and historical circumstances must be brought into the picture. The fact that circumstances made it necessary for the Negro to travel more, so that his rural, plantation background was gradually supplanted by a more urban, industrial life ... illiteracy was gradually passing ways ... and with the growth of the cultural life of the Negro, that brought about new self-respect. And economic growth, and also the tremendous impact of the world situation, with people all over the world seeking freedom from colonial powers and imperialism, these things all came together, and then with the decision of May 17, 1954, we gained the culminating point.[34]

In this interview, King masterfully connected the evolution of the cultural awakening of Blacks with freedom movements in Africa and beyond, given that, in his mind, colonialism, imperialism, and Jim Crowism were branches of the same tree. He further suggested, though without elaboration, that they had a symbiotic relationship. King's diverse leadership approaches and advocacy became even more apparent as he leveraged the SCLC to engage in local, state, national, and international issues.

On February 14, 1957, just four days after the NBC interview, King was elected President of the SCLC by its Executive Board of Directors. The SCLC was dedicated to nonviolent direct action in the pursuit of racial justice and organizing local groups in the South to confront the realities of racial segregation. It helped organize, advise, align, and coordinate with other organizations, essentially serving as an umbrella body and brain trust preoccupied with arming local groups in, among other things, the doctrine, methods, and tactics of nonviolent direct action. Arguably, the SCLC was the brainchild of Bayard Rustin, who explored how to build upon the successes of the Montgomery Bus Boycott throughout the South through a series of writings. In doing so, he suggested creating a umbrella organization to support local groups fighting Jim Crowism. The scope of the SCLC's activities evolved over time, and with King at the helm, expanded to include poverty and racial discrimination in the North and Africa's decolonization struggles.

At the time, President Lyndon B. Johnson and his National Security Council staff were sorely "concerned over the prospect of an imminent Negro leadership conference to set up an organization to influence US policy on Africa."[35] Johnson, who was viewed by many as liberal on civil rights issues, feared King and Black America's growing influence in foreign affairs. Since Johnson believed that he was

---

[34] Richard D. Heffner, *Interview with Martin Luther King Jr. and Julius Waties*, The Open Mind (February 10, 1957).
[35] *Memorandum From Robert W. Komer and Ulric Haynes of the National Security Council Staff to the President's Special Assistant for National Security Affairs (Bundy)*, March 30, 1965 (on file with the Office of the Historian, Foreign Relations of the United States, [1964–1968], Volume XXIV, Africa). See also, Johnson Library, National Security File, Country File, Africa, General, Vol. II, Memos & Miscellaneous, 7/64–6/65. Secret. A copy was sent to Clifford L. Alexander, Jr., Associate Special Counsel to the President.

working hard to "make the American Negro fully a part of American society," he didn't "think it at all a good idea to encourage a separate Negro view of foreign policy," despite recognizing "the American Negro Community's 'natural interest' in African affairs."[36] Of course, the American government has always been wary of Black America's special relationship with Africa. The Johnson administration did not want Black Americans to consider Africa a "special province"; he wanted them to be "interested in the totality of U.S. policy as Americans,"[37] and thus to ignore over 200 years of Black American foreign relations with other nations and peoples nestled in a complex history of struggle against enslavement, slavery, and racial segregation.[38]

Ulric Haynes, Johnson's Senior NSC Director on Africa, recommended to Robert Komer, Deputy National Security Advisor, that they interfere and "eliminate the *raison d'être*" for creating a "permanent organization" that would project Black American influence on US foreign policy towards Africa.[39] Not only did the Johnson administration try to disrupt the establishment of a private organization led by Blacks for this purpose, it was committed to steering any such organization "toward a non-racial outcome, i.e., it should include whites as well as Negroes."[40] By "whites," they of course meant white men, believing that their inclusion could drive out any radical machinations that might expose racialized contradictions in US policy on Africa, including US support of Apartheid in South Africa. These policies notwithstanding, US government efforts to stifle King and other Black leaders failed.

For his part, King believed that Black clergy and other leaders had "no moral choice, before God, but to delve deeper into the struggle – and to do so with greater reliance on non-violence and with greater unity, coordination, sharing and Christian understanding."[41] King resigned as minister of the Dexter Avenue Baptist Church in November 1959 to dedicate his efforts to the work of the SCLC and other like-minded organizations (including the American Committee on Africa [ACOA], which is discussed more substantively in a subsequent section). The SCLC served as his conduit for fighting Jim Crowism, while the ACOA was his means for confronting anti-Black racism, colonization, and Apartheid. King's battlefield was domestic and global – two inseparable war campaigns to liberate persons of African descent. Outside of his institutional relationships, King was heavily engaged in African affairs, and his activities and literary works, particularly *Stride*

---

[36] *Id.*
[37] *Id.*
[38] See generally, Elliott P. Skinner, AFRICAN AMERICANS AND U.S. POLICY TOWARD AFRICA, 1850–1924: IN DEFENSE OF BLACK NATIONALITY (Washington, DC: Howard University Press, 1992).
[39] *Memorandum From Robert W. Komer and Ulric Haynes of the National Security Council Staff to the President's Special Assistant for National Security Affairs (Bundy)*, supra note 35.
[40] *Id.*
[41] *Montgomery Improvement Association Press Release, Bus Protesters Call Southern Negro Leaders Conference on Transportation and Nonviolent Integration*, supra note 30.

Toward Freedom, were popular among African leaders, including Albert Luthuli, the president of South Africa's African Nation Congress.[42] From the invitations they extended to the pieces they read, African leaders were attracted to the power of nonviolent confrontation and the accompanying toolbox of strategies that were employed against America's white supremacist institutions and law.

3.3 BIRTH OF NEW NATIONHOOD: THE INTERNATIONAL LIBERATION OF BLACK PEOPLES

The year 1957 was a pivotal year in King's evolution as a Pan-African thinker. On April 7, 1957, before he resigned from the Dexter Avenue Baptist Church, Dr. King delivered one of his most radically insightful and edifying speeches, "The Birth of a New Nation," to his congregants in Montgomery, Alabama.[43] The sermon, oriented toward African independence, was presented shortly after his return from Ghana for the Independence Day celebrations on March 4, 1957.[44] It provides a window into King's African-centered consciousness. It fortified the theoretical framework that rooted his *Beloved Pan-Africanism*, which will be discussed in more detail in the following chapters.

"The Birth of a New Nation" was a tour de force in Black liberation discourse, drawing theoretical propositions from history, law, political science, sociology, and theology. King demonstrated mastery of the history of the Trans-Atlantic Slave Trade as well as the rapacious effects of enslavement, colonialism, and racial discrimination on all persons of African descent. His speech offered bold critiques of colonial oppression in Ghana, which was unique for Black American Christian leaders during this period. King argued:

> From 1850 to 1957, March sixth, the Gold Coast [now Ghana] was a colony of the British Empire. And as a colony she suffered all of the injustices, all of the exploitation, all of the humiliation that comes as a result of colonialism. But like all slavery, like all domination, like all exploitation, it came to the point that the people got tired of it.[45]

King understood that enslavement and colonialism led to various forms of protest, including civil war, rebellion, insurrection, protest, boycotts, domestic legal claims (e.g., the *Dred Scott* suit), and claims to outside law, including international human rights law, internal self-determination norms, and self-defense claims and actions

---

[42] From G. McLeod Bryan (October 10, 1959), in Clayborne Carson et al. (eds.), *King Papers, Volume V: Threshold of a New Decade* (January 1959–December 1960), 307.

[43] Martin Luther King Jr., *The Birth of a New Nation*, Sermon Delivered at Dexter Avenue Baptist Church (April 7, 1957), in Clayborne Carson et al. (eds.), *King Papers, Volume IV: Symbol of the Movement* (January 1957–December 1958), 156.

[44] King returned from Ghana by way of Nigeria, where he claims to have "stopped for a day or so," but the author has found no further information about the stop.

[45] Martin Luther King Jr., *The Birth of a New Nation*, supra note 43.

guaranteed under international law.[46] Said claims were informed by and/or incorporated lines of reasoning from African customary law and the African natural law rights-based traditions. One example is the prohibition against insults because "customary law rigorously discourages any conduct, whether by word or deed, that is likely to lead to a disturbance of the peace of the community" owing to "the overriding importance of the maintenance of social equilibrium in African society."[47] King challenged the morality and legality of the colonial encounter and drew inspiration and strategic direction from Black Ghana's nonviolent approaches against British colonialists. Ghana's path reconfirmed – and fortified – the utility of his use of nonviolent direct action to end Jim Crowsim in the American South.[48]

In "Birth of a New Nation," King evolved his thinking about freedom and justice. Studies of his speech need to be more represented in scholarly literature. His bold analyses crystallized his global vision, empathy for human suffering, and dedication to Africa and persons of African descent oppressed by the three evils of racism, poverty, and militarism, as well as their horrid consequences. King recounts "weeping" when Nkrumah addressed Ghanaians during independence celebrations, which may be the only time he explicitly acknowledged joyfully sobbing during the entirety of the civil rights era. I liken King's emotional state in Ghana to the reaction of millions of African Americans when Senator Barack H. Obama was elected the 44th president of the US on November 4, 2008. Nkrumah's empowering address to a polo stadium filled with people desperate for freedom and independence profoundly moved King. As the following statement indicates, King did not distinguish between Black Americans and Africans or Ghanaians, with whom he directly and unequivocally identified. He declared, opening by repeating a phrase of Nkrumah:

> "We are no longer a British colony, we are a free, sovereign people," all over that vast throng of people we could see tears. And I stood there thinking about so many things. Before I knew it, I started weeping. I was crying for joy. And I knew about all of the struggles, and all of the pain, and all of the agony that these people had gone through for this moment.[49]

---

[46] *We Charge Genocide: The Historic Petition to the United Nations for Relief from a Crime of the United States Government against the Negro People*, New York, [publisher not identified] (1951). In Henry J. Richardson III, THE ORIGINS OF AFRICAN AMERICAN INTERESTS IN INTERNATIONAL LAW (Durham, NC: Carolina Academic Press, 2008).

[47] T. Olawale Elias. Insult as an Offence in African Customary Law. AFRICAN AFFAIRS, Vol. 53, No. 210 (1954), 66. JSTOR, www.jstor.org/stable/718728. See also Taslim Olawale Elias. THE NATURE OF AFRICAN CUSTOMARY LAW (Manchester: Manchester University Press, 1956), Muna Ndulo, African Customary Law, Customs, and Women's Right, INDIANA JOURNAL OF GLOBAL LEGAL STUDIES, Vol. 18, No. 1 (Winter 2011), 88–89. http://scholarship.law.cornell.edu/facpub/187, and Oba Abdulmumini (2011). The Future of Customary Law in Africa, in J. Fenrich, P. Galizzi, & T. Higgins (eds.), THE FUTURE OF CUSTOMARY LAW IN AFRICA (Cambridge: Cambridge University Press, 2011), 58–80.

[48] Martin Luther King Jr., *The Birth of a New Nation*, supra note 43.

[49] Martin Luther King Jr., *The Birth of a New Nation*, supra note 43 at 160.

King's use of the first-person pronoun "we" is significant, as he used it to signify racial unity and the shared freedom experience of the Black race. King wept because he empathized with the plight of Ghanaians, and Ghana showed King what Black freedom might feel like in the US. Thus, while feeling the same sense of jubilation shared by Ghanaians, King painfully understood that African Americans had yet to reach the freedom threshold.

This stirring reality fueled his support of Africa and his growing understanding of the vital roles that Black Americans could play in Africa's development. In 1957, four years before President John F. Kennedy established the US Agency for International Development, "King did what so many Pan-Africanists before him had done" – he called for African Americans to return to Africa to assist in its development, arguing:[50]

> Right now is the time that American Negroes can lend their technical assistance to a growing new nation. I was very happy to see already, people who have moved in and making good. The son of the late president of Bennett College, Dr. Jones, is there, who started an insurance company and making good, going to the top. A doctor [Dr. Robert Lee] from Brooklyn, New York, had just come in that week and his wife [Dr. Sara Lee] is also a dentist, and they are living there now, going in there and working, and the people love them.[51]

King's pronouncement was consistent with the recovery and reclamation ideas of John Henry Clarke's description of Pan-Africanism: "'Pan' movements are not new in the world. These movements existed long before the use of the preface 'Pan' was a part of a group's organizational name. Any movement by an ethnic group to recover and reclaim their history, culture, and national identity, after slavery, war, or migration, forced or otherwise, can be called a 'Pan' movement."[52] Indeed, a recurring theme in King's thinking was his merging of the histories of Blacks in Ghana and America as intertwined and interdependent. He recognized their common heritage and history and argued and advocated for African American emigration to Ghana – an idea inspired by those who had done so years before the arrival of W. E. B. Du Bois. Dr. Robert Lee and his wife Sara (the first Black dentists in the country) and David Jones (son of David Dallas Jones, president of Bennett College,

---

[50] Jeremy I. Levitt, *Beyond Borders: Martin Luther King, Jr., Africa and Pan-Africanism*, TEMPLE JOURNAL OF INTERNATIONAL AND COMPARATIVE LAW, Vol. 31, No. 1 (Spring 2017), 315. Although Pan-Africanism has ancient roots, in the modern era, Henry Sylvester Williams organized the first Pan-African Congress in London in 1900.

[51] Martin Luther King Jr., *The Birth of a New Nation*, supra note 43 at 161. See also King, *Birth of a New Nation*, 57, n. 10 ("David Dallas Jones was president of Bennett College from 1926 to 1956. His son David established the Ghana Insurance Company in Accra.").

[52] John Henrik Clarke, Pan-Africanism: A Brief History of an Idea in the African World, PRÉSENCE AFRICAINE, Nouvelle série, No. 145 (1er TRIMESTRE 1988), 26. See also, Jeremy Levitt, Pan-Africanism, ENCYCLOPEDIA OF GLOBALIZATION, Vol. 3, N to T (Routledge, 2007), available at SSRN: https://ssrn.com/abstract=2221627.

3.3 Birth of New Nationhood

and founder of the Ghana Insurance Company) are among Black America's earliest arrivals to Ghana.[53]

In July 2007 and July 2008, I had the honor and pleasure of interviewing Dr. Robert Lee twice about Dr. King's 1957 visit to Ghana. He was gracious, generous, wise, and insightful – a pragmatic Pan-Africanist elder and one of the earliest Black Americans to officially become legally and culturally Ghanaian. The Lees first traveled to Ghana in 1953 and emigrated there in 1956. Known as Black America's elder statesman and an unofficial African American Ambassador to Ghana, Lee became a naturalized Ghanaian citizen in 1963 and lived in Ghana until his death on July 5, 2010. King and Lee met in Accra, and the former relied on Lee to navigate Ghana's political and cultural landscape. As an advocate of Black American emigration to Africa, King assured African Americans that President Nkrumah welcomed them, claiming, "Nkrumah made it very clear to me that he would welcome any persons coming there as immigrants and to live there."[54] Nkrumah and King's communication on this issue was, in fact, extraordinary: a Pan-African sorbet of sorts. Nkrumah respected and trusted King enough to personally "anoint" him to serve as a conduit of Pan-African engagement with Ghana, and perhaps more importantly, he recognized King's credentials as an emerging Pan-African leader. By age twenty-nine, King possessed the political savvy, intellect, consciousness, and courage to encourage African Americans to meaningfully contribute to Ghana's development, arguably situating him into the radical Pan-African tradition of Du Bois and Marcus Mosiah Garvey.

King embraced Pan-African ideals throughout his global human rights ministry, as evidenced by speeches such as "Birth of a New Nation" (1957),[55] "Let My People Go" (1965),[56] and "Honoring Du Bois" (1968, which, coincidentally, was one of King's last major speeches before his assassination).[57] These ideals also suffused his stalwart advocacy for African freedom. African American Pan-Africanist pioneers such as Dr. Robert Lee significantly influenced these Pan-African inclinations. In Ghana, for example, Lee organized a dinner with King, Bill Sutherland, and fellow Pan-Africanist Julius Nyerere, who in 1960 became Tanzania's first Prime Minister

---

[53] Upon his and Sara's arrival in Ghana, only one expatriate dentist (Lebanese) was in the country. Subsequently, many Black American emigrants to Ghana fled after Nkrumah was overthrown in 1966. Per Dr. Lee, who was a classmate of Nkrumah's at Lincoln University, Lee himself "received King in Ghana and tended to him when he fell ill." In a July 2007 interview in Accra, Dr. Lee shared with author that during his visit to Ghana, King stayed at Achimota School and became "ill or very frustrated" when he realized his access to Nkrumah was limited given the large number of visiting dignitaries.
[54] Martin Luther King Jr., *The Birth of a New Nation*, supra note 43 at 161.
[55] Martin Luther King Jr., *The Birth of a New Nation*, supra note 43 at 156.
[56] Martin Luther King Jr., *Let My People Go*, Address at the Southern Africa Benefit of the American Committee on Africa, Hunter Coll., N.Y.C. (Dec. 10, 1965) (on file with author)
[57] Martin Luther King Jr., *Honoring Dr. DuBois*, Address at Carnegie Hall, N.Y.C. (Feb. 23, 1968), pmeaye.tripod.com/kingondubois.pdf. The occasion was the International Cultural Evening sponsored by *Freedom Ways Magazine* on the 100th birthday of Dr. W. E. B. DuBois.

and one of the great Pan-African leaders of the decolonization era. King encircled himself with leading pan-African thinkers and leaders such as these, and through these interactions (between 1956 and his death in 1968), he infused his civil rights ministry with Africanized human rights precepts that crystallized his thinking and messaging. As King stated in his "Birth of a New Nation" sermon:

> Ghana has something to say to us. It says to us first, that the oppressor never voluntarily gives freedom to the oppressed. You have to work for it. And if Nkrumah and the people of the Gold Coast had not stood up persistently, revolting against the system, it would still be a colony of the British Empire. Freedom is never given to anybody. For the oppressor has you in domination because he plans to keep you there, and he never voluntarily gives it up. And that is where the strong resistance comes.

As noted in Chapter 2, he concludes, privileged classes never give up their privileges without strong resistance.[58]

King led his Alabamian audience beyond the "Dark Continent" myth and described Africa – through the lens of Ghana – as a revolutionary marketplace pregnant with freedom and opportunity. He didn't romanticize Africa like many Pan-Africanists who never pilgrimed to the continent; instead, he wove together the historiographies and modern veracities of Black subjugation in Ghana and the US into nesting dualities or interdependent emulations: colonial rule alongside de jure segregation, and decolonization beside desegregation. In "Birth of a New Nation," King reminds us that "if there had not been an Nkrumah and his followers in Ghana, Ghana would still be a British colony. If there had not been abolitionists in America both Negro and white, we might still stand today in the dungeons of slavery."[59] He considered colonization and segregation as twin evils necessitating revolt. However, King perceived Ghana's pathway to liberation as a "beautiful thing" because it achieved independence nonviolently:[60]

> Here is a nation that is now free, and it is free without rising up with arms and with ammunition. It is free through nonviolent means. Because of that the British Empire will not have the bitterness for Ghana that she has for China, so to speak. Because of that when the British Empire leaves Ghana, she leaves with a different attitude than she would have left with if she had been driven out by armies. We've got to revolt in such a way that after revolt is over we can live with people as their brothers and their sisters. Our aim must never be to defeat them or humiliate them.[61]

King's observation is noteworthy and consistent with his theory that social evil comprises three parts – poverty, racism, and militarism – which re-confirms and

---

[58] Martin Luther King Jr., *The Birth of a New Nation*, supra note 43 at 162.
[59] Id.
[60] Id.
[61] Id.

personifies his reinterpretation of Pan-Africanism, or Beloved Pan-Africanism. Beloved Pan-Africanism is anchored in love, global Blackness, radical nonviolent resistance, empathy, grave personal sacrifice, and divine justice. These forward-leaning principles helped Ghana shed the yolk of colonialism while peacefully allowing it to coexist with Britain.

King strengthened his point about Ghanaian independence with Black Baptist storytelling about what he witnessed during Ghana's Independence Day celebration dinner: "On the night of the State Ball ... Prime Minister Kwame Nkrumah was there dancing with the Duchess of Kent. And I said, 'Isn't this something? Here it is the once-serf, the once-slave, now dancing with the lord on an equal plane. And that is done because there is no bitterness.'"[62] Ostentatious language aside, King's observation was spot-on. However, he may have underestimated the extent of the bitterness derived from the over 300 years of colonial oppression that lay beneath Ghana's Independence Day pleasantries. After all, following Holland's brutal enslavement and colonization of the Gold Coast, Britain viciously took possession of it, murdered its traditional leaders, dismantled and corrupted its conventional authority structures, exploited its natural resources, and violently relegated Ghanaians to servitude.

Yet inspired by Ghana's example, King believed that the "aftermath of nonviolence is the creation of the beloved community," accompanied by redemption and "reconciliation, not its nemesis, violence, which only breeds emptiness and bitterness."[63] He called on African Americans to "fight passionately and unrelenting for the goals of justice and peace" with clean hands.[64] Love, he argued in "Birth of a New Nation," was the most potent weapon, and he wanted Blacks to radically employ nonviolent direct action against oppression, arguing that "if we wait for it to work itself out, it will never be worked out! Freedom only comes through persistent revolt, through persistent agitation, through persistently rising up against the system of evil."[65] These are revolutionary claims, not the rhetoric of a passive dreamer. King warned that integrated buses were "just the beginning" and that Blacks must persistently push for change or risk being placed in "the dungeons of segregation and discrimination for another hundred years ... where our children's children will suffer all of the bondage we have lived under for years."[66] King's radical phraseology was premeditated: freedom, justice, peace, agitation, and revolt – all included recourse to outside law and principles enshrined in international human rights law to encourage Black humanity and resistance against all forms of racial oppression.

King seemed to believe that Ghanaian independence was a marker that the forces of racism, poverty, and war were falling to the divine order of freedom, justice, and

---

[62] *Id.*
[63] *Id.*
[64] *Id.*
[65] *Id.* at 161.
[66] *Id.* at 162.

equality. King's faith in Black freedom was first and foremost tied to his faith in divine justice, which DuBois's sometimes secular intellect did not embrace. King believed that racial oppression, poverty, and militarism were rooted in universal patterns of white domination, which is why, by the age of twenty-nine, he began to expand his global ministry to confront the three evils at home and abroad. This view was undoubtedly exemplified in his famous claim that "injustice anywhere is a threat to justice everywhere."[67]

It was, perhaps, inevitable that King's radical Black consciousness would lead him to Ghana four years before W. E. B. DuBois immigrated to the newly independent West African nation in 1961. His visits to Kwame Nkrumah's Ghana, like his visit to Nnamdi Azikiwe's Nigeria in 1960 (discussed below), substantially impacted his Pan-African awareness and his understanding of the interplay between international relations, racial justice, international human rights, and civil rights (affixed in domestic law). His 1957 sojourn to Ghana brought world affairs closer to King – it internationalized him and provided the scholar–activist with comparative insights not attainable in classrooms and boardrooms. Ghana was King's first major trip abroad. It served as a gateway to other nations as he "trekked across West Africa, stopping over in Monrovia, Dakar, and Kano, and he crisscrossed Western Europe, exploring Lisbon, London, Paris, Rome, and Geneva."[68] In 1959, King made a pilgrimage to the land of Gandhi at the request of India's Prime Minister Jawaharlal Nehru.[69] India had a transformative impact on King in that his understanding of and commitment to nonviolence deepened greatly. Before returning to the US from India, King made stops in Karachi, Beirut, Jerusalem, and Cairo. His "overseas travels allowed him to participate in major global events, provided him respite from the day-to-day toils of the Southern struggle, and gave him the ability to forge stronger transnational ties with other liberation movements."[70] King read profusely about foreign affairs, and the exposure from these trips dramatically enhanced his knowledge base.

While King was raised in a home with a formidable African American history library, Lewis Baldwin rightly notes that "by the early 1960s, King had accumulated many books on 'Africa' and was collecting news on the subject from the *Pittsburgh*

---

[67] Martin Luther King Jr., *Remarks Delivered at Africa Freedom Dinner at Atlanta University* (May 13, 1959), in Clayborne Carson et al. (eds.), *King Papers, Volume V: Threshold of a New Decade* (January 1959–December 1960), 203 (on file with The Martin Luther King Jr. Research and Education Institute, Stanford University), available at https://kinginstitute.stanford.edu/king-papers/documents/remarks-delivered-africa-freedom-dinner-atlanta-university.

[68] Timothy H. Lovelace, *Martin, Ghana, and Global Legal Studies*, INDIANA JOURNAL OF GLOBAL LEGAL STUDIES, Vol. 25, No. 2 (2018), 624.

[69] Martin Luther King, Jr., *My Trip to the Land of Gandhi*, in Clayborne Carson et al, (eds.), *Volume V: Threshold of a New Decade* (January 1959–December 1960), 231, 231. Martin Luther King Jr., *Chronology*, in Clayborne Carson et al. (eds.), *King Papers, Volume V: Threshold of a New Decade* (January 1959–December 1960), 231, 47.

[70] Timothy H. Lovelace, *Martin, Ghana, and Global Legal Studies*, supra note 68. See also, Martin Luther King, Jr., My Trip to the Land of Gandhi, in Clayborne Carson et al. (eds.), *King Papers, Volume V: Threshold of a New Decade* (January 1959–December 1960), 231.

Courier, The New York Age, The New York Herald Tribune, and several African newspapers and journals,"[71] including local publications such as Ghana's *The Voice on Africa*. Moreover, King maintained an expansive network of friends and associates in Africa, particularly in Ghana, India, Kenya, Nigeria, and South Africa, keeping him abreast of the continent's issues.

3.4 THE AMERICAN COMMITTEE ON AFRICA

The American Committee on Africa had been founded in 1953. However, as King's influence grew apace with his involvement in African affairs, he felt inspired to engage with the organization upon his return from Ghana. On June 24, 1957, John Gunther, Honorary Chairman of the ACOA, invited King to join its National Committee, which he did on July 8, 1957.[72] Cofounded by George Houser, the ACOA's central aim was to advocate for an "American policy toward Africa designed to help the African peoples achieve national independence, justice and equality."[73] The ACOA was an anticolonial and antiracist, globally centered organization dedicated to "supporting African liberation struggles and informing the American public about African issues."[74] Based in New York, the organization was interracial and nonpartisan. It operated on the belief that US security and world peace would be significantly enhanced by a more enlightened US foreign policy toward Africa, mainly related to Apartheid South Africa and African demands for decolonization.[75]

From the outset, the ACOA was established with radical zeal and cooperated with various groups that opposed Apartheid in South Africa. The ACOA grew out of the Americans for South African Resistance Movement championed by civil rights activists such as George Houser, Bayard Rustin, and Bill Sutherland. The group lobbied the US government and the UN, met with African leaders inside and outside the US, crafted policy positions, and issued reports primarily focused on independence and liberation activities. Finally, the ACOA encouraged African leaders to take nonviolent approaches to independence and democratization. Fundraising that supported freedom movements, liberation-minded institutions such as churches, and African students studying in the US eventually led Houser to create the Africa Defense and Aid Fund within the ACOA.

Despite encouraging nonviolent decolonization approaches, the ACOA was pragmatic. It supported the National Liberation Front of Algeria, which engaged in bloody

---

[71] Lewis V. Baldwin, TO MAKE THE WOUNDED WHOLE, supra note 19 at 163.
[72] *John Gunter to Rev. Martin Luther King, Jr.* (June 24, 1957) (on file with Howard Gotlieb Archival Research Center, Boston University, Martin Luther King, Jr. Collection, Box 83, Folder 3, [loose document on file with author]).
[73] *Id.*
[74] American Committee on Africa (ACOA), *Biography* (on file with The Martin Luther King Jr. Research and Education Institute, Stanford University), available at https://kinginstitute.stanford.edu/encyclopedia/american-committee-africa-acoa.
[75] *Id.*

guerilla warfare against French colonization. It later backed the African National Congress, which included a military wing, *Umkhonto we Sizwe* (Spear of the Nation), led by former South African president Nelson Mandela. Primarily, the ACOA aimed to sway US policy and global actors and inform the public about Africa's anticolonial freedom struggles without endorsing violent tactics and solutions. For his part, King openly supported the anticolonial movement in Algeria, which was violent and revolutionary, even signing a 1959 petition that advocated for a local Algerian "referendum to determine Algeria's future."[76] He never spoke publicly about Algeria's violent pathway toward freedom, however, leading one to conclude that King understood that, in some cases, there was no peaceful pathway to freedom and independence.

King's decision to join the ACOA was based on his sincere interest and dedication to Africa and her people, as well as his belief in the moral responsibility of Black Americans to assist Africa and positively shape US policy toward her. The ACOA provided him with a platform, information portal, and structure to conduct his liberation agenda systematically and institutionally. King's attitude toward US policy in Africa was sensible and in line with his moral philosophy of racial justice and nonviolence, prominently articulated in the ACOA's campaign against Apartheid, for which he was vice-chair. This stance led to the 1957 "Declaration of Conscience Against Apartheid."[77]

The ACOA's leaders chose December 10, 1957, as the Universal Day of Protest against South Africa's racist policies, which coincided with Human Rights Day. The Declaration brought global attention to the racist and oppressive South African regime, which instituted Apartheid "into the economic, educational, religious and other areas of life" in South Africa, resulting in "countless indignities inflicted on millions of South African people."[78] These horrid mortifications included murder, rape, forcible displacement, false imprisonment, land grabs, exploitative taxation, low wages, dilapidated housing, marginalization of traditional leaders and law, and racial segregation and persecution with the goal "to prepare Africans for a subservient role in a white man's society."[79] The Declaration argued through the lens of international human rights law to address racial discrimination, equality before the law, the right of citizens to return to their country, freedom of opinion and expression, and the right of self-determination. Four hundred and fifty world leaders were asked to support the Declaration of Conscience, and by September 9, 1957, sixty

---

[76] *Id.*

[77] International Sponsoring Committee, *Declaration of Conscience on South Africa and Day of Protest* (December 10, 1957) (TLS, 1 p., on file with Martin Luther King, Jr. Papers, Morehouse Coll., Atlanta, Ga., Doc. No. 57210-000).

[78] *Declaration of Conscience: An Appeal to South Africa*, Day of Protest, Human Rights Day, supra note 78. See also *Minutes of the Executive Board Meeting of the American Committee on Africa*, September 9, 1957 (on file with African Activist Archive, PETER WEISS PAPERS, Michigan State University Libraries Special Collection), available at https://projects.kora.matrix.msu.edu/files/210-849-24904/PWACOAEB9-9-570pt.pdf.

[79] *Declaration of Conscience: An Appeal to South Africa*, supra note 78.

leaders had accepted the invitation. This support propelled the ACOA's nationwide campaign for the Declaration as well as global opposition to the racist policies of the Government of the Union of South Africa (the Apartheid government).[80] Ultimately, 123 leaders from thirty-eight nations signed the "Declaration of Conscience Against Apartheid," aimed at opposing colonial and racist rule in Africa. King was one of them, and his open support of the Declaration undoubtedly influenced other leaders.

The ACOA's success was partly due to King's willingness to serve on its various boards and committees. King was acutely aware of how his influence would shine a spotlight on the nefarious conduct of colonial regimes, including Germany's and the Union of South Africa's roles in committing genocide against and oppressing the people of Southwest Africa (today Namibia), particularly the Herero and Nama people.[81] South West Africa was subject to a League of Nations mandate but under the care, custodianship, and control of Apartheid South Africa, which was supposed to promote the inhabitants' material, moral, and social well-being. The South African government governed it as a fifth province of South Africa, boasting a white minority (12%) that predominated over Black Africans (85%, inclusive of Ovambos, Hereros, Namas, and Bushmen) and "Coloreds" (3% mixed-race people). Instead of promoting the inhabitants' well-being, however, South Africa persecuted the people of South West Africa – an international territory – and attempted to annex it in the wake of World War II. Through the ACOA's activities, including a publication titled *Southwest* [sic] *Africa: The UN's Stepchild*, King, who wrote the introduction and contributed to its content, challenged the UN's mishandling of South West Africa and South Africa's "nightmarish" and "tragic" expression of "man's inhumanity to man" propagated by the "regime of oppression and segregation."[82] As with racial segregation in the US and South Africa, King also opposed the South African government's racial oppression of Blacks in South West Africa and its various indignities, including travel passes.

The ACOA kept King engaged in the significant issues impacting Africa, and his burgeoning African network placed him in constant contact with Africa's most progressive leadership. His critique of European colonization and its impact on Africa was global. He argued, for example, that it was "impossible for Angola to stand in Africa and not be affected by what [was] happening in Nigeria, Kenya, and Rhodesia."[83] In response to his dismay with South Africa's Apartheid and Portugal's

---

[80] *Minutes of the Executive Board Meeting of the American Committee on Africa*, supra note 79.
[81] *Germany officially recognizes colonial-era Namibia genocide*, BBC, May 28, 2021, available at www.bbc.com/news/world-europe-57279008.
[82] Martin Luther King Jr., *Introduction to Southwest Africa: The UN's Stepchild*, October 1, 1959 to October 31, 1959 (on file with The Martin Luther King, Jr. Research and Education Institute, Stanford University), available at https://kinginstitute.stanford.edu/king-papers/documents/introduction-southwest-africa-uns-stepchild.
[83] Martin Luther King Jr., *To Deolinda Rodrigues* (July 21, 1959), in Clayborne Carson et al. (eds.), *King Papers, Volume V: Threshold of a New Decade* (January 1959–December 1960), 250 (on file with The Martin Luther King, Jr. Research and Education Institute, Stanford University), available at https://kinginstitute.stanford.edu/king-papers/documents/deolinda-rodrigues-0.

violently repressive policies in Angola, King decided to serve as Honorary Chairman of the ACOA's 1960 Africa Freedom Day celebration aimed at raising funds for the Africa Defense and Aid Fund.[84] King turned a blind eye while knowingly raising funds used to support militarized liberation movements in Southern and Central Africa. While King firmly believed in the power of nonviolence and employed nonviolent direct action during America's civil rights movement, he nonetheless felt duty-bound to support forceful freedom movements in other nations. His activism during the time even extended into the area of nuclear nonproliferation, and he was often asked to condemn colonial powers for atom bomb testing in Africa's Sahara.[85] In King's mind, freedom also meant liberation from the colonizers' weapons of mass destruction.

3.5 RETURN TO AFRICA

The year 1960 was challenging for King. Africa was calling, but to his chagrin, King could not fully embrace her triumphs. Although the Government of Ghana invited the Kings (including Coretta) to return to Ghana in April 1960 to witness the Inauguration of the Republic of Ghana through the adoption of its constitution, for example, other travel commitments prevented him from going.[86] In addition, the Government of Cameroon invited King and Reverend Edler Hawkins of New York to "attend the festivals of our Independence Day on January 1st, 1960,"[87] even volunteering to pay for King's travel expenses. The Cameroonians wanted King to preach and visit churches in Yaounde during their Independence Day celebrations. In his invitation letter to King, F. Akoa, Secretary General of l'E. P. C. [*Église Presbytérienne Camerounaise*], shared that "the era of inequality of humanity has come to an end, the Black-White Adjustment time has come, and it is a new

---

[84] *Letter from Donald Harrington to Martin Luther King, Jr. on Africa Freedom Day*, The Martin Luther King, Jr. Collection (on file with Howard Gotlieb Archival Research Center, Boston University, Box 83, Folder 3, February 16, 1960). See also, *Response Letter from Martin Luther King, Jr. (Mrs. Maude L.W. Ballou Secretary to Martin Luther King, Jr.) to Donald Harrington on Africa Freedom Day* (on file with Howard Gotlieb Archival Research Center, Boston University, Box 83, Folder 3, February 16, 1960).

[85] Positive Action Conference, Ghana (March 14, 1960) (on file with Howard Gotlieb Archival Research Center, Boston University, Martin Luther King, Jr. Collection, SPE-127, Box 70, Folder 3; see also Ministry of Foreign Affairs, Ghana, *Telegram to Martin Luther King, Jr. Inviting Participation in Conference on Nonviolent Positive Action* (March 14, 1960) (on file with author).

[86] *Invitation from the Government of Ghana to Rev. & Mrs. Martin Luther King* (on file with Howard Gotlieb Archival Research Center, Boston University, The Martin Luther King, Jr. Collection, Box 70, Folder 3, Envelop, Ghana, January 14, 1960). See also *A Letter from K.A. Gbedemah to Martin Luther King*, Jr (on file with Howard Gotlieb Archival Research Center. Boston University, The Martin Luther King, Jr. Collection, Box 70, Folder 3, Ghana, April 23, 1960).

[87] *Government of Cameroon Invitation to Martin Luther King – (October 31, 1959)* (on file with Howard Gotlieb Archival Research Center, Boston University, The Martin Luther King, Jr. Collection, Box 70, Folder 3, XVIII. French Cameroon [Akoa]).

Philosophy as well as a new Theology of these days, and Dr. Martin Luther King, Jr is the apostle and the champion of it."[88]

While Akoa's comments demonstrate the significant influence King had on the thinking and approaches of African independence leadership, King had to decline the invitation. "I know nothing that would delight me more than the opportunity of being a part of this great experience," he expressed, but "long-standing previous commitments" in the US "make it impossible for me to accept this invitation."[89] The American civil rights movement was boiling, and King was deeply engaged in what he referred to as fighting "a great struggle for freedom and human dignity," including "several protest rallies around the first of the year which I feel obligated to attend and guide."[90] It was unusual for King to respond to such invitations with total personal transparency, even indicating his deep regret for not being able to attend. He understood the historical importance of Cameroonian independence and how his attendance as a representative of African Americans among 102 state representatives would have been monumental.[91] Still, given his interest in and support of African independence movements, King hoped that the Government of Cameroon would invite him to visit later to explore "creative possibilities" with his people.[92]

In November 1960, however, King managed to take a trip to the inauguration of Nnamdi Azikiwe as Nigeria's first Indigenous Governor General. In a letter dated October 26, 1960, addressed to "My dear Reverend King," Governor General designate Nnamdi Azikiwe of Nigeria himself invited King to the inauguration celebration.[93] Marguerite Cartwright, the sociologist, Africanist, and famed African American *Pittsburgh Courier* columnist, helped organize the invitation. She wrote to King in October 1960 and reminded him of her role in assisting his sojourn to India in 1959, stating: "It seems to me that while one government wants to honor you, it is ironic that our own government permits you to go to jail."[94] Unfortunately, although King visited Nigeria between November 14 and 18, 1960, very little is known about the trip; however, King's evolution as an Africanist continued during his time there. When King arrived in Lagos, he commented:

> As I got off the plan in Africa, I thought of the fact that there are 27 independent countries in Africa. Within less than three years, more than 18 countries have

---

[88] *Id.*
[89] *Martin Luther King to the Government of Cameroon Invitation to* – (December 10, 1959), (on file with Howard Gotlieb Archival Research Center, Boston University, The Martin Luther King, Jr. Collection, Box 70, Folder 3, XVIII. French Cameroon [Akoa]).
[90] *Id.*
[91] *Government of Cameroon Invitation to Martin Luther King* – (October 31, 1959), supra note 87.
[92] *Id.*
[93] *From Nnamdi Azikwe*, October 26, 1960, Lagos, Nigeria, in Clayborne Carson et al. (eds.), *King Papers, Volume V: Threshold of a New Decade* (January 1959–December 1960), 533–534 (on file with The Martin Luther King, Jr. Research and Education Institute, Stanford University), available at https://kinginstitute.stanford.edu/king-papers/documents/nnamdi-azikiwe.
[94] Jason Miller, *Langston Hughes and Martin Luther King, Jr.*, SOUTH ATLANTIC REVIEW, Spring 2018, Vol. 83, No. 1, Special Issue: The Global Hughes, 24.

received their independence in Africa. They are looking over here. The wind of change is blowing all about, all throughout the age. They want to know what we are doing about democracy and they are making it clear that racism and colonialism must go.[95]

King recognized the importance of Nigeria to decolonization movements throughout Africa. He contended that Britain's power over Africa was waning and that the freedom of 40 million Nigerians evidenced its weakening grip on the continent. He noted that in 1930, only three countries (Liberia, Ethiopia, and South Africa) in Africa were independent. By 1962, however, he predicted that "there may be as many as thirty independent nations in Africa" – circumstances, he suggested, that have "influenced the thinking of Negroes."[96] King noted that, at the time, freedom was contagious and that Black Americans were encouraged by events in Africa. These positive influences emboldened his understanding that the fight for "human dignity is not an isolated event."[97] He believed that the independence of African states like Nigeria triggered a reset in African Americans, a boost in racial pride from the "color of his skin or the texture of his hair" to a "growing self-respect" and "determination to struggle and sacrifice until first-class citizenship" was achieved.[98]

Nevertheless, this was not King's first trip to Nigeria, the Kings traveled to Kano, Nigeria, in 1957 on a return flight from Accra, Ghana, and sojourned to Lagos in 1960 and attended various events, including luncheons, traditional dance performances, and private meetings. The 1957 trip to Kano seems to have given the Kings a bird's-eye view of rural Africa and African customary law and structures. Unfortunately, because the archival record of his Nigerian travel is lacking and scholars have largely failed to unearth documentation, King's Nigeria trips may be one of the most essential untold travel tales in African American history.[99] Notwithstanding, we know, for example, that in November 1960, he traveled to Lagos, Nigeria, on the same flight as Langston Hughes, who attended Lincoln University with Nnamdi Azikiwe – whom they were there to celebrate – as well as Kwame Nkrumah.

While his trip to Ghana was a form of awakening, the Kings' visit to Kano, Nigeria was bittersweet. In her seminal book, *My Life with Martin Luther King, Jr.*, Coretta Scott King discussed the "appalling poverty" the Kings observed in Kano, which

---

[95] Martin Luther King Jr., *Speech at a Rally*, Savannah, Georgia (on file with Howard Gotlieb Archival Research Center, Boston University, Martin Luther King, Jr. Collection, January 1, 1962, p. 6).
[96] Martin Luther King Jr., *Rising Tide*, a speech to the National Urban League (on file with Howard Gotlieb Archival Research Center, Boston University, Martin Luther King, Jr. Collection, September 6, 1960, 1ff).
[97] Id.
[98] Martin Luther King Jr., *Rising Tide of Racial Consciousness*, Address at the Golden Anniversary Conference of the National Urban League (September 6, 1960), New York, NY, *King Papers, Vol. IV: Threshold of a Decade* (January 1959–December 1960), 499.
[99] Jason Miller, *Langston Hughes and Martin Luther King*, Jr., supra note 94 at 22–41.

they believed "exceeded" the "worst state of Negroes in America."[100] The living conditions in Nigeria took them aback. King blamed Great Britain for its "exploitation of Africans," but at the same time, took great pride in Nigerians throwing off the yolk of their oppressors.[101] The Kings' trip to Nigeria ultimately reinforced King's belief that anti-Black racism and poverty were global evils that had to be defeated.

Indeed, the more King engaged the world outside of America, particularly Africa, the more unrelenting he became about equality in the US. In November 1960, King commented: "Now more than ever before America is challenged to bring her noble dream into reality. The shape of the world today does not permit America the luxury of exploiting the Negro and other minority groups. The price that America must pay for the continued oppression of the Negro is the price of its own destruction."[102] These are not the revelations of a passive idealist. Even a cursory glance at race relations in America in the 21st century makes one wonder whether King was right.

Racial segregation and its toolbox of discriminatory tricks even concerned the leadership of the United Nations, headquartered in New York. Soviet Premier Nikita Khrushchev, for example, was mainly concerned with the impact of racial segregation and racial discrimination on African and Asian representatives of the organization. In a 1960 speech to the United Nations General Assembly, Khrushchev commented: "Practice shows ... that the United States restricts and infringes upon the rights of the representatives of various States. There have been cases, for instance, where the representatives of young African and Asian States have been subjected to racial discrimination in the United States and even to attacks by thugs."[103] In a blistering critique of America's treatment of African Americans, King elevated Khrushchev's concern to make his penultimate point that racial injustice in America has and will continue to diminish the nation's global standing. He noted:

> My recent travel in Asia, Africa, the Middle East and South America have convinced me that America is at its lowest ebb in international prestige; and most of this loss of prestige is due to our failure to grapple with the problem of racial injustice. We must face the painful fact that we are losing out in the struggle to win the minds of the uncommitted peoples of the world. Just this week the most eloquent spokesman of the Communist bloc, Nikita Khruschev, suggested in his speech to the U.N., among other things, that the headquarters of this great organization be moved from the United States. The American press generally was very careful to

---

[100] Coretta Scott King, MY LIFE WITH MARTIN LUTHER KING, JR., supra note 6 at 166.
[101] Id.
[102] Martin Luther King Jr., *The Negro and the American Dream* (September 25, 1960), Excerpt from Address at the Annual Freedom Mass Meeting of the North Carolina State Conference of Branches of the NAACP, in Clayborne Carson et al. (eds.), *King Papers, Volume V: Threshold of a Decade* (January 1959–December 1960), 509.
[103] *Speech by Mr. Khrushchev, Chairman of the Council of Ministers of the Union of Soviet Socialist Republics, at the 869th Plenary Meeting of the 15th Session of the United Nations General Assembly*, September 23, 1960 (on file with History and Public Policy Program Digital Archive, United Nations Document A/PV.869:65–84), available at: http://digitalarchive.wilsoncenter.org/document/155185.

conceal one of the reasons Mr. Khruschev gave for suggesting this move. His direct words were: "Facts are known ... of representatives of young African and Asian states being subjected to racial discrimination in the United States." While we are used to Mr. Khruschev's intemperate and sometimes irresponsible words, we cannot dismiss these as totally false. The hour is late: The clock of destiny is ticking out. We must act now! It is a trite yet urgently true observation that if America is to remain a first-class nation it cannot have second-class citizens.[104]

King's apparent identification with Khrushchev's thinking worried US government officials. The sophisticated way he framed his thoughts is noteworthy because, in the Black International Tradition (BIT), they combine racial justice precepts with human rights concepts while invoking international law and public opinion.[105] First, King provided personal testimony about the negative way in which colored nations and peoples perceived America in the wake of persistent racial injustice. Second, he made claims to outside law and norms (the UN's human rights law or antiracism and antidiscrimination regimes) and pronouncements (e.g., Khrushchev's remarks) to highlight American hypocrisy, and he called out the media for being complicit. The US Government wanted the world to believe that America was a multiracial democracy where equality and a just rule of law reigned supreme. King exposed it for what it was: a racist nation governed by racist law, norms, and policy where the US Supreme Court regularly waged lawfare against Black Americans in a series of wicked legal decisions such as *Dred Scott v. Sandford* and *Plessy v. Ferguson*. King's call to action to end de jure segregation and other related inequalities was aligned with the BIT of Pan-African activism.

---

[104] *Id.* See also Martin Luther King Jr., *The Negro and the American Dream*, supra note 103. Khrushchev addressed the United Nations General Assembly on (September 23, 1960). A complete transcript of his speech also appeared in the *New York Times* the following day.

[105] The BIT is broadly defined as the "historiography of Black perspectives, claims, demands, and actions to 'outside law' or alternative norms of law derived from the internal logic and vocation of African customary law and international legal doctrine (e.g., human rights law, norms, jurisprudence, and practice) as a pathway to freedom that uncovers an African American jurisprudence about international law." Jeremy I. Levitt, *Beloved Pan-Africanism: Martin Luther King's Stride toward Africa, International Human Rights, and the Black International Tradition*, Z. Yihdego et al. (eds.), ETHIOPIAN YEARBOOK OF INTERNATIONAL LAW 2019, https://doi.org/10.1007/978-3-030-55912-0_8.

4

King Embraces Africa, 1961–1968

FIGURE 4.1 1960: civil rights leader Martin Luther King Jr. (left, rear) sits next to African nationalist leader (and future first President of Zambia, 1964–1991) Kenneth David Kaunda, who gestures as he speaks with two unidentified men, Atlanta, Georgia. Shutterstock.

4.1 THE CONTINENT CALLS

King's beliefs, thoughts, philosophy, influence, and impact on Africa, Africans, and the Black diaspora are the focus of this chapter. The eminent King scholar Louis Baldwin is the only intellectual to address this issue substantively and concretely. He was the first and, until this study, the only scholar to authoritatively examine the importance of King's thoughts on Africa and the Black world. In *To Make the Wounded Whole: The Cultural Legacy of Martin Luther King, Jr.*, Baldwin argues, "King's thoughts on Africa and the [B]lack world as a whole is an important aspect of any study of how his vision transcended the American South and the nation to assume international implications."¹ I agree. The global implications of King's work were profound. Although he was recognized as a world leader, and even though his global ministry was primarily aimed at combatting racism, poverty, and war, "most literature on King has either explicitly or implicitly limited him to the American context, presenting him as a southern [B]lack leader, a civil rights activist, an 'American Gandhi,' or a 'national symbol."² The international human rights and African dimensions of King's work have been largely ignored. Baldwin has noted his disappointment with the lack of intellectual inquiry about King's "attitude toward Africans and blacks in the diaspora" and his "experiences in various parts of the black world and of his activities on behalf of universal black liberation."³ His regret is rooted in the knowledge that few have documented the history of Africa's call to King and the latter's thunderous roar in response.

King seamlessly combined the American civil rights movement with Africa's freedom and independence movements into a transnational theory of change and doctrine. This was not a simple task, given that Africa's liberation movements varied from forceful to nonviolent. Yet King's transnational theory of change was simple: Black liberation demands organizing and empowering Black people in the US, Africa, and beyond to disrupt and dismantle white supremacy, whether it be European colonization, imperialism, racial segregation, Apartheid, or their antecedents. King's human rights stream of consciousness – confronting the three evils of racism, poverty, and militarism – anchored his theory of change and ministry. Baldwin posits that King's "giant triplets," for example, "were probably more characteristic of South Africa than most other parts of the world in the early 1990s."⁴ This might explain his bold support of the African National Congress and his willingness to take concrete action against South Africa's Apartheid regime before most American civil rights leaders showed any interest.

King understood that Black America's "growing awareness of his world citizenship is an earmark of his developing maturity," and he acknowledged that Blacks should concern themselves with "America's foreign policy as it relates to emergent African nations in Africa."⁵ He believed that Black Americans would be more powerful if African nations were stronger. He argued that advancements in racial justice in the US "have brought with it a healthy break with provincialism" or parochial thinking (i.e., wokeness).⁶ Referring to the American Negro Leadership Conference

---

[1] Louis Baldwin, To Make the Wounded Whole: The Cultural Legacy of Martin Luther King JR. (Minneapolis: Fortress Press, 1992), 162.
[2] Louis Baldwin, Toward the Beloved Community: Martin Luther King, JR., and South Africa (Cleveland, OH: Pilgrim Press, 1995), 1.
[3] Louis Baldwin, To Make the Wounded Whole, supra note 1 at 163.
[4] Louis Baldwin, Toward the Beloved Community, supra note 2 at 145.
[5] Martin Luther King Jr., *The Negro Looks at America, People in Inaction*, New York Amsterdam News, December 8, 1962.
[6] Id.

on Africa (ANLCA) and its goal of projecting African American political influence over US foreign policy toward Africa, King recognized that "the future of the emergent African nations (particularly those below the Sahara) and the American Negro are intertwined."[7] King argued that colonialism and segregation had a common root in global white supremacy and that they were grounded in the same spiritual, political, cultural, and economic forces. He highlighted the choices and contradictions in American foreign policy, which favored political expediency over moral imperatives: "the choice between advantageous economic aid and military alliances versus the establishment of racial and political justice."[8]

King was not simply a Pan-African minded human rights activist; he was a genuine Black Africanist, an African American expert on Africa. Africa was the backbone of his global ministry. He wanted the world to know that the histories of African nations, Africans, and American Negroes were interconnected because "colonialism and segregation" were kissing cousins and that "their common end is economic exploitation, political domination, and the debasing of the human personality."[9] King challenged the American foreign policy establishment and shared a powerful antidote from Kwame Nkrumah to America: "Beautiful words and extensive handouts cannot be substitutes for the simple responsibility of treating our colored brothers in America as first-class human beings. So, if we are to be a first-class nation, we cannot have second-class citizens."[10]

On April 18, 1959, Tom Mboya, a trade unionist, faithful Pan-Africanist, revered Kenyan independence leader, and close ally of King, addressed a crowd of more than 20,000, predominantly African American, marching in the Youth March for Integrated Schools to demand the implementation of the US Supreme Court's groundbreaking *Brown v. Board of Education* decision intended to dismantle racial segregation in schools. Mboya befriended King and the other core organizers of the march, including A. Philip Randolph and Bayard Rustin, as well as notables such as Roy Wilkins and Harry Belafonte. Mboya's support of the Black American civil rights movement in the US was novel and indicative of King's strategy to globalize and merge liberation movements in Africa and Black America.

On May 13, 1959, Southern Christian Leadership Conference (SCLC) organized a large, 250-person Africa Freedom Dinner at Atlanta University in honor of Mboya.[11] King shared with Mboya that colonialism and racial segregation were synonymous,

---

[7] Id.
[8] Id.
[9] Martin Luther King Jr., Press Statement regarding "Stand-ins," (February 19, 1962), (on file with The King Center Archives). See also, Baldwin, TO MAKE THE WOUNDED WHOLE, supra note 1 at 172. See also Dr. Martin Luther King Jr., *The Negro Looks at America, People in Inaction*, supra note 5.
[10] Martin Luther King Jr., *A View of the Dawn*, INTERRACIAL REVIEW, No. 30 (May 5, 1957), 84. See also, Nkrumah, Kwame, Biography (September 21, 1909 to April 27, 1972) (on file with The Martin Luther King, Jr. Research and Education Institute), available at https://kinginstitute.stanford.edu/encyclopedia/nkrumah-kwame.
[11] Martin Luther King Jr., *Remarks Delivered at Africa Freedom Dinner* at Atlanta University (May 13, 1959), in *King Papers, Volume V: Threshold of a Decade* (January 1959–December 1960), 203–204.

both being "based on a contempt for life, and a tragic doctrine of white supremacy."[12] King argued, "As long as segregation and discrimination exist in our nation, the longer the chances of survival are for colonialism and vice versa, for the very same set of complex politico-economic forces are operative in both instances."[13] Mboya agreed with King. He acknowledged being influenced by their friendship and King's influential book, *Stride Toward Freedom*. Mboya observed that he had "never found himself so completely captured by a book and ideas," especially King's ability to champion "our coloured people's cause," and to successfully defeat Jim Crow "without emotion, hate, or fear."[14] This was especially noteworthy because Kenya's liberation path had been violent. Mboya's use of the word "our" acknowledges his embrace of Black Americans as Africans and underscores his understanding and acceptance of King's Pan-African philosophy. In a 1962 letter to King, Mboya further demonstrated his (and Kenya's) solidarity with Black Americans in unequivocal terms, essentially condemning the US for violating the human rights of African Americans and reminding King that Blacks "have the right to equality, but [like Kenyans] have a duty to free yourselves."[15] He continued, employing the possessive adjective "our" and the pronoun "us" once again, claiming, "History and justice is on our side, so let us fight on till victory is achieved."[16]

King and Mboya developed a close friendship. Mboya was keenly aware of the "hard campaign" King was waging for freedom, justice, and equality in the US, pledging the "entire support" of the Kenyan people.[17] As Baldwin noted, King "always regarded Mboya as one who symbolized the Black struggle worldwide."[18] Mboya shared that King's non-violent leadership would inspire Kenyans and Africa, a meaningful gesture given the various trials associated with Kenya's bloody struggle for independence, which was not achieved until December 1963. Like the invitations he received from the governments of Ghana, Nigeria, and Cameroon, King was invited to celebrate Kenyan independence in 1963 but could not attend due to increasing demands on his personal and professional lives.[19] King could not travel

---

[12] Baldwin, TO MAKE THE WOUNDED WHOLE, supra note 1 at 174. See also, quoted in David J. Garrow, BEARING THE CROSS: MARTIN LUTHER KING, JR. AND THE SOUTHERN CHRISTIAN LEADERSHIP CONFERENCE (New York, NY: William Morrow Paperbacks, 2004). *Martin Luther King, Jr. to Tom Mboya* (July 8, 1959), MLKP-MBU, in *Martin Luther King, Jr., Papers [1954–1968]* (on file with Martin Luther King, Jr. Collection, Box 71, Folder 1, XXX. Kenya, P. Tom Mboya).

[13] Martin Luther King Jr., Press Statement regarding "Stand-ins," supra note 10. See also, Dr. Martin Luther King Jr., *The Negro Looks at America*, supra note 5.

[14] *A Letter from Tom Mboya to Martin Luther King, Jr.* (July 16, 1959), MLKP-MBU, in *Martin Luther King, Jr., Papers [1954–1968]* (on file with Martin Luther King, Jr. Collection, Box 71, Folder 1, XXX. Kenya, P. Tom Mboya). See also Baldwin, TO MAKE THE WOUNDED WHOLE, supra note 1 at 174.

[15] Baldwin, TO MAKE THE WOUNDED WHOLE, supra note 1 at 175.

[16] Id.

[17] *A Letter from Tom Mboya to Martin Luther King, Jr.* (October 22, 1962), MLKP-MBU (on file with Martin Luther King, Jr., Papers [1954–1968], Martin Luther King, Jr. Collection, Box 71, Folder 1, XXX. Kenya, P. Tom Mboya).

[18] Baldwin, TO MAKE THE WOUNDED WHOLE, supra note 1 at 175.

[19] Id.

given his numerous movement-related institutional responsibilities and obligations, including combatting state violence against demonstrators in Birmingham (which resulted in his jailing), helping to organize the August 1963 March on Washington for Jobs and Freedom, which attracted more than 250,000 persons, and his need to eulogize the child victims of the bombing of the Sixteenth Street Baptist Church in Birmingham in September 1963. Black liberation in America was a key priority.[20]

Nonetheless, King's global ministry crossed the African continent. As president of the SCLC, King's antiwar philosophy organically led him into international human rights law and conflict prevention. In a 1961 letter George Houser, executive director of the American Committee on Africa (ACOA), invited King to serve as a member of an unofficial commission of inquiry into the "tragic problem in Angola," referring to Portugal's violent and genocidal activities in the country.[21] The commission intended to ascertain the "extent of death and destruction" in Angola, including the killing of 50,000 persons, the destruction of entire villages in the north, and the creation of "80,000 refugees in the Congo."[22] In particular, Houser wanted to employ prominent Americans to pressure Portugal, a US ally and member of NATO, to "end its repression in Angola" by establishing the unsanctioned commission to "make first-hand observations" of the situation in the country and to provide recommendations for action to US government officials and the international community through the UN.[23]

King was acutely aware of and concerned about Portuguese savagery in Angola, commenting, "I know of no situation in the world that concerns me more than the brutality and barbarity taking place in Angola today."[24] King believed that the world should "rise up and protest ... [the] unbelievable atrocities perpetrated by the Portuguese government against the people of Angola."[25] He supported sending an unofficial commission of Americans to assess the situation and desired to be a part of it; however, he reluctantly declined Houser's invitation to be part of the delegation. King reasoned that the freedom movements in the US were at a critical juncture and that he had a moral obligation to spend the next few months focused on

---

[20] Coincidentally, King and Mboya were born in 1929 and 1930, respectively, and were gunned down by assassins within a year of one another. Mboya was murdered on July 5, 1969, one month before his thirty-ninth birthday, while still mourning the April 6, 1968 assassination of King.

[21] *Letter from George Houser to Martin Luther King, Jr.* (June 21, 1961), in *King Papers* (1954–1968) (on file with Howard Gotlieb Archival Research Center, loose document on file with author).

[22] Id.

[23] Id.

[24] *Letter from Martin Luther King, Jr. to George Houser* (July 19, 1961), in *King Papers, Volume VII: To Save the Soul of America* (January 1961–August 1962), 255. King also received various communications from Angolans, asking him to assist them in their struggles against Portuguese colonization. For example, Deolinda Rodriques Francisco de Almeida, a twenty-year-old student activist fighting for Angolan independence, sent him letters in 1959. *King to Rodriques* (July 21, 1959), in *King Papers, Volume V: Threshold of a New Decade* (January 1959–December 1960), 250–251.

[25] *Letter from Martin Luther King, Jr. to George Houser*, supra note 24, p. 255.

fortifying gains made in the Southern struggle. King felt it would be "impossible" to spend several weeks traveling abroad given the daily momentum in the US civil rights struggle that he was leading in defiance of Jim Crow.

Still, through ACOA and later ANLCA, King's interest in the Angolan situation expanded. ANLCA condemned Portuguese forced labor of Black Angolans and the denial of the latter's civil, political, economic, social, and cultural rights. By November 1962, the Portuguese bombing of Angolan villages resulted in nearly 200,000 refugees, and Angola's freedom struggle became more violent and protracted. As a founding member of ANLCA, King wholeheartedly agreed with the organization's efforts to influence US actions against Portuguese injustices, including mobilizing international action in the form of a peacekeeping mission. Most important was ANLCA's argument that African Americans have a "special responsibility" to lobby the US government for a change in policy on Angola.[26] Consistent with King's thinking, ANLCA's position was that Black Americans "cannot separate this struggle at home from that abroad."[27] Thus, they held vital meetings and conferences to consider the situation in Southern Africa and determine "what the Afro-American community can do to create a more vigorous American policy towards these problems."[28]

Martin Luther King Jr. enjoyed strong bonds of brotherhood with Africa's liberation class. His relationships with Oliver Tambo, Kwame Nkrumah, Nnamdi Azikiwe, Tom Mboya, and Premier Ben Bella, Algeria's first elected president and leader of Algeria's War of Independence against France, were reflective of his radical intellect, activism, and knowledge of African affairs. King and Bella met on October 27, 1962, when Bella was prime minister (1962–1963) – less than a year before he was elected President of Algeria. The meeting was opportune because, at this juncture, Algeria was the newest African nation to shed the yoke of colonial rule. Although the Algerians had engaged in a brutal war of independence, King and Bella discussed various issues, from the "efficacy of nonviolence to the Cuban missile crisis."[29] But they spent most of their time conversing about racial justice (Figure 4.2). King was impressed with Bella's "complete familiarity with the progression of events in the Negro struggle for full citizenship."[30] King recognized Bella's repeated reference to King and African Americans as brothers. Like King, Bella believed in the reciprocal relationship between colonialism and segregation. King argued that the "battle of

---

[26] *Preamble*, The American Negro Leadership Conference on Africa: Resolutions, Arden House Campus of Columbia University, Harriman, New York (November 23–25, 1962) (on file with African Activist Archivist) (available at https://africanactivist.msu.edu/recordFiles/210-849-28596/african_activist_archive-a0a0l4-a_12419.pdf.
[27] *Id.*
[28] *Id.*
[29] Leonardo Campus, *Martin Luther King's Reaction to the Cuban Missile Crisis*, EUROPEAN JOURNAL OF AMERICAN STUDIES, [online] 5 | (2017), available at http://ejas.revues.org/12186.
[30] Martin Luther King Jr. "My Talk with Ben Bella." Draft article (originally prepared for an unknown publication) in Clayborne Carson (ed.), *The Papers of Martin Luther King, Jr.*, Volume VII: *To Save the Soul of America* (January 1961–August 1962).

FIGURE 4.2 October 10, 1962: Algerian Premier Ahmed Ben Bella shakes hands with Martin Luther King Jr. in New York.

the Algerians against colonialism and the battle of the Negro against segregation is a common struggle" against evil systems designed to oppress humanity.[31] One of the reasons King and Bella's comments, statements, and conversations are valuable is because Bella was one of the first "Afro-Arab" and Muslim leaders with whom King developed close relations and who clearly viewed the African world beyond strict racial constructs. Bella seemed to view all persons of African descent as African, including Blacks in the diaspora. Indicative of the BIT, King argued that "racial segregation in America has international implications" and, referencing Bella, believed that our failure to solve it would undermine America's "moral and political voice in the world community."[32] According to King, "racism in our nation must go or we will be relegated to a second-rate power in the world."[33] He further asserted that our

[31] Id.
[32] Id.
[33] Id.

"anemic democracy" will destroy itself if it continues to oppress Blacks.[34] Racism, he argued, was a "cancerous, domestic problem" that must be surgically removed not "merely to meet the Communist challenge" or "appeal to Asian and African peoples"; rather, he stated, "in the final analysis, equal opportunity without regard to race must be established in America *because it is right*."[35] On these issues, King and Bella were kindred souls, a bonding that emboldened King's commitment to defeating Jim Crow.

Black students throughout the US were also invigorated by Africa's freedom movements, which, combined with the broader American civil rights movement and diverse calls for Black power, encouraged them to fight for change. As Baldwin notes, King was acutely aware of the influence of African freedom fighters on Black American youth and young radicals in the Caribbean. King opined that the "liberation struggle in Africa has been the greatest single international influence on American Negro students."[36] He noted that Black students firmly believed that if Africans can break colonialism, the "American Negro can break Jim Crow."[37] Black Americans respected Africa's new leadership class, including Nkrumah, Azikiwe, Mboya, and Dr. Hastings Banda of Nyasaland (Malawi), the first prime minister (1963) and president of Malawi (1964–1993). These leaders were "heroes," especially at America's Historically Black Colleges and Universities (HBCUs). This was why, for example, there were nationwide protests when the Congolese President Patrice Lumumba was assassinated.[38]

Unfortunately, the Pan-African and democratic inclinations that brought these leaders into power and their nations into independence from colonial rule were eventually undermined and marred by internal turmoil, civil conflict, corruption, external interventionism, and dictatorships. And, while King joined and aligned with them in the global fight against white supremacy, he likely would have condemned and disassociated himself from the socialistic and strongman politics that ensued, including Nkrumah's socialism and Banda's "president for life" politics.

These eventualities aside, King embraced (and was embraced by) leaders in the Caribbean, recognizing their influences on the "civil rights movement and on the black struggle worldwide."[39] He possessed a unique ability to connect with African and Caribbean leaders alike. For example, while there is scant information about King's view of Marcus Garvey, who was Jamaican, Baldwin argues that

---

[34] Id.
[35] Id.
[36] Martin Luther King Jr., THE AUTOBIOGRAPHY OF MARTIN LUTHER KING JR., Clayborne Carson (ed.), 1998, at 138. Martin Luther King Jr., The Time for Freedom Has Come, NEW YORK TIMES MAGAZINE, September 10, 1961, 25. See also, Martin Luther King Jr., A Speech Regarding the Influence of African Movements on U.S. Students (on file with The King Center Archives, [May 1962], 3, loose document on file with author).
[37] Leonardo Campus, *Martin Luther King's Reaction to the Cuban Missile Crisis*, supra note 29.
[38] Id.
[39] Baldwin, TO MAKE THE WOUNDED WHOLE, supra note 1 at 177.

4.1 The Continent Calls

King believed Marcus Garvey represented the "fullest bonds and obligations that existed between Africans, West Indian blacks, black Americans, and others in the black diaspora."[40] The author agrees with this sentiment, as it reflects the famous but unsourced statement attributed to King that Garvey "was the first man of color to lead and develop a mass movement. He was the first man on a mass scale and level to give millions of Negroes a sense of dignity and destiny. And make the Negro feel he was somebody."[41] Some of King's closest advisors, operatives, and supporters were also of Caribbean descent, including Harry Belafonte (Jamaica), C. L. R. James (Trinidad), Stokely Carmichael (Trinidad), George Padmore (Trinidad), and Sidney Potier (Bahamas), demonstrating the symbiotic relationship between Blacks in the Caribbean and in the US in the global struggle against colonialism and white supremacy. King's Caribbean connections and influences were bolstered, in particular, by strong ties to Norman W. Manley, first Premier of Jamaica, and Dr. Francois Duvalier (Papa Doc), President of Haiti, with whom, as Baldwin notes, King "shared the vision of universal black freedom and independence."[42] Baldwin further observed that "Manley and Duvalier also had a high regard for King, viewing him as a voice for oppressed blacks everywhere."[43] Duvalier even referred to King as the leader of Black African peoples who "shall remain for us Negroes the Mahatma of the Western Hemisphere."[44] In other words, he viewed King through a Pan-African lens.

King was not naïve, however. He listened to African American students' concerns and questions about the "bitter irony in the picture of his country championing freedom in foreign lands and failing to ensure that freedom to twenty million of its own."[45] King acknowledged that Black Americans "watched the decolonization and liberation of nations in Africa and Asia since the end of World War II" and, he seemed to argue, this caused them to inwardly reflect and conclude they had "been too passive, unwilling to take strong measures to gain [their] freedom."[46] King's observation

---

[40] Id.
[41] Although the above quote is often attributed to King, the author was unable to independently verify the source of this quote.
[42] Baldwin, TO MAKE THE WOUNDED WHOLE, supra note 1 at 177–178.
[43] Id.
[44] Notwithstanding, unlike the politics of Kenya and Malawi, among others, had King lived long enough to observe the political regression of Duvalier in Haiti, he would likely have condemned Duvalier's strongman politics and violent regime. What's more, when King was assassinated, Duvalier, a phony Pan-Africanist and self-appointed president-for-life, organized a large funeral that appeared to be a veiled attempt to attach himself to the apostle of nonviolence to divert attention away from and cover-up rapid corruption, human rights violations against Haitians, and the violent and repressive nature of his dictatorial government. Dr. Francois Duvalier, A TRIBUTE TO THE MARTYRED LEADER OF NONVIOLENCE, REVEREND DR. MARTIN LUTHER KING, JR., trans. John E. Pickering (Prot-au-Prince, Haiti: Presses Nationales, 1968), 20. See also, Baldwin, TO MAKE THE WOUNDED WHOLE, supra note 1 at 176.
[45] Martin Luther King Jr., WHY WE CAN'T WAIT (New York, NY: Signet Classics, 2000), 11.
[46] Id. at 10.

is interesting and perhaps indicative of Black American sentiments during Ghana's independence in 1957, three years after *Brown v. Board of Education*. However, one would be hard-pressed to apply his "passive" reasoning to a history of over 250 uprisings, rebellions, and multiple civil rights movements.[47] In the same way that Black American freedom struggles moved the justice needle forward, African independence movements were largely successful – thirty-four countries had shed the yoke of colonialism by 1963 – heightening the burgeoning calls for freedom among African Americans. The global order was changing: Whites were losing their stranglehold on Black and brown nations, and new international bodies such as the UN emerged that granted the Global South a chance to foray into global governance.

King fully understood that independent nations in Africa and the West Indies had strategic influence in the one venue inaccessible to African Americans: the UN. King observed:

> The Negro saw black statesmen voting on vital issues in the United Nations – and knew that in many cities of his own land he was not permitted to take that significant walk to the ballot box. He saw black kings and potentates ruling from palaces – and knew he had been condemned to move from small ghettos to larger ones. Witnessing the drama of Negro progress elsewhere in the world, witnessing a level of conspicuous consumption at home exceeding anything in our history, it was natural that by 1963 Negroes would rise with resolution and demand a share of governing power, and living conditions measured by American standards of colonial impoverishment.[48]

King's observation was astute. Essentially, Black Americans were witnessing the "dream" of liberation for persons of African descent all over the world, but not for themselves. In addition, freedom for Africa entailed sovereignty and independence from white rule; it meant new constitutional frameworks and rules of law, and it naturally ushered in new socioeconomic realities for Africans. Many Black Americans were both empowered by and conflicted about these new realities because they continued to be beset by the uncertainties of Jim Crow. They were a minority oppressed by the world's leading hegemonic power and, despite any rights-based advances, would never take possession of or govern it. Hence, their general aspirations and activism were curbed by the reality that they could not even vote unmolested in their own country.

As such, African Americans had no standing to bring or to address grievances before the UN. In addition, the old and newly independent nations of Africa and the Caribbean were either unwilling or unable to advocate for an end to racial segregation in the US, as few openly defended African American equality and human rights before the New York-based UN. This lack of reciprocity was sobering, considering that Black Americans had been boldly advocating for an end to

---

[47] See generally, Herbert Aptheker, AMERICAN NEGRO SLAVE REVOLTS (New York: International Publishers, 1974).
[48] Martin Luther King Jr., WHY WE CAN'T WAIT, supra note 45 at 11.

colonization, Apartheid, US interventionism, and other forms of inhumane treatment of their brethren in Africa for over a century. The failure of African nations to resolutely support Black American freedom and equality in some ways legitimized Negro isolationism on the world stage, further stoking community frustration and disenfranchisement. Ultimately, deadly police violence and racial segregation lit this simmering frustration triggered social rebellion that culminated in a historic number of race riots throughout the US, beginning in Birmingham, Alabama (1963), Harlem, New York City (1964), Watts in Los Angeles, California (1965), Chicago, Illinois (1966), and in numerous other cities in 1967.[49]

By 1962, King had traveled to Africa multiple times, befriended Africa's leadership class, joined ACOA, become a leading figure in the organization, and amplified efforts to oppose colonization and global white supremacy in Africa in various writings, speeches, and interviews. He also supported and organized scholarships for many African students to attend university in the US. His speeches on Africa's sociopolitical and economic conditions, particularly related to liberation movements and their connection to Black America's civil rights movement, were written and delivered with precision and substance uncommon in the civil rights community, let alone at American universities. During this period, King operated with complex duality; after developing strong bonds of kinship with African leaders and bona fide expertise on African issues, he shifted his attention to the brewing race pot that was America – but without relinquishing his African stripes. His ability to simultaneously address domestic and international matters individually and institutionally at the highest levels separated King from other civil rights leaders. From a doctoral student who began as a young pastor in Montgomery, he became a local civil rights leader who progressed into a formidable national civil rights organizer and activist – only to transform into an international human rights icon and Pan-African thinker and spokesman for the Black race. However, this conversion maintained its duality; King functioned domestically and internationally with equal force and recognition, ultimately knowing his legacy was rooted in freeing Black Americans.

The American civil rights movement inspired a new generation of Black high school and college students to challenge the racial status quo. Black leaders like King competed in a marketplace of progressive ideological norms to influence them. He was impressed with the "intensity and depth of their commitment" and willingness to "die" if necessary.[50] Baldwin rightly notes that King was similarly excited about African students because they represented the "brightest hope for full African independence."[51] This enthusiasm provides insight into why, as early as

---

[49] In 1967, Tampa, Florida; Cincinnati, Ohio; Atlanta, Georgia; Newark, Plainfield; New Brunswick, New Jersey; and Detroit, Michigan all experienced race riots.
[50] Baldwin, TO MAKE THE WOUNDED WHOLE, supra note 1 at 179. See also, Martin Luther King, Jr., A Speech Regarding the Influence of African Movements on U.S. Students, supra note 36 at 3.
[51] Baldwin, TO MAKE THE WOUNDED WHOLE, supra note 1 at 179.

1957, he eagerly assisted in educating African students in the US by providing them with scholarships to, among other places, Tuskegee Institute and Alabama State College. Even before working with Tom Mboya's Airlift Africa scholarship program for Kenyan students to attend university in the US, King provided scholarships for Ghanaians to attend Tuskegee.[52] King also fielded numerous requests for scholarship assistance from African students. As the world's leading human rights figure, he carefully reviewed and responded to hundreds of letters from foreign students with extraordinary decorum, empathy, and brotherhood.

King genuinely sought to help African students attend university in the US and was frustrated that he could not do more. He organized scholarships with assistance from "college presidents and some governmental officials"[53] and, in the fall of 1959, recommended that the SCLC provide an annual scholarship to an African student as part of Black America's "deep sympathy with our African brothers in the struggle for freedom and human dignity, and in order to reveal our awareness of the oneness of our struggle."[54] King's efforts were monumental, as he sincerely believed in the racial oneness of Black Americans and Africans and the intersected fight for freedom and equality that bonded them together. He also understood the importance of taking affirmative actions that would "do a great deal to develop a sense of self-respect within African students and contribute in some little way toward developing persons to take over leadership responsibilities in that great continent."[55] King's ideas on the topic were, in many ways, forward-thinking. He was acutely aware that developing the next wave of African leadership at HBCUs, where they would become conversant in Black America's history, culture, and social mores, would fortify and sustain relations between African Americans and the continent. This had been the case, after all, for Nkrumah, Azikwe, and Tolbert.

Although resources were scarce, the scholarships that King supported through his various organizations (e.g., Dexter Avenue Baptist Church, SCLC, and ACOA) and networks (including Tom Mboya's Airlift Africa) were intended to encourage and strengthen Black liberation. Baldwin correctly notes that "King's efforts on behalf of African students, and for black freedom worldwide, earned him the respect and

---

[52] *A Letter from Martin Luther King, Jr. to Maurice K. Amekuji* (August 8, 1959) (on file with Howard Gotlieb Archival Research Center, Martin Luther King, Jr. Collection, Box 70, Folder 3, Ghana).

[53] *A letter from Martin Luther King, Jr., to Mr. John Cleopas Miyengi* (June 1, 1959) (on file with Howard Gotlieb Archival Research Center, Martin Luther King, Jr. Collection, The King Papers, bulk: June 1, 1959, Box 71, Folder 1, SPE-127). For more information on the plethora of letters that King received from African students, please see Baldwin, TO MAKE THE WOUNDED WHOLE, supra note 1 at 179–182.

[54] Martin Luther King Jr., *Recommendations to the Board of the S.C.L.C.*, THE SOUTHERN CHRISTIAN LEADERSHIP CONFERENCE MEETING, COLUMBIA: SOUTH CAROLINA (on file with The King Center Archives [September 29–October 1, 1959], 3). See also, *Letter from Martin Luther King, Jr. to Amin Msowoya* (September 19, 1960) (on file with Howard Gotlieb Archival Research Center, Martin Luther King, Jr. Collection, Box 71, Folder 3, loose document on file with author).

[55] *Id.*

admiration of Africans everywhere – a level of respect and admiration enjoyed by very few black American leaders in our history."[56]

King's generosity and courteousness to African and Caribbean leaders and students attracted organizers, activists, and advocates who regularly visited him in Atlanta. King was a celebrity. His numerous invitations to the continent from governments and civic organizations in Africa and the Caribbean indicated his global stature, not excluding many naming opportunities in schools, streets, and lectures. For example, despite decades-long political tension between the US and Cuban governments, Cuban Christians established the Dr. Martin Luther King Jr. Memorial Center (CMMLK) in Havannah, Cuba, in 1987. The Center aims to engage in social transformation and promote ecumenical values within the "Cuban socialist project." In 2018, I had the opportunity to visit the CMMLK, where I met with Pastor Raúl Suárez Ramos, one of its founders and the executive director at the time. He shared that promoting Liberation Theology and offering critical and liberating intersectional education under the rubric of Christianity had consumed the Center's work. Still, today, Ramos and most Cubans have enormous respect for the life and legacy of Martin Luther King Jr. and for most revolutionary African American civil rights leaders. Nevertheless, Christians in Uganda (82 percent of the population) were among the first to honor King. In 1961, with his full knowledge and consent, they built and named a technical school after him in Uganda. School organizer and noted educator and trade unionist Ouma Namwambe sought to name the school after King in honor of his supporting African students studying in the US.

King consistently spoke with groups of Africans studying in the US or simply visiting America, and he was the most sought-after and popular speaker for African student organizations. These students sought civil rights education and training to make social change nonviolently in their home countries. Students in the Caribbean similarly embraced King. In June 1965, King visited the University of the West Indies in Mona, Jamaica, as a keynote speaker for their valedictory service. As Baldwin states, "The address was clearly representative of his view that people of African descent everywhere shared a common condition and struggle. This view became the foundation stone of King's activities on behalf of black people."[57] This "foundation stone" formed as early as 1957, and every international trip to Africa and the Caribbean fortified it.

4.2 KING RESPONDS TO AFRICA

In 1962, King doubled down on his efforts to support newly independent African states and those seeking to shed the yoke of colonial rule. His work with ACOA from 1957 onward provided keen insights into how African Americans could influence US foreign policy toward Africa. ACOA provided a powerful multiracial platform to

---

[56] Baldwin, TO MAKE THE WOUNDED WHOLE, supra note 1 at 181.
[57] Id.

advocate for the liberation of African states and peoples. However, King wanted to create a more formidable African lobby group that recognized the historical kinship bonds between Black Americans and Africans. He and others launched the new initiative in November 1962 while the UN, where the subjects of African decolonization, independence, and development would be discussed, was in session. A host of prominent Black leaders founded ANLCA, including King; Roy Wilkins, Executive Secretary of the National Association for the Advancement of Colored People (NAACP); A. Phillip Randolph, President of the Brotherhood of Sleeping Car Porters; James Farmer of the Congress of Racial Equality; and Dorothy Height, President of the National Council of Negro Women, among others.[58] They "were deeply concerned about the developments in Africa ... [and] the struggle for freedom in Africa" and genuinely believed that the Black American "struggle at home is made much easier to the extent that equality and freedom are achieved in Africa."[59]

ANLCA was birthed out of a conference on "The Role of the American Negro Community in U.S. Policy toward Africa" at the Arden House campus of Columbia University. Theodore E. Brown was hired as ANLCA's first Director. Like ACOA, ANLCA focused on empowering Africa and Africans through varied advocacy and racial, economic, and political aid. ANLCA distinguished itself, however, in that it was founded and governed by Blacks with an anti-Black racism, anticolonial, anti-imperial, and anti-Apartheid Pan-African mandate. ANLCA sought to aggressively influence US government policy toward Africa to eliminate "colonialism and its evils" and to repatriate African Americans to Africa "for official and unofficial American jobs of all categories."[60] This position was cemented further in a critical statement penned by King in the *New York Amsterdam News* on November 8, 1962:

> Colonialism and segregation are nearly synonymous; they are children in the same family, for their common end is economic exploitation, political domination, and the debasing of human personality. In many ways, the future of the emergent African nations (particularly those below the Sahara) and the American Negro are intertwined.[61]

Here, King's thinking embodied and combined two Pan-African conceptions: first, that racial segregation in the US and colonialism in Africa are linked, if not interdependent; and second, that Black Americans had a moral obligation to lobby for a US foreign policy favorable to Africa and Africans. Doing so, he argued, "would be

---

[58] Another responsible for the founding of the ANLCA includes Whitney M. Young, Jr., Executive Director of the National Urban League.
[59] Draft, *Letter to Support*, The American Negro Leadership Conference on Africa (loose document on file with author).
[60] *The American Negro Leadership Conference on Africa: Resolutions*, Arden House Campus of Columbia University, Harriman, New York (November 23–25, 1962).
[61] *Statement by Martin Luther King, Jr.*, NEW YORK AMSTERDAM NEWS, New York (December 8, 1962).

beneficial for both Africa and America."[62] As scholar James Meriwether rightly notes, King "advanced the bonds of connection" thesis throughout ANLCA's activities.[63]

As members of ANLCA's Policy Committee, King and others called for a "Marshall Plan for Africa" in December 1962.[64] They advocated for more significant political, economic, and technical assistance to newly emerging African states and those still under colonial rule. This included levying sanctions against South Africa, instituting arms and munitions sanctions against Portugal,[65] and "more extensive use of qualified Black Americans in the foreign service and the State Department policymaking."[66] Unfortunately, the US government had no interest in recruiting and training Black diplomats. Where the ANLCA Policy Committee believed that African American diplomats would be more stalwart and effective advocates for African liberation and development and serve as the bridge for expanding relations between Black America and Africa, the US Foreign Service was the exclusive domain of white men with only a few Blacks and women sprinkled in between. ANLCA's aims were bold and threatening to Washington. In 1962, only 17 out of 3700 (or 0.45 percent) Foreign Service Officers were Black,[67] and nearly all dispatched to Africa and Latin America.

ANLCA presented its plan to President John F. Kennedy without measurable success.[68] The *Baltimore Afro-American* dubbed the 1962 meeting notable; the "historic White House meeting" signified the "first time" that a "significant group of Black leaders" met "at length in the Oval Office to discuss the nation's relationship with Africa" let alone to discuss foreign policy on any level.[69] What made the lengthy meeting particularly unique was its location in the Oval Office and its exclusive focus on US relations with Africa – perhaps representing the apex of ANLCA's growing influence. In January 1965, they also met with President Lyndon B. Johnson, though unfortunately with the same results. Indeed, neither the Kennedy nor the Johnson administrations supported Black American engagement in foreign affairs, particularly related to African liberation, and they actively sought to interfere with

---

[62] James H. Meriwether, TEARS, FIRE, AND BLOOD: THE UNITED STATES AND THE DECOLONIZATION OF AFRICA (Chapel Hill: The University of North Carolina Press, 2021), p. 124.

[63] *Id.*

[64] The Marshall Plan was an economic and political development program to assist Western European nations rebuild after World War II.

[65] Portugal was a violently brutal colonizer of Angola and Mozambique that actively supported the ideology of white supremacy, including South Africa's Apartheid government.

[66] James H. Meriwether, TEARS, FIRE, AND BLOOD: THE UNITED STATES AND THE DECOLONIZATION OF AFRICA, supra note 62 at 124.

[67] Heather Hansen, At the Crossroads of History, Williams, Magazine, Spring 2024, at https://today.williams.edu/magazine/at-the-crossroads-of-history/. See also, Brandon Grove, BEHIND EMBASSY WALLS: THE LIFE AND TIMES OF AN AMERICAN DIPLOMAT (University of Missouri Press, 2005).

[68] *Africa "Marshall Plan" Asked by Negro Leaders*, THE WASHINGTON POST (Tuesday, DECEMBER 18, 1972), and in *King Papers (Series I–IV)* (on file with Center for Nonviolent Social Change, Martin Luther King, Jr., Box 3, folder 5).

[69] James H. Meriwether, TEARS, FIRE, AND BLOOD: THE UNITED STATES AND THE DECOLONIZATION OF AFRICA, supra note 62 at 125.

the establishment of ANLCA and mute any prominent African American voices in US foreign policy and foreign affairs.[70]

Nevertheless, King was determined to galvanize tangible and human resources to fight colonization and Apartheid, promote development in Africa, and educate, organize, and train African Americans "to relate the American Negro with Africa and its many problems."[71] He employed ACOA, and a battery of civic groups to finance and politically bolster ANLCA's mission, including his fraternity (Alpha Phi Alpha, Inc.), churches like Dexter Avenue Baptist Church, civil rights organizations such as the SCLC, various foundations, trade unions, and HBCUs like Morehouse College and the Tuskegee Institute. All agreed that the US government should assist with the political and economic development of newly independent African states, "help liberate the remaining colonial territories," and "instill within the Negro population of the United States a conscious identification with the Africans."[72] They also sought to influence the masses of Blacks in the US to become more connected with African freedom struggles and forthrightly "cultivate African diplomats and their families in this country."[73] This cultivation was intended to provide African diplomats with a firm understanding of the plight of the Negro in America and to explore the various ways African Americans could assist in Africa's development.

One hundred Black leaders attended the first meeting at Arden House. Notably, many expressed displeasure with the understanding that African diplomats and politicians demonstrated about the "United States power structure and the relationship of the American Negroes to it."[74] These leaders rightly felt that Africans too often "did not understand the social and economic progress achieved by the Negroes, and also failed to understand that the political power of a minority of 19 million, although important, was necessarily limited in what it could achieve."[75] The truth of the matter was that some African diplomats and politicians were not dissimilar from European and Canadian diplomats and leaders in their naïveté about the plight of Black Americans and the structural dynamics of race relations in America.

During this first meeting at Arden House, King argued for a "Marshall Plan for Africa" to address the enormity of the problems facing newly independent

---

[70] *Memorandum From Robert W. Komer and Ulric Haynes of the National Security Council Staff to the President's Special Assistant for National Security Affairs (Bundy)* (Mar. 30, 1965), in Foreign Relations of the United States, 1964–1968, vol. XXIV, Africa (Office of the Historian, U.S. Dep't of State). See also Johnson Library, National Security File, Country File, Africa, General, Vol. II, Memos & Miscellaneous, 7/64–6/65. Secret. A copy was sent to Clifford L. Alexander, Jr., Associate Special Counsel to the President.

[71] A *Letter from Martin Luther King, Jr., to Mr. Theodore E. Brown*, in *King Papers* (1954–1968) (on file with The King Center Archives, Box 20, folder 10, April 1, 1963).

[72] M.S. Handler, *U.S. Negroes Link Aid to Sub-Saharan African Nations with Rights Struggle*, THE NEW YORK TIMES (November 25, 1962).

[73] *Id.*

[74] *Id.*

[75] *Id.*

African states. President Truman had instituted the Economic Recovery Act of 1948 on April 3, 1948, known as the Marshall Plan in honor of its architect, US Secretary of State George Marshall. It was passed with the sole aim of rebuilding the physical and economic infrastructure of postwar Europe in the wake of World War II, including the establishment of "markets for American goods, creat[ing] reliable trading partners, and support[ing] the development of stable democratic governments in Western Europe."[76] King believed that if the US could invest nearly $14 billion to rebuild Europe, America should also help rebuild African states emerging from the claws of colonialism and Apartheid, especially since the US supported the repressive regimes in South Africa and Angola.

King wanted Black Americans to be recruited for "official and unofficial American jobs of all categories in Africa."[77] This is why ANLCA urged the US to "abandon the practice of excluding ... American Negroes from its missions" in South Africa and barring Africans from activities and programs sponsored by the US embassy and consulates in South Africa. King understood that African American employment in Africa would lead to repatriation and immigration, marriage between African Americans and Africans, technical cooperation with African governments, and business and entrepreneurship opportunities. He, along with the other ANLCA leaders, rejected the false presumption held by some in the US State Department that African leaders preferred dealing with white American diplomats. All 100 leaders attending the ANLCA meeting actively sought to "link the integration struggle in the United States with the fate of sub-Saharan African states, thereby initiating a 'new phase in the civil rights struggle.'"[78]

This new phase was global – an authentic movement toward Pan-Africanism that sought to reshape US policy in Africa. At the time, the *New York Times* misunderstood King and misinformed the public by claiming that he believed the new phase was part of a "worldwide struggle for freedom rather than a specific interest focused in Africa," a framing that appeased white fear and constituted a false dichotomy at best.[79] The *New York Times* was mistaken for two reasons: first, one may credibly argue that King's central global ministry was focused on Africa. Second, King's ministry was essentially centered on persons of African descent facing colonial and/ or racist oppression domestically and globally, making it a worldwide struggle. He understood that the ancestral place of origin for all Black people was Africa and that no Black person could genuinely be free if colonialists and Apartheidists ruled Africa. This type of Pan-African thinking was reflected in his activities as an organizer and

---

[76] *Act of April 3, 1948, European Recovery Act (Marshall Plan)*; Enrolled Acts and Resolutions of Congress, 1789–1996; General Records of the United States Government; Record Group 11; National Archives. See also, National Archives, Milestone Documents, *Marshall Plan* (1948), available at www.archives.gov/milestone-documents/marshall-plan.

[77] Handler, *U.S. Negroes Link Aid to Sub-Saharan African Nations with Rights Struggle*, supra note 72.

[78] *Id.*

[79] *Id.*

sponsor of ANLCA, which, in its solicitation for participation among Black leaders, offered the following statement:

> We believe the 19 million American Negro citizens must assume a greater responsibility for the formation of United States policy in sub-Saharan Africa. Negroes are of necessity deeper concerned with developments in Africa because of the moral issues involved and because the struggle here at home to achieve in our time equality without respect to race or color is made easier to the extent that equality and freedom are achieved everywhere. The advancement of individual freedom and human dignity in this key area demands affirmative action and help by our government through the normal channels of international diplomacy and in the councils of the United Nations.
>
> We believe that a meeting of Negroes in positions of leadership in organizations that are active in, and a part of the Negro community would be fruitful in terms of supplying information, crystalizing opinion, developing a program to activize the masses of Negro citizens, and in providing a continuing channel through which our voices can be heard by our own government.[80]

ANLCA and King's thinking reflected that of most African Americans during this era. He subscribed to the view that there was no clash between focusing on Africa and the nonwhite world outside of the US, given that people of African descent were being oppressed globally. Since King's focus was political and economic, he understood that "the real problem is to bring about economic independence along with the political independence for the Africans."[81] He acknowledged that African development provided "American Negroes inspiration for their struggle here."[82] It was a struggle, he believed, would have had more gravitas domestically and globally if there had been more "African study centers at Negro institutions of learning" to train "cadres for work in Africa sustainably."[83] Most American foundations and grantmaking institutions funded African Studies at predominantly white institutions, which is why, even today, there are far more white "Africanists" than Black ones. Hence, ANLCA argued that American foundations operating in and focused on African affairs, which during this period were predominated by whites, had failed to invest in the development of African Studies programs at HBCUs. This disparity might explain why there are still very few formidable African Studies programs at HBCUs.

King leveraged his positions in ACOA and ANLCA to influence US foreign policy in Africa regarding economic development, racial equality, and political freedom. The all-Black led ANLCA firmly embraced the racial and ethnic bonds of kinship between African Americans and Africans and reaffirmed Black American

---

[80] African Activist Archive, *American Negro Leadership Conference on Africa Invitation Letter*, in *Peter Weiss Papers*, Michigan State University Libraries Special Collections (August 31, 1962), available at https://africanactivist.msu.edu/recordFiles/210-849-28613/african_activist_archive-a0a015-a_12419.pdf.
[81] *Id.*
[82] *Id.*
[83] *Id.*

solidarity with the peoples of Africa and their "aspirations for freedom, human rights, and independence."[84] ANLCA focused heavily on educating and organizing African American leaders and groups to embrace and empower Africa and change American approaches and thinking about the continent. In the Preamble of the ANLCA Resolutions, drafted at Arden House on Columbia University's campus, participants agreed that the "American Negro community has a responsibility in simple terms of historical continuity" to combat the evils of colonialism, Apartheid, and other forms of oppression.[85] Furthermore, conference participants unabashedly identified the unique obligation of the American Negro Community to Africa:

> The American Negro community in the United States has a special responsibility to urge a dynamic African policy upon our government. Although we have a serious civil rights problem which exhausts much of our energy, we cannot separate this struggle at home from that abroad. If the United States cannot take vigorous action to help win freedom in Africa, we cannot expect to maintain the trust and friendship of the newly independent and soon-to-be independent peoples of Africa and Asia.[86]

This was not the only expression of pragmatic Pan-Africanism in the ANLCA Resolutions worthy of examination. ANLCA's appeal to the binding authority of the UN Charter to promote human rights and democracy in Africa fits well within the Black International Tradition (BIT) of advocacy. As Baldwin rightly notes, "The A.C.O.A. and the ANLCA gave impetus and continuity to King's idea that black Americans, in particular, and Americans, in general, had a contribution to make to the awakening and uplift of Africa."[87]

As a founder and member of ANLCA's Call Committee, King fully endorsed its resolutions and positions concerning US actions in Africa. He strongly opposed the continued exploitation of Africans in the Congo and the continued subjugation of Africa and Africans. Moreover, ANLCA called for foundations operating in Africa with predominantly white staff to employ African Americans and to fund Black American organizations seeking to assist in Africa's development:

> We are disturbed by the failure of American foundations to include Negro citizens in policy posts handling African affairs. We call upon them to appoint distinguished and competent American Negroes to their Boards and to top staff positions.
>
> We view with disapproval the policy of philanthropic foundations in ignoring predominantly Negro institutions and organizations which have demonstrated an abiding interest in Africa and Africans, and Negro scholars versed in African affairs.

---

[84] Preamble, *The American Negro Leadership Conference on Africa: Resolutions*, supra note 26.
[85] *Id.*
[86] *Id.*
[87] Louis Baldwin, TO MAKE THE WOUNDED WHOLE, supra note 1 at 186.

We urge, therefore, foundations to include Negro institutions, organizations, and scholars more adequately in their grants and endowments. We call upon the President's Committee on Equal Employment Opportunity to enforce the non-discrimination clause in contracts between our government and corporations and educational institutions operating in Africa.[88]

ANLCA also called upon the organized religions in the US to reexamine their missionary activities in Africa, particularly concerning the incorporation of Africans as trainers and the reconstruction of their goals to meet the needs of the "African people for education and for training in modern-day skills and techniques, and in terms of the Africans' aspiration for freedom and independence."[89] Additionally, the Preamble to the ANLCA Resolutions focuses explicitly on the US government's covert actions in support of the racist regimes in the Congo, Angola, South Africa, South West Africa, and Mozambique, as well as the years of "economic and cultural deprivation" of African states and peoples. They especially highlighted the need to review the continent's development aid to align it with what the US had allocated for Europe.[90]

King's Pan-African activities were originally channeled through his relationships with African leaders and states, but they became more robust through ACOA and ANLCA. He helped frame, advocate for, and politically support the overall missions of ACOA and ANLCA, including procuring significant resources for them by directly contributing support from the SCLC. For example, the SCLC supported ACOA's Africa Defense and Aid Fund, which George Houser created in 1958 to support opponents and victims of Apartheid facing emergencies in South and Central Africa and to support "Africa's struggle for greater democracy."[91] Indeed, King's commitment to ACOA was tied to his respect and admiration for its director, George Houser, a white Methodist minister who dedicated much of his life to Africa's liberation struggles. King allowed Houser to use the King "name and influence" to support its various "appeals, petitions, declarations, and conferences," including ACOA's annual Human Rights Day ceremonies (held annually on December 10) and Africa Freedom Day events (held annually in April).[92] As if King were not busy enough, he often served as an honorary chairperson or speaker at these events. He is the main reason that the ACOA's profile increased among African leaders and the American foreign policy establishment.

---

[88] *American Negro Participation in the United States Programs in Africa*, ANLCA RESOLUTIONS, Arden House Campus Columbia University (November 23–25, 1962).
[89] Preamble, *American Negro Participation in the United States Programs in Africa*, supra note 26.
[90] *Id.*
[91] *A Letter from Martin Luther King, Jr., to Potential Contributors to the Africa Defense and Aid Fund* (November 12, 1959), MLKP-MBU, in *King Papers* (1954–1968), available at https://kinginstitute.stanford.edu/king-papers/documents/friend#ftnref2.
[92] Baldwin, TO MAKE THE WOUNDED WHOLE, supra note 1 at 186.

Baldwin accurately reports that King invited several high-ranking African leaders to the US and coordinated their trips in the 1950s and 1960s, including "Tom Mboya of Kenya and Kanyama Chiume and Joshua Nkomo of Central Africa," earning him an excellent reputation among Africa's preeminent leaders.[93] King also joined organizations such as The Africa League. He was invited to various meetings and conferences throughout Africa, including Ghana, in March 1960 – a meeting he could not attend – to nonviolently challenge atomic tests in the Sahara as part of Africa's peace and security framework.[94] King's nonviolent approach to domestic and global issues was admired, desired, and even adopted by activists and leaders facing vital challenges to state security, including civil conflicts and decolonization. For instance, in 1966, as a member of ANLCA's Call Committee, King worked with Roy Wilkins to raise funds and galvanize support for President Kenneth Kaunda of the Republic of Zambia to deliver a keynote address at ANLCA's third biennial conference. Kaunda admired King and sought a peaceful resolution to white rule in Rhodesia, but to no avail (Figure 4.1).[95] One of the rationales for inviting Kaunda, a significant stakeholder in seeking to resolve the Rhodesian (Zimbabwe) crisis, was to inspire him to find a peaceful pathway to independence and encourage the US to adopt a proactive policy that would empower the people of Rhodesia by recognizing its leadership rather than following Britain's colonial "non-policy."[96]

The leadership of ANLCA, including King, was concerned about the state of affairs in Southern Africa, including the continued white-minority rule in Rhodesia, South African Apartheid, and the "recent tragic decision of the World Court in the South-West African case."[97] Concerning the latter, Ethiopia and Liberia filed suit in the International Court of Justice (ICJ) claiming that South West Africa, a former German colony under a League of Nations Mandate, remained under a Mandate

---

[93] *Id.*

[94] *Western Union Telegram from C.D. of Accra, Ghana, to Martin Luther King, Jr.* (March 14, 1960), MLKP-MBU (on file with King Papers, Box 70, Folder 3, Ghana, 1954–1968, 1–2, loose document on file with author). "The Positive Action Conference in Accra, Ghana was associated with Kwame Nkrumah and led a protest against the French government's testing of atomic weapons in the Sahara." *Id.*

[95] On May 5, 1960, Kenneth Kaunda visited King at Ebenezer Baptist Church in Atlanta, Georgia, four years before he became President of Zambia. At the time, Kaunda was an anticolonial leader in Northern Rhodesia (now Zambia) and was dedicated to ensuring that Zambia played a pivotal role in combating Apartheid in South Africa, Southwest Africa, Portuguese Angola, and Rhodesia.

[96] *Papers of the NAACP, Part 28: Special Subject Files, 1966–1970,* Group IV, Series A-14: "Africa," Reel 1, 0388, *Africa-General, 1966–1969,* at 1–71. See also, *Letter from Roy Wilkins to Martin Luther Jr. Concerning Invitation to President Kenneth Kaunda* (July 22, 1966), AMERICAN NEGRO LEADERSHIP CONFERENCE ON AFRICA (loose document on file with author).

[97] *From Theodore E. Brown to Martin Luther King, Jr.* (October 12, 1966) (on file with Martin Luther King, Jr. Collection: Subseries 1.1: Correspondence: General A-D, 0000–0000–0000–0131a. Robert W. Woodruff Library of the Atlanta University Center, Inc., Morehouse Coll.). See also, *Letter from Theodore E. Brown to Martin Luther King, Jr.* (July 28, 1966) (loose document on file with author).

and that, because of that, South Africa was still bound to its obligation to allow the UN – the successor to the League of Nations – to exercise executive authority over it.[98] Ethiopia and Liberia claimed that the Apartheid government in South Africa, which was mandated to assist and develop South West Africa, instead introduced Apartheid, exploited its natural resources, established military bases in the country, and denied Blacks the right to participate in the constitution of order. On July 18, 1966, a divided court (7–7) determined that Ethiopia and Liberia did not establish any legal right or interest in whether South West Africa remained a territory under a UN Mandate or whether South Africa breached its obligation as a Trustee of the Mandate in its treatment of Africans in South West Africa (today Namibia).[99] King and the leadership of ANLCA were disillusioned with the ICJ's determination, which led to the continued repression of Black Namibians and South Africa's racist grip in the region. Southern Africa was important to King. He saw no distinction in the suffering of Black South West Africans and Black Rhodesians. For example, he explicitly condemned the white minority Government of Rhodesia for "blocking representation on the part of the African people themselves."[100] He believed that the UN should send a force that would support the British government's denial of independence to any version of a Southern Rhodesia established undemocratically, arguing for a one-man-one-vote approach rather than a white-minority rule system.[101]

Another interesting example of King's involvement in peace-making concerns the Nigerian Civil War (July 6, 1967–January 15, 1970). The war began when Biafra, in the Eastern Region of Nigeria, largely inhabited by members of the Igbo (Ibo) nation, sought to secede from Nigeria after approximately 20,000 Igbo were killed in Northern Nigeria by government forces and militia in September 1966.[102] Under the auspices of ANLCA, which had been seeking ways to end secessionist civil conflict in Nigeria since March 1967, King, A. Phillip Randolph, Roy Wilkins, and Whitney M. Young Jr. were preparing a peace mission to the region before King was assassinated.[103] King dispatched Theodore Brown, then president of ANLCA, to Nigeria

---

[98] South West Africa (Ethiopia v. South Africa; Liberia v. South Africa), 1962 I.C.J. 319 (Dec. 21). See also, *South-West Africa Cases (Ethiopia v. South Africa; Liberia v. South Africa); Second Phase*, International Court of Justice (ICJ), July 18, 1966, www.refworld.org/jurisprudence/caselaw/icj/1966/en/90239

[99] *Id.*

[100] Martin Luther King Jr., *On the World Taking a Stand on Rhodesia: An Interview*, Paris, France (on file with The King Center Archives, October 25, 1965, Roll #35 Sync Sound #73, 1, loose document on file with author).

[101] *Id.*

[102] See generally, Alexander A. Madiebo, THE NIGERIAN REVOLUTION AND THE BIAFRAN WAR (Enugu, Nigeria: Fourth Dimension Publishers, 1980). See also, Ntieyong U. Akpan, STRUGGLE FOR SECESSION, 1966–1970: PERSONAL ACCOUNT OF THE NIGERIAN CIVIL WAR (London: Frank Cass, 1972). and Heerten, L., & A.D. Moses (2014), The Nigeria–Biafra War: Postcolonial Conflict and the Question of Genocide, JOURNAL OF GENOCIDE RESEARCH, Vol. 16 (2014), 169–203.

[103] See generally, JA Farquharson, *To the Benefit of Africa, the World, and Ourselves: The American Negro Leadership Conference on Africa (ANLCA) Mission to Nigeria, 1966–1968*, JOURNAL OF GLOBAL HISTORY, Vol. 17 (2022), 457–476.

4.2 *King Responds to Africa* 97

twice to help lay the groundwork for his engagement as a mediator "to aid in the resolution of the Nigerian crisis."[104] In a letter from Nigerian intellectual Simon Obi Anekwe to King, Anekwe asked King to "bring the moral strength of 22 million black Americans" to lobby the US government, the Organization of African Unity (OAU), and the UN to end the armed conflict in Nigeria.[105] The pre-planning documentation reveals that King was going to play a vital role in negotiations between the two rival leaders, Lieutenant General Yakubu Gowon (Biafra) and Lieutenant Colonel Chukwuemeka Odumegwa Ojukwu, which may have led to a peaceful cessation of conflict. With King as the most prominent and respected member of the ANLCA mission, their efforts enjoyed broad support from President William Tubman of Liberia, a member of the OAU delegation on the Nigerian conflict, and Lieutenant General Joseph A. Ankrah of Ghana, who was the lead mediator for the OAU delegation. Tubman strongly encouraged ANLCA's "American Negro leaders," namely King, Wilkins, Randolph, and Young, to organize a "peace mission" that would help "end the suffering caused by the Civil War in Nigeria."[106] Lieutenant General Ankrah likewise supported an African American peace delegation to try and resolve the crisis in Nigeria, believing that "American Negro Leaders" were "very important in this endeavor."[107]

On November 24, 1967, ANLCA Executive Director Theodore Brown met with Ethiopian Emperor Haile Selassie in Nigeria to lay the groundwork for the ANLCA peace mission. He quotes Selassie as saying, "Nothing could be more helpful and produce a sense of hope for all Nigerians and all Africa in general, than to have distinguished American Negro leaders come to Africa specifically on a humanitarian mission to help end the bloodshed in Nigeria."[108] Emperor Selassie welcomed the "opportunity to confer and explore ways in which the OAU and the American

---

[104] Simon Anekwe, Africa Today – The Leadership, NEW YORK AMSTERDAM NEWS, January 27, 1968, 15. See also, *Letter from Simon Obi Anekwe to Member of the American Negro Leadership Conference on Africa* (August 18, 1967) (on file with The King Center Archives, document on file with author).

[105] *Id.*

[106] *Memorandum From Theodore E. Brown to Dorothy Height, Martin Luther King, A. Philip Randolph, Roy Wilkins, Whitney Young* (March 21, 1967), Box A42, File NAACP Administration 1966 – General Office File American Negro Leadership Conference on Africa 1966–69, The Records of the National Association for the Advancement of Colored People (TRNAACP) (Library of Congress (LOC), Washington, DC), See also, *4 Top Rights Leaders Consider Africa Trip*, THE CHICAGO DEFENDER, December 23, 1968, 32; *Civil Rights Leaders May Go to Nigeria*, NEW YORK AMSTERDAM NEWS, January 13, 1968, 26.

[107] *Emissary Trip to Africa in November 1967 Regarding the Nigerian Civil War: A Statement from Theodore E. Brown to Roy Wilkins, Whitney Young, A. Phillip Randolph, and Martin Luther King, Jr.* (January 10, 1968) (on file with The King Center Archives); *Memorandum from T.E. Brown to R. Wilkins, W. Young, A.P. Randolph, M.L. King, "RE: Nigeria"* (June 14, 1967), Box A42, File NAACP Administration 1966 – General Office File American Negro Leadership Conference on Africa 1966–69, TRNAACP, LOC.

[108] *Memorandum from T.E. Brown to R. Wilkins, W. Young, A.P. Randolph, M.L. King, "RE: Nigeria"* (June 14, 1967), Box A42, File NAACP Administration 1966 – General Office File American Negro Leadership Conference on Africa 1966–69, TRNAACP, LOC.

Negro leaders could be successful in this effort."[109] This was quite an endorsement by one of the intellectual founders of the OAU and one of Africa's most famous and respected leaders. Selassie clearly understood that the proposed ANLCA delegation represented the concerns of 22 million Black Americans on African issues, and he even invited the delegation to Ethiopia during their African travels. Had King lived, he would have played a pivotal role in seeking to end Nigeria's bloody civil war.

King's work with ANLCA's Call Committee and Policy Committee gave him the institutional gravitas to speak forthrightly to US officials on African issues. Moreover, his ability to identify the intersections between morality and foreign policy was unique, especially as it related to America's moral obligations to the continent of Africa and her people. From fundraising for Africa's liberation and development to policy speeches and advocacy to US officials and the American public writ large, King regularly compared, contrasted and drew inspiration from the problems faced by African Americans and Africans.

This was how King pragmatically harmonized Africa and Black America's freedom movements – which included outspokenly supporting forceful and non-violent self-determination movements in the continent. Again, King supported the nationalist movements in Angola, Mozambique, and Algeria, which violently struggled for freedom and independence. His knowledge and understanding of the interplay between African Affairs and global governance were formidable. Algeria, in particular, became a priority. Working through ACOA and ANLCA, King lobbied the US government to take progressive action to bring peace to Algeria by encouraging the UN General Assembly to organize peaceful negotiations between France and Algerian nationalists seeking freedom from colonial oppression.[110] His recourse to international law, including UN law, supporting Algerian independence demonstrated his knowledge of international human rights law and the UN's role as an arbiter and enforcer of international peace and security.

King's anticolonial activism was truly Pan-African, not just in the racialized substance of his advocacy but also because of the geographical breadth of his engagements. For example, he openly advocated for the freedom of the people of Nyasaland (Malawi) from British colonial rule, administered by its cruel colonial governor, Sir Robert Armitage. He argued that at least 500 Africans (ultimately 1,300) were being held as political prisoners, specifically members of the Nyasaland African Congress, and thousands of others were being detained by what was clearly a police state.[111] His remarks were made while colonial authorities declared a state of emergency in the small nation, during which time colonial security forces killed at least fifty Malawians.

---

[109] Id.

[110] American Committee on Africa, *A Call for Peace in Algeria*, November 20, 1959, MLKP-MBU (on file with King Papers [1954–1968], Box 18, Folder 2, 1, loose document on file with author).

[111] *A Letter from Martin Luther King, Jr., to Supporters of the American Committee on Africa*, November 12, 1959, MLKP-MBU (on file with King Papers [1954–1968]), available at https://kinginstitute.stanford.edu/king-papers/documents/friend.

King also spoke passionately of South Africa. In his 1965 speech "Let My People Go," King deemed US support of South Africa "the shame of our nation" and called on the international community to boycott it.[112] He was a fervent opponent of Apartheid in South Africa and South West Africa and seems to have understood the Apartheid government's perverse nature through the lens of his experiences fighting racial segregation in the US. It was one thing to be taken from your homeland and systematically enslaved and oppressed as a racial minority in North America. It was quite another to be relegated to servitude and racially oppressed in your homeland as the racial and cultural majority. Like many Black Americans, King was genuinely mortified by the wickedness of the Apartheid state and, as Baldwin documents, he spent nearly his entire adult life fighting it.

4.3 KING AND APARTHEID

King's anti-Apartheid advocacy deserves special attention because it represents one of his earliest and prolific African engagements.[113] King's antimaterial class consciousness made him a formidable adversary, as did his slavocratic heritage, which allowed him to understand the dynamics of racial oppression and race-based class warfare and simultaneously become bonded to the African world, its people, and its struggles. This deliberate bonding fortified his robust anti-Apartheid activism, which, in December 1965, ultimately led him to call for an international boycott against South Africa to "demonstrate the international potential for non-violence."[114] On December 10, 1965, Human Rights Day at Hunter College in New York, he delivered his blistering "Let My People Go" speech. The speech represented only his second lecture on the situation in South Africa despite having been working closely with leaders of the African National Congress (ANC) to dismantle Apartheid since the late 1950s. In the speech, King posited that, despite having "volumes of facts" to the contrary, whites continued to depict Africa "as the home of black cannibals and ignorant primitives" in "books, motion pictures, and other media of communication."[115] Offering a paradigm shift, King argued:

> Africa does have spectacular savages and brutes today, but they are not black. They are the sophisticated white rulers of South Africa who profess to be cultured, religious and civilized, but whose conduct and philosophy stamp them unmistakably as modern-day barbarians.

---

[112] Martin Luther King Jr., *Call for an International Boycott of Apartheid South Africa, Let My People Go*, Address at Hunter College, New York City, Human Rights Day (December 10, 1965), African Activist Archive, https://africanactivist.msu.edu/recordFiles/210-849-20874/mlkspeechopt.pdf.

[113] Lewis Baldwin comprehensively documented King's anti-Apartheid ministry in his seminal book, TOWARD THE BELOVED COMMUNITY: MARTIN LUTHER KING, JR. AND SOUTH AFRICA. His treatment of the subject is by far the most comprehensive and insightful. Lewis V. Baldwin, TOWARD THE BELOVED COMMUNITY: MARTIN LUTHER KING, JR. AND SOUTH AFRICA, supra note 2.

[114] Martin Luther King Jr., *Call for an International Boycott of Apartheid South Africa*, supra note 112.

[115] Id.

> We are in an era in which the issue of human rights is the central question confronting all nations. In this complex struggle an obvious but little appreciated fact has gained attention –the large majority of the human race is non-white – yet it is that large majority which lives in hideous poverty. While millions enjoy an unexampled opulence in developed nations, ten thousand people die of hunger each and every day of the year in the undeveloped world.[116]

King believed that the "issue of human rights was the central question confronting all nations" and that white supremacy and white domination in Africa and beyond could lead to an "international race war," noting in the above passage that the "large majority of the human race is non-white."[117]

In "Let My People Go," King analytically employed a form of comparative humanitarianism. He criticized US foreign policy in South Africa and its abject failure to condemn the Apartheid government, let alone levy sanctions against it. He used the example of the brutal and crooked US intervention in the Dominican Republic in April 1965 – when President Lyndon B. Johnson sent American troops to thwart the removal of a corrupt military junta that overthrew the nation's first freely elected government – to highlight the nation's hypocrisy. King referred to US military action in the Dominican Republic as an "overwhelming force shocking the world with our zealousness and naked power," interrogating, by contrast, the US's muted response to the violent oppression of Black South Africans. He reasoned: "Our protest is so muted and peripheral it merely mildly disturbs the sensibilities of the segregationists, while our trade and investments substantially stimulate their economy to greater heights."[118] Going further, King offered critical economic insights. He argued that the US gave the Apartheidists:

> Massive support through American investments in motor and rubber industries, by extending some forty million dollars in loans through our most distinguished banking and financial institutions, by purchasing gold and other minerals mined by black slave labour, by giving them a sugar quota, by maintaining three tracking stations there and by providing them with the prestige of a nuclear reactor built with our technical cooperation and fueled with refined uranium supplied by us.[119]

King's leadership and support for ACOA ensured his engagement on all issues in South Africa, as did his relationship with leaders in the ANC, such as Oliver Tambo (President of the ANC, 1967–1991) and Albert Luthuli (President of the ANC, 1952–1967). Tambo and King had communicated since 1957, when the former appealed to King to politically and financially support the first International Day of Protest against Apartheid. King did. Luthuli, meanwhile, considered King to be

---

[116] Id.
[117] Id.
[118] Id.
[119] Id.

his "hero."[120] King similarly admired Luthuli. During his acceptance speech for the Nobel Peace Prize, King specifically acknowledged Luthuli, the first African to win the Nobel Peace Prize (1960), while connecting the Black American civil rights movement with the anti-Apartheid struggle, noting that Luthuli's "struggles with and for his people are still met with the most brutal expressions of man's inhumanity to man."[121] Baldwin rightly notes that while he and Luthuli never physically met, "the impelling spiritual, moral, and intellectual power they drew from each other must have reinforced their convictions about the need for Africans and African Americans to join forces in the struggle against racism and colonialism."[122]

In his actions, King operated in the BIT by appealing to outside law and norms (e.g., UN law) and seeking an audience with the UN Special Committee Against Apartheid to condemn the South African government. On June 10, 1963, as a member of ACOA's National Committee and a founding member of ANLCA, King requested to appear before the "Committee, at its convenience, to testify on the policies of apartheid of the Government of the Republic of South Africa." It was highly unusual for Black people to give testimony at the UN and even more rare for African Americans. Nevertheless, E. S. Reddy, Principal Secretary of the Special Committee on the Policies of Apartheid of the Government of the Republic of South Africa, granted King's request,[123] but King was unable to testify due to scheduling conflicts.[124]

The ANLCA also received requests for assistance from the Pan-Africans Congress in mobilizing American resources to "wipe out apartheid and all of its evils in South Africa."[125] In addition, King contributed to numerous ACOA campaigns, even acting as vicechair of the 1957 "Declaration of Conscience" against Apartheid. Then, in December 1962, Luthuli and King cosponsored the "Appeal for Action against Apartheid," which, among other things, appealed to "all men of goodwill to take

---

[120] *A letter from James W. King to Martin Luther King, Jr.*, March 25, 1964, MLKP-MBU (on file in King Papers [1954–1968], loose document on file with author). See also, *Lutuli, Albert J., January 1, 1898 to July 21, 1967* (on file with The Martin Luther King Jr. Research and Education Institute), available at https://kinginstitute.stanford.edu/lutuli-albert-j#:~:text=Although%20Lutuli%20and%20Martin%20 Luther,(Papers%205%3A307.

[121] Martin Luther King Jr., *Acceptance Speech in the Auditorium of the University of Oslo, on the Occasion of the Award of the Nobel Peace Prize*, December 10, 1964, The Nobel Prize, available at www.nobelprize.org/prizes/peace/1964/king/acceptance-speech/.

[122] Louis Baldwin, TO MAKE THE WOUNDED WHOLE, supra note 1 at 203.

[123] *Letter from E.S. Reedy to Martin Luther King, Jr.*, PO 230 SOAP (2-1-2) (June 28, 1963). (loose document on file with author). E.S. Reddy prepared the communication at the behest of H.E. M. Diallo Telli (Guinea), Chairman of the Special Committee on the Policies of Apartheid of the Government of the Republic of South Africa.

[124] Martin Luther King Jr. and Albert John Luthuli, *Appeal for action against apartheid*, Published by the United Nations at the request of the Special Committee against Apartheid in a pamphlet in tribute to Dr. King (New York: UN Center against Apartheid, 1984). See also, Boutros Boutros-Ghali, THE UNITED NATIONS AND APARTHEID, 1948–1994, UN blue book series (New York, NY: Department of Public Information, UN 1994), 19.

[125] Martin Luther King Jr. and Albert John Luthuli, *Appeal for action against apartheid*, supra note 124.

actions against Apartheid" by organizing demonstrations on Human Rights Day, lobbying for economic and trade sanctions, urging the UN Mission to the United Nations to adopt resolutions condemning South Africa, boycotting South African products, and educating the public to engage in public action to build an "international quarantine of Apartheid."[126]

By this time, King was an internationalist who worked with and through local, national, and international organizations and bodies to liberate Black people, particularly Africans and "Negroes." Thus, he strongly condemned US support of the South African government and chastised the US for not "sacrificing trade and profit to oppose" South Africa effectively.[127] By allying with the "monstrous government in its grim war with black people," he argued that the US continued its legacy of participating in the "infamous African slave trade" and the "rape of Africa."[128] In "Let My People Go," King remarked that "there are few parallels in human history of the period in which Africans were seized and branded like animals, packed into ships' holds like cargo and transported into chattel slavery," describing the Middle Passage as "a holocaust reminiscent of the Nazi slaughter of Jews, Poles, and others."[129] South African Apartheid, he argued, was one of those parallels. He went on to describe Apartheid as the "world's worst racism."[130] Still, he suggested that it could be solved nonviolently given the massive economic leverage held in South Africa by the major powers like the U.S.S.R., Great Britain, France, the US, Germany, and Japan. King was clear that he wanted the US, which he viewed as an enabler of Apartheid, to boycott South Africa. Even though Black Americans are not descendants of Southern Africa, he considered America's debt to the African world as "an obligation of atonement that is not canceled by the passage of time."[131]

These are hardly the ruminations of a passive reformist; instead, they were the thoughts and actions of a radical – a militant for global justice, unafraid to inform the white man that his racist worldview devolved him from "human to pre-human."[132] King seemed to resent the fact that "Negroes were dispersed over thousands of miles and over many continents."[133] However, he proclaimed, "[we] have found each other again," in full realization of the "powerful unity of Negro with Negro."[134] King was called to confront the abomination that was Apartheid in South Africa and, in doing so, indicted the moral character of mankind with the

---

[126] *Id.*
[127] Martin Luther King Jr., *Call for an International Boycott of Apartheid South Africa*, supra note 112.
[128] *Id.*
[129] *Id.*
[130] *Id.*
[131] Martin Luther King Jr., *Call for an International Boycott of Apartheid South Africa*, supra note 112. See also, Marcus Rediker, *Atonement*, LOS ANGELES TIMES, January 21, 2008, available at www.latimes.com/archives/la-xpm-2008-jan-21-oe-rediker21-story.html.
[132] *Id.*
[133] Martin Luther King Jr., *Call for an International Boycott of Apartheid South Africa*, supra note 112.
[134] *Id.*

immense suffering of Black South Africans.[135] In a March 1960 letter to President Dwight Eisenhower, King and other Black leaders applauded the US government's condemnation of the Sharpeville massacres in South Africa while wondering when Eisenhower would publicly condemn Jim Crow in the American South. The letter asks a simple but remarkable question, highlighting the sophistication of King and its authors: "Africans are turning to the UN for moral support and encouragement: must we?" This suggestive threat to the Eisenhower administration reveals that King understood how to leverage outside or international law and institutions to challenge domestic policy.[136] His dedication to fighting Apartheid was absolute, and despite being overwhelmed by the civil rights movement in the US, he accepted an invitation from the Students' Visiting Lecturers Organization of the University of Cape Town to serve as the T. B. Davie Memorial Lecturer for 1965; however, he was denied an entry visa because of his global recognition as a racial justice activist who opposed Apartheid.[137] During the same period, King was also invited by the National Union of South African Students to deliver a keynote address to its 1966 Congress.[138] He was popular among Black South African youth and progressive whites, which is why the Apartheid regime detested him. Although these invitations were a testament to his global standing as a racial justice and peace advocate, the Apartheid government feared him, especially King's moral courage and power to challenge their regime.[139] But for his assassination, King was primed to accelerate efforts to end Apartheid, help mediate an end to the Nigerian Civil War, and encourage Cameroon's transition to democracy. He was poised to author a new conflict prevention, management, and resolution paradigm rooted in two of Beloved Pan-Africanism's core tenets: love, global Blackness, and nonviolence.

4.4 KING HONORS DU BOIS

King's strong Pan-African inclinations were reflected in the many forms of his advocacy, from his sermons, speeches, and writings to his travels, friendships, and participation in liberation-orientated organizations. The analysis above situates King

---

[135] *Letter from Martin Luther King, Jr. to Dr. Raymond Hoffenberg* (July 11, 1965), (loose document on file with author).

[136] *Letter to Dwight D. Eisenhower*, March 26, 1960 (on file with The Martin Luther King, Jr. Research and Education Institute), available at https://kinginstitute.stanford.edu/king-papers/documents/dwight-d-eisenhower-3.

[137] *South African Visa Denied to Dr. King*, THE NEW YORK TIMES, March 25, 1966, 4. *Letter from Monica Wilson on Behalf of the Students' Visiting Lecturers Organization of the University of Cape Town to Martin Luther King, Jr.* (November 12, 1965), (loose document on file with author). *Letter from Martin Luther King, Jr. to the South African Embassy in New Orleans, Louisiana* (February 9, 1966) (loose document on file with author).

[138] *Letter from Martin Luther King, Jr. to the South African Embassy in New Orleans, Louisiana* (February 9, 1966), (loose document on file with author).

[139] *Letter from Martin Luther King, Jr. to Dr. R. Hoffenberg*, supra note 135.

in the Pan-African tradition. However, his relationship with Du Bois, the "father" of Pan-Africanism, merits examination given that they communicated, greatly admired one another, and thought similarly about the Black world. It is perhaps unsurprising that King offered a resounding tribute to the famous Pan-Africanist forefather, W. E. B. Du Bois (1868–1963). Through Du Bois, King's Pan-African thoughts are illuminated. Like Du Bois, King had a deep connection and love for Africa and persons of African descent, irrespective of their nationality or place of origin. Like DuBois, his thinking on Africa was radical. As far back as 1956, King addressed the indignities of political and economic exploitation, segregation, and the disenfranchisement of Africa, King opined that "for centuries, Africa has been one the of most exploited continents in the history of the world" and has "suffered all of the pain and affliction that could be mustered up by other nations.[140] Unlike Du Bois, he was driven first by ecclesiastical rationale and then by liberation politics. As a Pan-Africanist, King highlighted and shared Du Bois's recognition of the "importance of the bonds between American Negroes and the land of their ancestors."[141] Again, King believed that Africans were "our brothers," African Americans were "a part of Africa," Africa's problems were "our problems,"[142] and that Africa was the Motherland. King and Du Bois both believed that people should be free to live peacefully with whomever they choose, thereby embracing two core principles of Pan-Africanism: self-determination and non-discrimination. In lockstep with Du Bois, King proclaimed:

> In conclusion, let me say that Dr. Du Bois' greatest virtue was his committed empathy with all the oppressed and his divine dissatisfaction with all forms of injustice. Today we are still challenged to be dissatisfied. Let us be dissatisfied until every man can have food and material necessities for his body, culture and education for his mind, freedom and human dignity for his spirit.[143]

By the age of twenty-eight, King was fully immersed in African affairs, having already visited Ghana, befriended South African anti-Apartheid leaders, and delivered his famous "Birth of a New Nation" speech. By contrast, Pan-Africanism's father, Du Bois, didn't sojourn to Africa (Liberia) until age fifty-five, nor did he intellectually engage the continent with as much fervor as early in his life as King did.

King respected Du Bois and agreed with his philosophical ideas about white America and the interdependent plights of Blacks in America and Africa. In

---

[140] Martin Luther King Jr., *The Birth of a New Nation*, Sermon Delivered at Dexter Avenue Baptist Church (April 7, 1957), in *King Papers, Volume IV: Symbol of the Movement* (January 1957–December 1958), 156.

[141] Martin Luther King Jr., Honoring DuBois, *Published speech in* FREEDOMWAYS 8 (1968), 6.

[142] Martin Luther King Jr., *Recommendations to the SCLC Executive Committee*, September 30, 1959, available at https://kinginstitute.stanford.edu/king-papers/documents/recommendations-sclc-executive-committee.

[143] Martin Luther King Jr., *Honoring DuBois*, supra note 141 at 13.

Honoring DuBois, King expressed a belief that whites benefited by learning the truth about Black Americans, arguing:

> In closing, it would be well to remind white America of its debt to Dr. Du Bois. When they corrupted Negro history they distorted American history, because Negroes are too big a part of the building of this nation to be written out of it without destroying scientific history. White America, drenched with lies about Negroes, has lived too long in a fog of ignorance. Dr. Du Bois gave them a gift of truth for which they should eternally be indebted to him.[144]

Concerning African American relations with Africa, King dedicated one of his last significant speeches to Du Bois's work in this area during the International Cultural Evening celebrating the 100th birthday of Du Bois at Carnegie Hall on February 23, 1968. In this radically insightful speech, King commented that "after World War I he [Du Bois] called Pan-African Congresses in 1919, 1921, and 1923, alarming imperialists in all countries and disconcerting Negro moderates in America who were afraid of this restless, militant, black genius."[145] King's reference to moderate Negroes was bold and indicative of his black radical consciousness, which too often is lost in the "dreamer narratives" that surround him.

King argued that Black Americans have a deep connection with Africa because it is the land of their origin.[146] Like Du Bois, King embraced this close bond built on racial ancestry, affinity, political unity, cultural connectedness, and liberation-orientated activism. He identified with and recognized Africa and her people as ancestral kin and, like Du Bois, considered the defeat of racism in the US as inseparable from and interdependent with the fight against colonialism and apartheid. Of course, the BIT did not start with King. However, his efforts built on a voluminous history of African Americans and their assistance to African states and freedom movements.[147] One granular example was Black American support to Ethiopia during Emperor Selassie's reign after the League of Nations turned its back on it.[148] After Benito Mussolini, Prime Minister of Italy, invaded Ethiopia in 1935, African Americans were incensed and provided moral and material support to the African nation during the war effort despite being crushed themselves by America's Great Depression.[149] Additionally, Emperor Selassie commissioned two Black American

---

[144] *Id.* at 9–10.
[145] Martin Luther King Jr., *Honoring Dr. DuBois*, The Centennial Address Delivered at Carnegie Hall in New York City (February 23, 1968), available at http://pmeaye.tripod.com/kingondubois.pdf. The occasion was the International Cultural Evening sponsored by Freedom Ways Magazine on the 100th birthday of Dr. W. E. B. DuBois.
[146] Martin Luther King Jr., *Call for an International Boycott of Apartheid South Africa, Let My People Go*, supra note 112. See also, Marcus Rediker, *Atonement*, supra note 131.
[147] See generally, Elliott P. Skinner, AFRICAN AMERICANS AND U.S. POLICY TOWARD AFRICA, 1850-1924: IN DEFENSE OF BLACK NATIONALITY (Washington, DC: Howard University Press, 1992).
[148] *Id.* at 8.
[149] See generally, William R. Scott, *Black Nationalism and the Italo-Ethiopian Conflict 1934–1936*, THE JOURNAL OF NEGRO HISTORY, Vol. 63, No. 2 (Apr. 1978), 118–134. Nearly 2000 Black Americans

pilots (Tuskegee airmen), Hubert Fauntleroy Julian (Harlem's "Black Eagle") and John C. Robinson, to build and command its small Air Force against the Italian military.[150] Black Americans have consistently supported anticolonial movements in Africa. As such, King would agree with Du Bois's view that "economic exploitation and racism was 'the program of the white world,'"[151] because his antiracist and anticolonial activism was the *sine qua non* of his Pan-African identity.

From this background, George Houser's apparent distinction between Pan-Africanist and universalist (or integrationist) ideals seems trivial as a means of denying King his rightful place as a Pan-African leader, especially given that the two ideals intersect and complement the antiracist, antipoverty, anticolonial, and antiwar values in Pan-Africanism. As scholar James Cone states, King's dream "was not limited to racial equality in the United States but was defined by its universality and eternity," a dream that complemented the global thinking, advocacy, and interests of twentieth-century Pan-Africanists in the developing world and beyond.[152] King's appreciation of Du Bois's work as a human rights leader reinforced the view that Du Bois fortified King's global ministry and attentiveness to Beloved Pan-Africanism. King's Pan-African inclinations were well developed long before the Montgomery Bus Boycott (December 5, 1955 –December 20, 1956), and his notion of Beloved Pan-Africanism honed nearly a decade before delivering his "I Have a Dream" speech in front of the Lincoln Memorial during the March on Washington (August 28, 1963). On the topic of Black American unity with Africa, King explained:

> For the American Negro there is a special relationship with Africa. It is the land of his origin. It was despoiled by invaders; its culture was arrested and concealed to justify white supremacy. The American Negro's ancestors were not only driven into slavery but their links with their past were severed so that their servitude might be psychological as well as physical. In this period when the American Negro is giving moral leadership and inspiration to his own nation, he must find the resources to aid his suffering brothers in his ancestral homeland. Nor is this aid a one-way street. The civil rights movement in the United States has derived immense inspiration from the successful struggles of those Africans who have attained freedom in their own nations. The fact that black men govern States, are building democratic institutions, sit in world tribunals, and participate in global decision-making gives every Negro a needed sense of dignity.[153]

King's bold grasp on the domestic and international impacts of white supremacy and his recognition that African Americans have always served as America's moral compass and as self-healers might be the ultimate example of self-help. Moreover,

---

volunteered for a Black expeditionary force to fight in the Ethiopian armed forces against the Italian invasion but were thwarted by the US Government.

[150] *Id.* at 129–130.
[151] *Id.* at 122.
[152] James Cone, *Martin Luther King Jr., and the Third World*, supra note 2 at 459.
[153] Martin Luther King Jr., *Call for an International Boycott of Apartheid South Africa*, supra note 112.

King's acknowledgment of the influence of African freedom struggles and independence on the civil rights movement in the US and Africa's recognition of King's influence on African independence movements typifies the Du Boisian view of Pan-African cooperation.

Unfortunately, Du Bois's passive mentorship of King as a Pan-Africanist abruptly ended. On August 27, 1963, to the dismay of King and the Pan-African world, Du Bois died at the age of 95 in Ghana, one day before the March on Washington. One wonders whether King's most celebrated moment as a global human rights leader was emboldened by Du Bois's death. Before King's "I Have a Dream" speech, Roy Wilkins, who was not a supporter of Du Bois because of his socialist views, asked all participants at the March on Washington to honor Du Bois with silence. King declared that Du Bois "was one of the most remarkable men of our time" and revered him as the father of Pan-Africanism, proclaiming that Du Bois "died at home in Africa among his cherished ancestors."[154]

---

[154] *Id.*

5

Beloved Pan-Africanism

FIGURE 5.1 July 16, 1963: Dr. Martin Luther King Jr. (left), civil rights leader, talks with President Julius Nyerere of Tanganyika at a reception given by Nyerere in honor of President Kennedy, in Washington, DC. Dr. King arrived after President Kennedy had departed. People in the background are unidentified. (AP Photo/Henry Burroughs.)

5.1 KING, PAN-AFRICANISM, AND THE BLACK INTERNATIONAL TRADITION

By 1966, thirty-six independent African states were struggling with new identities, imperial relationships, and evolving ethnic relations. While there have always been diverse interpretations of Pan-Africanism, the confluence between "statis Pan-Africanism and its concomitant state-based nationalism, and people's Pan-Africanism based on solidarity and African identity" complicated Pan-Africanism's evolution as a predominant Africanism.[1] This reality weighed heavily on the hearts and minds of African, African American, and Caribbean leaders, including Julius Nyerere. As a leading Pan-Africanist and former President of Tanzania, Julius Nyerere opined:

---

[1] Issa G. Shivji, *What Is Pan-Africanism?*, INTERVENTIONS: CONTEMPORARY LEFT ISSUES IN AFRICA, Issue 1 (2023).

Indeed, I believe that a real dilemma faces the Pan-Africanist. On the one hand is the fact that Pan-Africanism demands an African consciousness and an African loyalty; on the other hand, is the fact that each Pan-Africanist must also concern himself with the freedom and development of one of the nations of Africa. These things can conflict. Let us be honest and admit that they have already conflicted.[2]

Nyerere's litmus test for what Pan-Africanism demands is instructive: It demands an African consciousness, African loyalty, and concern for the liberation and development of at least one African state. One can quibble with Nyerere's criterion for its concision, as "African" might be substituted for "Black" consciousness and loyalty, and any concern for freedom and development might equate to actions aimed at the liberation of Blacks in the diaspora or one or more nations of Africa. This begs the question whether King's actions, advocacy, and contributions to Black freedom struggles satisfy, validate, and or expand on Nyere's test or pioneer a new one (Figure 5.1).

This chapter examines how King's global ministry embodies Pan-African currents.[3] The study of King through the lens of Pan-Africanism is "intellectual territory that is terra nullius [a Latin phrase arguably meaning land belonging to no one] across the fields of law, social science, and the humanities."[4] Thus, *silehonemi inē yigebanyali* (an Amharic phrase meaning "therefore, I claim it"). It is somewhat curious why scholars have omitted King's Pan-African persona and ministry given that his thinking on Africa and the Black world is central to understanding his radical reasoning and how his human rights ministry transcended the racial injustice in the US and impacted the Global South and beyond.[5] King's commitment to Africa, Blacks in the Diaspora, and "his activities in support of "universal black liberation" have "not been seriously studied,"[6] which is quite unfortunate. As previous chapters demonstrate, King's thinking about Africa and her people significantly shaped his understanding of racism in America and the world.

King's timing was prophetic. His global ministry was birthed during Africa's decolonization period, at least a decade before the May 1963 founding of the Organization of African Unity (OAU). Hence, as King evolved his global ministry, which was primarily centered on ending Apartheid in South Africa and African

---

[2] J. K. Nyerere, The Dilemma of the Pan-Africanist, in J. K. Nyerere, FREEDOM AND SOCIALISM (Oxford: Oxford University Press, 1968), 208.
[3] This chapter draws inspiration from and incorporates content from two articles written by the author: Jeremy I. Levitt, *Beyond Borders: Martin Luther King, Jr., Africa, and Pan-Africanism*, TEMPLE INTERNATIONAL & COMPARATIVE LAW JOURNAL, Vol. 31, No. 1 (2017), available at https://ssrn.com/abstract=2973462; Jeremy I. Levitt, *Beloved Pan-Africanism: Martin Luther King's Stride toward Africa, International Human Rights, and the Black International Tradition* (December 1, 2020), available at https://ssrn.com/abstract=3806590.
[4] Jeremy I. Levitt, *Beyond Borders*, supra note 3 at 302.
[5] Lewis V. Baldwin, TOWARD THE BELOVED COMMUNITY: MARTIN LUTHER KING, JR., AND SOUTH AFRICA (Cleveland, OH: Pilgrim Press, 1995), 164.
[6] Id.

independence from the yoke of colonial rule, his transnational advocacy helped elevate the Black American civil rights movement and globalized the international human rights movement against racism, apartheid, colonization, and war. As Richardson observes, King was the first "modern black leader, after Du Bois, to most prominently embody" the unity of the civil rights and international human rights discourses and movements.[7] One may credibly argue that King's global ministry propelled him into national prominence, earning the 1964 Nobel Peace Prize for civil rights and social justice for his activism and modeling of nonviolent resistance in confronting America's oppressive system of racial discrimination and segregation.[8]

In July 1964, one year after the founding of the OAU, the Ethiopian government invited King to celebrate the seventy-third birthday of His Imperial Majesty Haile Selassie I (Emperor Selassie).[9] Interestingly, Emperor Selassie, who was an admirer of King's, was a candidate for the Nobel Peace Prize in the very year that King won. He was nominated for playing the predominant role in the establishment of the OAU while King won for his global human rights ministry. Both leaders (who were devout Christians raised in Black church traditions) were recognized by the international community for organizing movements aimed at fighting against and dismantling colonial and racist political and legal systems. While King's human rights ministry and Emperor Selassie's OAU embraced different forms of Pan-African crusading, both leaders claimed recourse to outside the law to effectuate their mandates, including the international law rights to self-determination, independence, and fundamental human rights guaranteed under the United Nations (UN) Charter.

In 1963–1964, the Philadelphia-based American Friends Service Committee Board of Directors (the Quakers) nominated King for the Nobel prize largely because his nonviolent direct-action approach significantly influenced African leaders, whom, they explained, "are perhaps most aware of racial tensions" and "in several striking cases seeking to create a spirit of reconciliation and to use methods that will not increase the likelihood of violence."[10] The nomination continued, "[t]hese leaders have been influenced and are being encouraged by the example of MARTIN LUTHER KING, Jr."[11] King's influence on African leaders may be the ultimate confirmation of the global impact and utility of the Kingsian brand of Pan-Africanism.

---

[7] Henry J. Richardson III, *Dr. Martin Luther King, Jr. as an International Human Rights Leader*, VILLANOVA LAW REVIEW. Vol. 52, No. 3 (2007), 471–486. https://digitalcommons.law.villanova.edu/vlr/vol52/iss3/2/.

[8] The Nobel prize was reserved for those who "conferred the greatest benefit on mankind," The Nobel Peace Prize, *History*, at www.nobelpeaceprize.org/History.

[9] *Invitation to Martin Luther King, Jr. from Emperor Haile Selassie I*, Box 7, folder 43, Martin Luther King, Jr., Papers, 1954–1968, Boston University, Boston.

[10] *Invitation to Martin Luther King, Jr. from Emperor Haile Selassie I*, supra note 9. See also, *MLK's Invitation from Haile Selassie in 1964*, TADIAS MAGAZINE (2016), available at www.tadias.com/index.php?s=martin+luther+king+quakers.

[11] *Id.*

5.1 King, Pan-Africanism, and the Black International Tradition

The Quaker's letter evidenced a sacrosanct principle of Pan-Africanism: mutual respect and recognition among freedom fighters in Africa and the Black Diaspora. The Quakers went on to argue that King's "work to resolve serious conflicts without violence is also helping to reduce in the United States the indiscriminate bitterness that condemns international organization, and in particular the United Nations, because of the participation of people of non-white races and of the concern to promote 'the dignity and worth of the human person' regardless of race."[12]

After winning the Nobel Peace Prize, King's global ministry rapidly advanced down a Pan-African superhighway, fortifying the legacy of African American interests in international relations,[13] international law, and the Black International Tradition (BIT). The BIT encompasses the historiography of Black perspectives, claims,[14] demands, and actions in relation to "outside law" or alternative norms of law anchored in African customary law.[15] Broadly defined, African customary law is an inherited or established normative order derived from the customs and usages of indigenous Africa – that is, customary patterns of thought, action, or social behavior (as a cultural and religious practice or social custom) observed by a people or peoples out of a sense of moral and legal obligation and, in the first instance, arbitered by traditional authority structures. It was the system of law that governed the internal logic, thinking, and vocation that framed Black American responses to the slave trade, enslavement, and racial segregation. Outside law in the form of African customary law has always been affixed to international law (e.g., human rights law and the law on self-determination).

5.1.1 African Natural Law and the Black International Tradition

Equality norms embedded in the US Constitution and civil rights jurisprudence and practice also offer a pathway to freedom that uncovers African American jurisprudence about and on international law.[16] In his seminal text *The Origins of African-American Interests in International Law*,[17] Richardson demonstrates that the BIT "stretches back to the very origins of our nation, preceding even the

---

[12] Id.
[13] For a seminal work on African Americans and US policy toward Africa, 1850–1924, see generally, Elliott P. Skinner, AFRICAN AMERICANS AND U.S. POLICY TOWARD AFRICA 1850–1924: IN DEFENSE OF BLACK NATIONALITY (Washington, DC, Howard University Press, 1992).
[14] The term "claim" embodies the notion of Black agency, and as a legal and historical construct, orders systematic decisions, demands, and actions that challenge white supremacist norms, constructs, systems, and approaches to ordering society.
[15] Nearly all precolonial Africa, including ancient precolonial Kemet, Nubia, Kush, Punt, and Ethiopia, as well as the medieval era empires of Ghana, Mali, Songhai, and Zimbabwe, adhered to a form of customary law.
[16] Jeremy I. Levitt, Beloved Pan-Africanism: Martin Luther King's Stride toward Africa, International Human Rights, and the Black International Tradition, in Z. Yihdego et al. (eds.), ETHIOPIAN YEARBOOK OF INTERNATIONAL LAW 2019, https://doi.org/10.1007/978-3-030-55912-0_8.
[17] See generally, Henry J. Richardson III, THE ORIGINS OF AFRICAN-AMERICAN INTERESTS IN INTERNATIONAL LAW (Durham, NC: Carolina Academic Press, 2008).

Constitution."[18] The said norms evolved from Black experiential and resistance perspectives predicated on African natural law and rights as well as adaptive African traditions and cultural norms, not on Eurocentricity or European notions of natural rights. After all, the US Supreme Court's infamous 1856 *Dred Scott v. Sanford* decision jurisprudentially and normatively identified the African distinctness of Black Americans while failing to recognize them as humans, let alone citizens. In the decision, Justice Taney opined, "A free negro of the African race, whose ancestors were brought to this country and sold as slaves, is not a 'citizen' within the meaning of the Constitution of the United States."[19] The Court reasoned:

> They had for more than a century before been regarded as beings of an inferior order, and altogether unfit to associate with the white race, either in social or political relations; and so far inferior, that they had no rights which the white man was bound to respect; and that the negro might justly and lawfully be reduced to slavery for his benefit. He was bought and sold, and treated as an ordinary article of merchandise and traffic, whenever a profit could be made by it. This opinion was at that time fixed and universal in the civilized portion of the white race. It was regarded as an axiom in morals as well as in politics, which no one thought of disputing, or supposed to be open to dispute; and men in every grade and position in society daily and habitually acted upon it in their private pursuits, as well as in matters of public concern; without doubting for a moment the correctness of this opinion.[20]

The BIT was constructed in response to this form of violent, dehumanizing, and racist worldview institutionalized and propagated by the white race against persons of African descent long before the "Negro" or "African" was a citizen of the US. The BIT was thus in many ways born and framed by Black American claims to outside law, whether it be African natural law and rights or international law. It was anchored in their propensity toward liberation-orientated cultural behaviors and norms that challenged America's slaveocracy and the Supreme Court classification of Africans in America as chattel.

King sought to nonviolently combat violent and totalitarian white supremacist law and policy by embracing the cultural perspectives of Americans of African origin, Black Africans, and Afro-Caribbeans. King understood that the white race's apparent hatred – seen in anti-Black pseudo-science, structural racism, and theories of inferiority – was rooted in the mythos of Africa and Africans as an inferior species of humanoid, arguably dating back to biblical times.[21] He also grasped the power of

---

[18] Henry J. Richardson III, *Dr. Martin Luther King, Jr. as an International Human Rights Leader*, supra note 7 at 471–486. https://digitalcommons.law.villanova.edu/vlr/vol52/iss3/2/.

[19] Roger Brooke Taney, and Supreme Court of The United States. *U.S. Reports: Dred Scott v. Sandford*, 60 U.S. 19 How. 393. 1856. www.loc.gov/item/usrep060393a/.

[20] Id.

[21] See generally, Cain Hope Felder, RACE, RACISM, AND THE BIBLICAL NARRATIVES: ON USE AND ABUSE OF SACRED SCRIPTURE (Minneapolis: Fortress Press, 2023); Steven Rodney Sadler, Jr., CAN A CUSHITE CHANGE HIS SKIN? AN EXAMINATION OF RACE, ETHNICITY, AND OTHERING IN THE HEBREW BIBLE (New York: T&T Clark, 2005).

domestic and international law, policy, doctrine, and norms in opposing systemic inequity, injustice, and inequality. This is why, perhaps more than any other Black leader, King was dedicated to uniting the African American civil rights movement with African independence movements. After all, Black American resistance movements were psychologically and spiritually rooted in African customary law and cultural norms that predated and rejected American and European chattel slavery, colonization, and invasion of Africa.

Black Africa's cultural, intellectual, and normative agency conceivably birthed the template for international law, human rights precepts, and Europe's natural rights traditions.[22] Africa's natural law and rights customs and practices were well conceived long before the emergence of prehistoric Europe (before 800 BCE).[23] They were anchored by deeply rooted Kemetic socio-legal norms such as MA'AT, a "'law of nature" that expresses itself through customary rules in the Egyptian pantheon.[24] Consequently, enslaved Africans and their progeny, African Americans, rejected "subordinating identity demands forced on them by the European/American slave system."[25] Why? African customary law opposes foreign aggression and oppressive orders. It prescribes revolutionary responses to the Transatlantic Slave Trade, enslavement, and consequent systems. It is law par excellence derived from "local customs and usages of traditional Africa" and rooted in people, peoples, and nations as reflected in their ethnic and cultural "common consciousness."[26]

African customary law is living law that does not comprise "a single uniform set of customs prevailing in any given country."[27] In the private sphere, most Africans have and continue to function daily by and subject to customary law, especially in marriage, inheritance, business, religious practice, and governance or traditional authority structures. Such norms have been codified into national constitutions, particularly traditional African authority structures, and serve as influential sources of law at the

---

[22] See generally, Jeremy I. Levitt, *The African Origins of International Law: Myth or Reality?*, UCLA JOURNAL OF INTERNATIONAL LAW AND FOREIGN AFFAIRS, Vol. 19, No. 113 (2015), available at https://ssrn.com/abstract=2645865.

[23] *Id.* at 18.

[24] In modern international law, customary international law and *jus cogens* norms are perhaps anatomically the most like MA'AT: They were fundamental, universally recognized, preemptory norms or principles of law from which no derogation was permitted. Pharaoh's primary purpose was to "make MA'AT, to make harmony, balance, reciprocity, justice, truth and righteousness." MA'AT was the "force" that ensured "'an ideal state of the universe'" and, accordingly, guided human and institutional behavior and informed the intellectual template from which morality, justice, and rule construction – including treaties – emanated. Jeremy I. Levitt, *The African Origins of International Law: Myth or Reality?*, supra note 22.

[25] Henry J. Richardson III, THE ORIGINS OF AFRICAN AMERICAN INTERESTS IN INTERNATIONAL LAW, supra note 17 at 449.

[26] See generally, C. Ogwurike, *The Source and Authority of African Customary Law*, UNIVERSITY OF GHANA LAW JOURNAL, Vol. 3, No. 1 (1966).

[27] Muna Ndulo, *African Customary Law, Customs, and Women's Rights*, 18 INDIANA JOURNAL OF GLOBAL LEGAL STUDIES (2011), 88.

local and national levels, evidencing their multi-millennial consistency and durability. African customary law generates streams of normative consciousness, behavior, and legal norms dictating that the legal status (e.g., free) and identity (e.g., trade, clan, tribe, or culture) of people and peoples is permanent and "travels with that person wherever he or she may go as a member" of a group.[28] This self-determining identity principle rooted in African natural law remained true irrespective of the jurisdictional or territorial authority claims of European and American colonists and slavocrats.

The epistemological underpinning of African customary law seeks to preserve African descendants' histories, authority, culture, languages, heritage, stories, and collective memories as a source of strength. This liberation promising standardizing authority generates a distinct jurisprudence that underwrites the BIT, broadly defined. Pan-Africanism was conceived by the BIT akin to other critical approaches such as Critical Race Theory, Third World Approaches to International Law (TWAIL), and Critical Race Feminism, all of "which seek to examine the question of whether and how the history of subordinated groups have been stolen by others through oppression and massive distortion, and to frame issues of authority to correct the present jurisprudential and legal consequences of such distortion."[29] King's approach or Pan-Africanism dispositions fit squarely into BIT's cosmogony.

5.2 WHAT IS PAN-AFRICANISM?

As a subset of BIT, Pan-Africanism's Black radical historiography may originate in David Walker's appeal and Martin Delaney's pro-Africa advocacy before its refashioning and refinement by towering intellectuals and activists such as George Washington Williams, John Jacob Thomas, William Edward Burghardt Du Bois (W. E. B. Du Bois), Cyril Lionel James (C. L. R. James), Cheikh Anta Diop, Léopold Sédar Senghor, George Padmore, Audely Moore, and Dara Abubakari.[30] As scholar Cedric Robinson aptly notes:

> Black radicalism is a negation of Western civilization, but not in the direct sense of a simple dialectical negation. It is certain that the evolving tradition of Black radicalism owes its peculiar moment to the historical interdiction of African life by European agents. In this sense, the African experience of the past five centuries is simply one element in the mesh of European history: some of the objective requirements for Europe's industrial development were met by the physical and mental exploitation of Asian, African, and native American peoples. This

---

[28] Henry J. Richardson III, THE ORIGINS OF AFRICAN AMERICAN INTERESTS IN INTERNATIONAL LAW, supra note 17 at 451.
[29] Henry J. Richardson III, The Origins of African American Interests in International Law, 17 BUFFALO HUMAN RIGHTS LAW REVIEW, 1 (2011), 13.
[30] Ashley Farmer, *Reframing African American Women's Grassroots Organizing: Audley Moore and the Universal Association of Ethiopian Women 1957–1963*, JOURNAL OF AFRICAN AMERICAN HISTORY, Vol. 101, Nos. 1–2 (2016), 69–96.

experience, though, was merely the condition for Black radicalism – its immediate reason for and object of being – but not the foundation for its nature or character. Black radicalism, consequently, cannot be understood within the particular context of its genesis. It is not a variant of Western radicalism whose proponents happen to be Black. Rather, it is a specifically African response to an oppression emergent from the immediate determinants of European development in the modern era and framed by orders of human exploitation woven into the interstices of European social life from the inception of Western civilization.[31]

In the mid twentieth century Black diaspora, Black radical approaches birthed a four-way struggle vacillating between 1) non-separatist civil rights activists, 2) Black nationalists, 3) Black Marxists, and 4) Pan-Africanists. These categories were not mutually exclusive; many activists fit into multiple categories. King wrestled with this reality during the civil rights movement, most prominently with the rise of the Black Power Movement, which he took exception to and believed was a confusing "emotional concept."[32] And, while this tetralogy often crisscrossed, or through human and theoretical agency evolved from one to the other, they remain distinct doctrines within the Black radical tradition of resistance[33] – or, for purposes of this analysis, the BIT.

According to reputed intellectual Ron Walters, the African continent was divided by the two-line struggle between Negritude and Marxism–Leninism for most of the twentieth century.[34] The most robust stream of consciousness between diaspora and continental Africans was Pan-Africanism; it provided a unity tent for the diverse array of philosophical positions. Simply put, therefore, Pan-Africanism may be defined as a movement for the globalization of African unity.[35] More specifically, as I have noted elsewhere, it is the "internationalization of African liberation philosophy, which seeks to unify and empower people of African descent all over the world to demand and attain freedom, equality, and justice from the domestic and global forces of white domination, and to maximize their human potential."[36] As a global liberation philosophy,

---

[31] Cedric J. Robinson, BLACK MARXISM: THE MAKING OF THE BLACK RADICAL TRADITION (Chapel Hill, NC: University of North Carolina Press, 1983), 73.
[32] Martin Luther King Jr., THE AUTOBIOGRAPHY OF MARTIN LUTHER KING JR, Clayborne Carson (ed.), 1998, 321–323.
[33] See generally, Cedrick J. Robinson, BLACK MARXISM, supra note 31. "The Black radical tradition is a collection of cultural, intellectual, action-oriented labor aimed at disrupting social, political, economic, and cultural norms originating in anticolonial and antislavery efforts. This tradition is not only resistance against structures rooted in slavery, imperialism, and capitalism, but maintenance of an ontology (cultural traditions, beliefs, values)." Dominiques Thomas and Tabbye Chavous, *The Black Radical Tradition of Resistance, A Series on Black Social Movements*, NATIONAL CENTER FOR INSTITUTIONAL DIVERSITY (February 6, 2019), available at https://medium.com/national-center-for-institutional-diversity/the-black-radical-tradition-of-resistance-7277f09ef396.
[34] Ronald W. Walters, PAN AFRICANISM IN THE AFRICAN DIASPORA: AN ANALYSIS OF MODERN AFROCENTRIC POLITICAL MOVEMENTS (Detroit, MI: Wayne State, 1993), 75.
[35] Jeremy I. Levitt, *Pan-Africanism* (2007). ENCYCLOPEDIA OF GLOBALIZATION, VOLUME III N to T (London: Routledge, 2007), 935–936, available at https://ssrn.com/abstract=2221627.
[36] Id.

Pan-Africanism was born of the effort to empower people of African descent – "whether Nigerian, African-American, or Black Australian – to dismantle the institutions of global white supremacy," including the slave trade, enslavement, colonialism, imperialism, racial segregation, and Apartheid.[37] This dismantling includes challenging the "contemporary and systemic institutional vestiges of these practices, such as neo-colonialism, global indebtedness, chronic underdevelopment, acute poverty, perpetual warfare, rapid disease progression" and the new Jim Crowism.[38] And, while I disagree with Rita Abrahamsen's position that "Pan-Africanism is not inherently progressive," given that its organizing logic and vocation is derived from African natural law and human rights precepts (i.e., liberating persons of African descent from white supremacist systems), I do agree with her supposition that "it is far from monolithic or unified, but contains internal tensions and fissures, multiple variations and inflections, all adapting and mutating in interaction with global events."[39]

Admittedly, the definition above is not a Black nationalist-separatist formulation of Pan-Africanism – which King, like Du Bois, openly rejected – because Pan-Africanism is not based on narrow and parochial idioms of exclusion. It seeks to unify and organize people of African origin and their allies wherever they are, regardless of the systems of governance they live under or racial stratifications at play. As Baldwin rightly notes, the "nationalist elements in King's thought … focused on specific problems faced by peoples of African ancestry throughout the world."[40] While it is true that some African American Pan-Africanists philosophically come out of the Black nationalist tradition with its various archetypes, like King, most did not subscribe to separatism as a foundational or governing principle because Black nationalism and Pan-Africanism are not mutually exclusive.

King essentially was a "Du Boisian," perhaps even a neo-Du Boisian, given that his global ministry was framed by what James Cone accurately refers to as the "black church tradition" (essentially, Black theology and moral activism) in contrast to W. E. B. Du Bois's more secular socialist inclinations.[41] King embraced Du Bois's "militant, self-respecting self-assertion directed against racial prejudice and racial injustice."[42] He thus dismissed strategies predicated on hate (e.g., escape or forced

---

[37] Id.
[38] Id. See generally, Michelle Alexander, THE NEW JIM CROW: MASS INCARCERATION IN THE AGE OF COLORBLINDNESS (New York: The New Press, 2010).
[39] Rita Abrahamsen, *Internationalists, Sovereigntists, Nativists: Contending Visions of World Order in Pan-Africanism*, REVIEW OF INTERNATIONAL STUDIES, Vol. 46, No. 1 (2020), 57.
[40] Louis V. Baldwin, TO MAKE THE WOUNDED WHOLE: THE CULTURAL LEGACY OF MARTIN LUTHER KING JR. (Minneapolis: Fortress Press, 1992), 165.
[41] James Cone, Martin Luther King Jr., *Black Theology–Black Church*, THEOLOGY TODAY, Vol. 40, No. 4 (January 1, 1984), 417.
[42] Brandon Terry and Tommie Shelby, Introduction: Martin Luther King, Jr., and Political Philosophy, in Brandon M. Terry & Tommie Shelby (eds.), TO SHAPE A NEW WORLD: ESSAYS ON THE POLITICAL PHILOSOPHY OF MARTIN LUTHER KING, JR. (Boston: Harvard University Press, 2018), 21.

repatriation), violence, and passive submission and adjustment to white power as well as forms of passive or submissive integration. Instead, as Brandon Terry and Tommie Shelby note, "King adopts both Du Bois's framing of political options and his social-theoretical analysis of the Negro problem," as illustrated in his seminal analysis of the Montgomery Bus Boycott in *Stride Toward Freedom*.[43] One stark difference between Du Bois and King is a key feature of King's Pan-African brand: his disdain for elitism and violence – a contempt driven by moral imperatives and anchored in the Gospel of Jesus rather than Du Boisian pragmatism.

From this background, it is somewhat intriguing that anyone who worked with King would question his Pan-African credentials. For example, George Houser's (Houser) opined that King was not "essentially a Pan-Africanist" because King's "starting point" (whatever that means) was not his African roots but his perspective that the "struggle was universal" (whatever that means).[44] Even if Houser's assertion were true – a conclusion not supported by a close study of King's positions and global ministry – Houser's "Pan-Africanist litmus test," clamoring to one's African roots, imposes curious subjectivity and rigidity. Embracing one's African roots as a defining characteristic of Pan-Africanism and/or viewing the struggle for racial justice and equality as universal are neither qualifiers nor disqualifiers of Pan-Africanism. Interestingly, Houser was white and had no African roots to embrace; subsequently, by his definition, he disqualified himself from being a Pan-Africanist despite having a prominent legacy of Pan-African-like engagement. Moreover, Houser wrongly claimed that "[b]efore the post-World War II upsurge in Africa, American blacks were ambivalent toward that continent. It was difficult to bolster black self-esteem by identifying with an area that was looked upon as backward and that was ignominiously dominated by foreign powers."[45] Houser's misinformed contention ignores Black American history and discounts Negro emigration and repatriation histories to Africa long before the "post-World War II upsurge with Africa."[46] Houser was not thinking about the post-Revolutionary War emigration of "Black Americans" to Sierra Leone following the example of Job Ben Soloman's repatriation to Senegal. Houser ignored free Black Boston shipowner Paul Cuffe's repatriation of thirty-eight formerly enslaved Blacks to Sierra Leone (1815), which captured the imagination of free and enslaved Blacks in the US. Moreover, American Blacks reluctantly established a settlement in Liberia in 1822, and the Republic of Liberia in 1847, with over 20,000 having originally relocated at the behest of the American Colonization Society, a southern association of

---

[43] Id.
[44] George Houser, Freedom's Struggle Crosses Oceans and Mountains: Martin Luther King, Jr. and the Liberation Struggles in Africa and America, in Peter J. Albert & Ronald Hoffman (eds.), WE SHALL OVERCOME: MARTIN LUTHER KING, JR., AND THE BLACK FREEDOM STRUGGLE (New York: Pantheon Books in cooperation with the United States Capitol Historical Society, 1990).
[45] Id.
[46] Id.

Slavocrats.⁴⁷ Some Blacks independently emigrated to Africa during slavery; however, the works of Marcus Garvey's Universal Negro Improvement Association (UNIA) Back to Africa programs began in 1915, and W. E. B. Du Bois's Pan-African activism, commencing in 1919, captured the hearts and minds of Black Americans across the country. All these movements were predicated on Black self-determination, colonial, anti-slavery, and anti-racist Negro American ideals, and migration efforts.

In addition, for the Pan-Africanist, universality – uniting with other oppressed people, peoples, groups, nations, and anti-racist allies irrespective of background – is essential to ending the subjugation of Black peoples by racial oppression, alien occupation, domination, and exploitation. Interestingly, universality was a foundational principle behind Third World solidarity, which reached "an apex with the Bandung Conference [April 18–24, 1955] of twenty-nine Afro-Asian nations representing more than half of the world's population."⁴⁸ All four of the genuinely independent African states attended the conference, including Egypt, Ethiopia, Liberia, and Libya – Apartheid South Africa was not invited. Leaders of African nations on the pathway to independence were also welcomed, including the Gold Coast (Ghana) and the Central African Federation (Malawi, Zambia, and Zimbabwe). Bandung demonstrated Africa's appetite and capacity for self-governance, as well as multilateral cooperation and organization under the umbrella of Pan-African unity. As pressure mounted on Britain, France, Portugal, Belgium, and Spain to decolonize, Bandung increased pressure on them and empowered African nations seeking freedom from their colonial yokes. One conference observer, Homer Jack, American clergyman, pacifist, social activist, and close friend to King, reflected that "Bandung somehow caught the world's imagination, and early on its leaders were conscious that history was looking over their shoulder."⁴⁹ It essentially conceived and gave expression to the "international nonaligned movement and the establishment of the Asia-Africa sub-grouping at the United Nations."⁵⁰

Prominent Black Americans, such as Congressman Adam Clayton Powell and the author Richard Wright, attended the Bandung Conference and wholeheartedly supported African unity. They viewed the Black American struggle for freedom as inseparable from African freedom movements. King's speeches reflected Bandung's predominant consensus that the colored people and nations of the world must fight racism, colonialism, and imperialism. Houser reminds us that the Bandung

---

⁴⁷ See generally, Jeremy I. Levitt, THE EVOLUTION OF DEADLY CONFLICT IN LIBERIA: FROM PATERNALTARIANISM TO STATE COLLAPSE (North Carolina: Carolina Academic Press, 2005).
⁴⁸ David Levering Lewis, W.E.B. DUBOIS BIOGRAPHY OF A RACE 1898–1919 (New York: H. Holt, 1994), 288.
⁴⁹ Homer A. Jack, *Toward Freedom*, a newsletter published in Chicago (March/April 1985) (on file with Swarthmore College Peace Collection, Homer A Jack Papers (SCPC-DG-063), Box: DG 063: Later Accessions: 16 (Mixed Materials)). See also Homer A. Jack (1916–1993), Congress of Racial Equality, available at www.thecongressofracialequality.org/homer-jack.html.
⁵⁰ George Houser, Freedom's Struggle Crosses Oceans and Mountains, supra note 44 at 170.

Conference took place at the beginning of the Montgomery Bus Boycott; hence, King certainly was influenced by it. For example, in a December 1963 speech at Western Michigan University, King heralded the waning influence of colonial powers in Africa and beyond, arguing that the wind of change is blowing in Africa and around the world. King believed that it was "sweeping away an old order and bringing into being a new order":

> Now we are all familiar with this old order that is passing away. We have lived with it and we have seen it in all of its dimensions. We have seen the old order in its international dimensions in the form of colonialism and imperialism. As you know, the vast majority of the peoples of our world live in Asia and Africa. For many, many years, people of these two continents were dominated politically, exploited economically, segregated and humiliated by some foreign power. But even there we notice change has taken place. I can remember when Mrs. King and I first journeyed to Africa to attend the independence celebration of the new nation of Ghana. We were very happy about the fact there were now eight independent countries in Africa. But since that night in March, 1957, some twenty-seven new independent nations have come into being in Africa. This reveals to us that the old order of colonialism is passing away, and the new order of freedom and human dignity is coming into being.[51]

The Asia-Africa or Bandung Conference's final communiqué "condemned racialism as a means of cultural suppression," promoted "cultural co-operation among Asia and African countries," and "discussed the problems of dependent peoples and colonialism and the evils arising from the subjection of peoples to alien subjugation, domination and exploitation."[52] This final communiqué was adopted one year after the US Supreme Court's iconic 1954 *Brown vs. Board of Education* decision declared that racial segregation or internal colonialism was illegal. The communique affirmed that all colonized people and nations should be free and independent;[53] promoted economic and cultural cooperation among Asian and African nations; declared its full support for fundamental human rights; and lamented the policies and practices of racial segregation and discrimination, defining them as gross violations of human rights and a denial of the fundamental dignity of man. Finally, the communiqué fully embraced the international law principle of self-determination and peaceful co-existence among colored nations.[54] It championed human rights precepts while appealing to international or outside law; that is, norms, doctrine, law, and jurisprudence intended to contest colonialism and racism.

---

[51] Martin Luther King Jr., speech at Western Michigan University (December 18, 1963), available at https://libguides.wmich.edu/mlkatwmu/speech.
[52] *Final Communique of the Asian-African Conference of Bandung* (April 24, 1955), in Ministry of Foreign Affairs, Republic of Indonesia. *Asia-Africa Speak from Bandung* 161, 161–169. Twenty-nine African and Asian countries met in Bandung, Indonesia, at the international conference.
[53] Id. at 161.
[54] Six of the twenty-nine nations participating in the Bandung Conference were from Africa, including Egypt, Ethiopia, Ghana (previously Gold Coast), Liberia, Libya, and Sudan.

King avidly supported the conference and wholeheartedly believed that the plight of people in Africa and the Black diaspora was intertwined. His universal human rights consciousness deepened his desire for all people of color to be free. In an address to the St. Louis Freedom Rally in April 1957, King called for an end to the "bondage of colonialism and imperialism" affecting the colored people of the world, who, he declared, comprised "two-thirds" of the world's population.[55] Fully aware that several anticolonial and self-determination movements involved violence, such as Algeria and Kenya, King argued that "[o]ne day these people got tired of being trampled over by the iron feet of oppression" and "decided to rise and protest."[56] King noted that "more than one billion three hundred million of the colored peoples of the world have broken loose from colonialism and imperialism." From the conference rooms of Bandung, they shouted, "[r]acism and colonialism must go."[57] And, while some might romanticize the anticolonial nostalgia of Bandung, King's acknowledgment and identification with its greater purpose was certainly illustrative of his growing Pan-African consciousness.

As the previous chapters have shown, King was motivated by the racial solidarity, recognition, and actions of African leaders such as Kwame Nkrumah and his finance minister, N. K. Gbedemah, whom King met during trips to Africa and Europe. Nkrumah and Gbedemah seem to have shared with King that they were "making it clear in the UN and other diplomatic circles around the world that beautiful words and extensive handouts cannot be substitutes for the basic simple responsibility of giving freedom and justice to our colored brothers [African Americans] all over the United States."[58] Nkrumah's radical consciousness was fortified by universal values and an abiding sense of racial solidarity with African Americans, making him one of few African heads of state to openly advocate for the plight of Black Americans – a plight that was internationalized by King's appeals to the United Nations and government of the US, as well as through his entreaties to outside law, norms, and doctrine. Indeed, King's internalization of Ghana's nonviolent transition to independence and his recognition of Nkrumah's Pan-African advocacy for Afro-Asiatic freedom influenced him to Africanize "The Great World House."[59] And, while the historiography, meaning, and context of Pan-Africanist discourses have changed

---

[55] *A Realistic Look at the Question of Progress in the Area of Race Relations*, Address Delivered at *St. Louis Freedom Rally* (April 10, 1957), in Clayborne Carson, et al. (eds.), *King Papers, Vol. IV: Symbol of the Movement*, 175 (January 1957–December 1958) (Berkeley: University of California Press, 2000).
[56] Id. at 176.
[57] Id.
[58] Id.
[59] King's concept of the "Great World House" contextualizes his ideas and social praxis for creating a brotherhood of mankind, a single neighborhood of the human family that is "globally connected, integrated, and united around a core of universal shared values." It focused on "eliminating the triple evils of racism, poverty, and war through nonviolent resistance." Vicki L. Crawford and Lewis Baldwin, Reclaiming the Great World House: The Global Vision of Martin Luther King Jr. (Athens, GA: University of Georgia Press, 2019), 1.

over time, this analysis clearly demonstrates that King was establishing a Pan-African legacy despite the sentiments of contrarians who argue that his divergence with Black nationalism or separatism was dispositive of his Pan-African identity.

Like King, Du Bois was not a Black nationalist or separatist. This raises the question of whether Black nationalism as an archetype was or is a prerequisite or interdependent component of Pan-Africanism as traditionally understood. Like Houser, various King commentators comingle these concepts (i.e., Black nationalism, separatism, and Pan-Africanism). Accordingly, they disassociate King and his distinctive contributions to Pan-African movements and Pan-Africanism writ large. This is tragic. For example, Brandon Terry seemingly argues that nationalism is the gateway to Pan-Africanism, opining that King's "weak cultural particularity thesis" did not "entail strong forms of nationalism, like a deep-rooted Pan-Africanism or black separatism."[60] The radical Black tradition, as expressed through the BIT, upends this casting of King, as it shows that Black nationalism and Pan-Africanism are not the same nor mutually exclusive. Terry does not define Pan-Africanism or its epistemology nor does he explain what he means by "weak particularity thesis" or what modifiers like "deep-rooted" mean. Rather, he argues that King's open aversion to separatist forms of Black nationalism bar him from membership in the Pan-African club. I'm afraid I must disagree. Terry's thesis erroneously contends that King "did not see a need to secure a strong cultural base for political unity" and supports this naked idea by arguing that King criticized "pan-African cultural nationalists" – whatever that classification means – "for fleeing the 'ambivalence' of African American identity in search of an illusory wholeness in expressive cultural practices they associate to Africa."[61] Nothing could be further from the truth. King's African consciousness derived from a solid cultural base nurtured in Sweet Auburn's radical search for racial justice, which he elevated into a political unity thesis rooted in the global struggle for Black freedom.

King understood that Black unity transcended territorial boundaries and necessitated Black solidarity – African American political and cultural oneness with continental African identity. After all, King grasped that African Americans were not continental Africans but rather their kin, though he acknowledged the multigenerational impacts of enslavement, slavery, Black codes, and Jim Crowism on African American identity, consciousness, and uniqueness. In fact, he acknowledged these distinctions despite the pseudo-African impulses and romanticism embraced by some cultural nationalists. Unlike most activists of his era, King traveled to Africa and had a learned understanding of its challenges. He boldly embraced his African heritage. And, while Terry acknowledges that King invoked "African Americans' connection to Africa, and [that King] suggested modes of

---

[60] Brandon Terry, Requiem for a Dream: The Problem-Space of Black Power, in Brandon M. Terry & Tommie Shelby (eds.), TO SHAPE A NEW WORLD, supra 42 at 315.
[61] Id.

transnational solidarity,"[62] he incorrectly argues that King's "formulations placed less emphasis on the idiom of 'racial' ancestry than resonant and shared features of racial oppression between colonialism and Jim Crow."[63] But King did not need to emphasize or debunk the obvious: He often opined that Negroes were of Black African racial ancestry and that their place of origin or homeland was Africa, not America. It is with this understanding that he focused on dismantling systems that sought to persecute, subjugate, and kill persons of African descent wherever they might live.

The historical record simply does not support Terry's framing of King's 'racial ancestry' thesis. King rightly found consistency between his strong embrace of Blackness and African racial ancestry on the one hand, and interracial unity on the other. Nevertheless, he did distinguish himself from other radicals who rejected the notion that racial allies (e.g., whites) could contribute to Black freedom struggles. This belief informed his human rights ministry and, with it, his stalwart opposition to racial oppression, colonialism, and Jim Crowism, which he believed orginated from the same evil source. King's Beloved Pan-Africanism – his global ministry – created a strong base for African and African American unity, and it was arguably predicated on racial and cultural ancestry, kinship, empathy, and unity with Africa, Africans, and other oppressed peoples. Global racial oppression fortified rather than diluted King's Pan-African consciousness and actions. He even encouraged Black Americans to emigrate to Africa to assist in her development,[64] not to "abandon" America or "escape American racism" like so many disillusioned Black nationalists and nationalist-minded Pan-Africanists. He believed in fighting domestically and globally, which made him more of a purist than many of his so-called revolutionary contemporaries. King's Pan-African advocacy helped reshape and internationalize Black American distinctiveness, oppression, and claims to outside law by refashioning international human rights law through the prism of African American interests in international law and Pan-Africanism. He worked tirelessly to humanize African identity and subjugation by openly contesting the legitimacy of national racism (e.g., Jim Crowism) and international racism (like Apartheid).

5.3 PAN-AFRICANISM, BLACK NATIONALISM, AND BLACK ZIONISM

In an April 1963 letter to Theodore E. Brown – with whom King closely collaborated to support anticolonial movements and the anti-Apartheid movement in South Africa – King provided vital insight into his vision about the relationship between

---

[62] Id.
[63] Id.
[64] Martin Luther King Jr., *The Birth of a New Nation*, Sermon Delivered at Dexter Avenue Baptist Church (April 7, 1957), in Clayborne Carson, et al. (eds.), *King Papers, Volume IV: Symbol of the Movement* (January 1957–December 1958), 161.

Black Americans, Africa, and Africans.[65] King observed: "I have no doubt that the question of the relationship of the American Negro to Africa is one of great importance. I am convinced that we have a moral and practical responsibility to keep the civil rights movement in America close to our African brothers."[66] King understood the symbiotic relationship and interplay between the human rights and liberation movements in the US and Africa, from fighting Jim Crowism and Apartheid to disrupting and dismantling racist regimes. Keeping the movement close to "our African brothers" was a part of King's broader global strategy to defeat white supremacy and its antecedents, or what he referred to as the three evils of poverty, racism, and war.[67] It was this intellectual openness and militancy, as well as his Pan-African inclinations, that attracted a variety of propositions from members of the public advocating for Black empowerment through concepts such as Black repatriation and Zionism.

In its original formulation, Zionism was and still is essentially a political, ideological, and cultural movement that established a Jewish state for Jews from around the world in Israel.[68] It has a long and complex history awash with violent conflict, clashing ideals, intricate divisions, and grievances, particularly from Palestinians and the Arab world. Zionism derives from the word "Zion," a hill and city in the Old City of Jerusalem where the sacred Temple Mount rests. It is a holy site in the Abrahamic religious traditions: Judaism, Christianity, and Islam. Zionism's roots date back to the late nineteenth century in response to violent anti-Semitism in Europe, as well as the brutal oppression of Jews in Africa, Asia, and the Middle East.[69] The World Zionist Organization was founded in 1897, and reached prominence under the leadership of Theodor Herzel, an Austrian journalist who believed that a Jewish nation-state was essential for the existence of the Jewish people and a solution to the global problem of anti-Semitism.[70] The Nazi Holocaust of Jews and others during World War II brought about the political will and international recognition for the need of a Jewish state. Consequently, the State of Israel was formed in 1948 in Palestine.

Although King is rarely thought about in the context of the century-old Israeli–Palestine conflict, he was arguably a traditional Zionist in that he supported the establishment, maintenance, and existence of a Jewish homeland and the State of Israel. He was well versed in the political dynamics of the Israeli–Palestinian divide

---

[65] Theodore Edward Brown was a protégé of A. Phillip Randolph and prominent labor leader. He worked closely with King during the civil rights movement and became president of the American Negro Leadership Conference on Africa in 1962.
[66] *Letter from Dr. Martin Luther King Jr. to Theodore E. Brown* (April 1, 1963) (on file with Center for Nonviolent Social Change, Inc., Atlanta, GA, Martin Luther King, Jr. Papers [Series I–IV], Martin Luther King, Jr., Box 3, folder 7).
[67] Id.
[68] Walter Laqueur, A HISTORY OF ZIONISM: FROM THE FRENCH REVOLUTION TO THE ESTABLISHMENT OF THE STATE OF ISRAEL (New York: Knopf Doubleday, 2003), 384.
[69] Milton Viorst, ZIONISM: THE BIRTH AND TRANSFORMATION OF AN IDEAL (New York: St. Martin's Press, 2016), chapter 1.
[70] Id.

and assessed it through the lens of a pastor, not a politician. King viewed all of Israel, including Palestine, as holy ground and, unlike many civil rights leaders, traveled to Israel with Coretta Scott King in March 1959. They visited eastern Jerusalem and the West Bank, which at the time was under the territorial control of Jordan. King posited that the 1967 Arab-Israeli War was "one of the most difficult problems of the world."[71] He was attuned to the fact that most persons in the Arab and Muslim worlds, including many in Africa, viewed the birth of the Jewish state as a form of colonialism masquerading as virtuous Jewish nationalism and self-determination. The internal dynamics of the Israeli-Palestinian conflict concerned King. And while he supported the Jewish homeland, King was troubled by its political, military, economic, and social impacts on Palestinians.[72] In a June 18, 1967, interview on ABC's "Issues and Answers," King opined that "for ultimate peace and security of the situation [1967 Arab-Israeli War] it will probably be necessary for Israel to give up this conquered territory because to hold on to it will only exacerbate the tensions and deepen the bitterness of the Arabs."[73] While King recognized Israel's right to survive and defend itself, and believed the United Nations should play the central role in ending the Six-Day War, he questioned Israel's continued occupation of Palestinian lands.[74]

It could be argued that the troubled histories of Jewish Zionism and the 1967 Arab-Israeli War might have skewed King's thinking about Black Zionism. However, he was arguably more concerned by the idea that after building America and suffering under its slaveocracy and the ensuing totalitarian anti-Black order, Black Americans "should turn around and run at this point in history."[75] To this, he declared, "I say that we will not run!"[76] However, while King appears to have rejected the Jewish model of Zionism for African Americans, he seemingly did not reject the concept itself. Black Zionism and Pan-Africanism are distant but interconnected dueling cousins that may have illuminated or fortified what King identified as the "inner transformation" of Blacks. He argued:

> Negroes today are experiencing an inner transformation that is liberating them from ideological dependence on the white majority. To lose illusions is to gain

---

[71] Martin Kramer, *Where MLK Really Stood on Israel and the Palestinians*, MOSAIC (March 13, 2019), available at https://mosaicmagazine.com/observation/2019/03/where-mlk-really-stood-on-israel-and-the-palestinians/.

[72] Interview with Dr. Martin Luther King, Jr. by Tom Jerriel & John Casserly, *ABC Issues and Answers* (June 18, 1967), transcript in The King Ctr. Digital Archive, https://web.archive.org/web/20150304113151/www.thekingcenter.org/archive/document/issues-and-answers.org/archive/document/abcs-issues-and-answers-mlk-interview.

[73] Id. See also, Martin Kramer, *In the Words of Martin Luther King*, THE WAR ON ERROR: ISRAEL, ISLAM, AND THE MIDDLE EAST (New Brunswick, NJ: Transaction, 2016), 253–267.

[74] Id. at 257, 259.

[75] Martin Luther King Jr., *Kings' Challenge to the Nation's Social Scientists*, Speech given at the American Psychological Association Annual Convention, JOURNAL OF SOCIAL ISSUES, Vol. 24, No. 1 (September 1, 1968).

[76] Id.

truth. Negroes have grown wiser and more mature, and they are hearing more clearly those who are raising fundamental questions about our society whether the critics be Negro or white. When this process of awareness and independence crystallizes, every rebuke, every evasion, become hammer blows on the wedge that splits the Negro from the larger society.[77]

In King's universe, this split might have been physical, psychological, spiritual, or any combination. Either way, he was committed to building a democratic multiracial society in the US that would disrupt Negro fragmentation while embracing endeavors to propagate African freedom movements and development, African/African American solidarity, Black American emigration to Africa, and efforts to export nonviolent approaches to conflict management in emerging African states and societies. All of these imperatives represent markers of Pan-Africanism. King was a practitioner of Pan-Americanism, not merely an ivory-towered critic. Unlike most Americans of African descent who were a part of the radical Black tradition, King trekked to Africa and was even called on by its leadership to help combat white supremacy and intra-African deadly conflicts such as the Nigerian Civil War (aka, the Biafran War of 1967–1970). Unfortunately, his assassination eclipsed any opportunity for him to help mediate an end to the civil war between Nigeria and the Republic of Biafra during its attempt at secession.

Pan-Africanism aims to maximize the human potential of people of African descent worldwide from the physical, historical, psychological, spiritual, social, cultural, political, economic, and industrial forces of white supremacy, domination, ideology, and systemic oppression.[78] Unlike Zionism, Pan-Africanism does not necessitate the establishment of a single nation-state, let alone a Black one. Unlike the World Zionist Organization, most Pan-Africanists did not strongly advocate for a Western hemispheric Black nation-state – although members of Africa's Casablanca group constituted one exception, advocating for a US of Africa. For most Pan-African activists and scholars, Africa was enough. And while, for many Black militants, Black nationalism was the intellectual and political gateway to Pan-Africanism, Black nationalism, "Black Zionism," and Pan-Africanism share a common thread: the total and complete freedom, liberation, and independence of African states, nations, peoples, and persons of African descent wherever they might exist. Pan-Africanists on the continent and in the diaspora historically prioritize African liberation from colonialism, neo-colonialism, and racist regimes above founding a Black nation in America or a supranational Black nation-state somewhere else in the diaspora.

King was a problem solver and a tactical pragmatist. King did not see the utility in racial separatism in America. Whereas, during Marcus Garvey's era, it was

---

[77] Id.
[78] Jeremy I. Levitt, Pan-Africanism, ENCYCLOPEDIA OF GLOBALIZATION, VOLUME III N to T, supra note 35.

hard to visualize Pan-Africanism through an integrated lens, given America's racist and segregated constitution of order. Although they differed in this regard, King embraced Garvey's thinking about racial pride, independence, and unity. And, like Garvey, King seemed to prioritize Black empowerment (e.g., voting rights and economic equality) over violently fighting white supremacy and its machinations. For King, the latter was a roadmap to the former. He did not fight integration for integration's sake. In the American context, he demanded racial equality and justice within a multiracial democracy without ignoring the importance of Black empowerment, arguing that Blacks should seek "political and economic power to reach ... legitimate goals."[79] He reasoned that Black Power "was born from the wombs of despair and disappointment. Black Power is a cry of pain. It is a reaction to the failure of White Power to deliver the promises and to do it in a hurry. ... The cry of Black Power is a cry of hurt."[80]

Garvey was a pragmatist as well. He shouldered the realities of America's violent racial caste system with its thorny satchel of sharecropping, Black codes, and Jim Crow segregation. By contrast, nearly four decades after Garvey, King sought to dismantle said social evil. Garvey's influence on progressive and radical African American thought and culture was and is enduring. As already noted, King himself embraced several ideas offered by Garvey, arguing that Blacks should embrace their cultural history, heritage, and roots to create a new sense of self-esteem while throwing "off the manacles of self-abnegation."[81] Borrowing from Garvey, King reasoned that the Black man should "say to himself and the world: I am somebody. I am a person. I am a man with dignity and honor. I have a rich and noble history, however painful and exploited that history has been. I am black and comely."[82] Finally, King continuously contended that the heritage of African Americans is African, rooted in Africa and that we should never sever our ties with our African brothers and sisters.[83] His thinking evolved over time, as did the various freedom prescriptions and proposals he contemplated.

Indeed, King regularly received extensive information from data, reports, and proposals about the challenges confronting colonial Africa and Jim Crowism. The following two sub-sections explore two intriguing proposals forwarded to King during a time when he was deeply involved in supporting African liberation

---

[79] Martin Luther King Jr., *It Is Not Enough to Condemn Black Power* (October 1966), in *Martin Luther King, Jr., Papers* [1950–1968] (on file with Martin Luther King, Jr. Center for Nonviolent Social Change, Inc., Atlanta, Georgia, loose document on file with author).

[80] Martin Luther King Jr., *King Address at SCLC Staff Retreat* (November 14, 1966) in *Martin Luther King, Jr., Papers* [1950–1968] (on file with Martin Luther King, Jr. Center for Nonviolent Social Change, Inc., Atlanta, Georgia loose document on file with author).

[81] Martin Luther King Jr, WHERE DO WE GO FROM HERE: CHAOS OR COMMUNITY? (Boston: Beacon Press, 1967), 43–44.

[82] *Id.*

[83] John J. Ansbro, MARTIN LUTHER KING, JR: THE MAKING OF A MIND (Maryknoll, NY: Orbis Books, 1984), 206.

5.3 Pan-Africanism, Black Nationalism, and Black Zionism

and independence movements and discovering global pathways to combat white nationalism in the US and abroad. The first proposal urged him to encourage Black Americans to emigrate to West and Central Africa,[84] while the second note asked him to adopt a Black Zionist organization that would empower Blacks in Africa and the US. Both were written by seemingly well-intended and advanced-thinking white men. The proposals, which embraced Pan-African concepts and complemented King's intellectual trajectory, provide a window into how others perceived the scope of King's interests and activities in Africa and an opportunity to further examine his thinking about Black liberation inside and outside the US.

5.3.1 Back to Africa?

The first proposal came from Attorney Leslie G. Johnson, who advocated to King that African Americans should return to the Congo (the Democratic Republic of the Congo) in the wake of the vacuum created by fleeing Belgians after Belgian decolonization.[85] Johnson was a prominent oil and gas lawyer from Logan, Ohio, and a World War II veteran of the Army Air Force. His letter to King was dated July 29, 1960, less than a month after Congolese independence (June 30, 1960). Johnson was abreast of decolonization movements in Africa, particularly in the Congo, and was inspired by Congo's independence from Belgium. He believed that Black Americans had a vital role to play in Africa's development and security. Johnson alleged that the "[w]hite man's era there has ended," and with Belgium's withdrawal, a political, economic, and social "vacuum" was created that should be filled with African American emigration and its accompanying technical expertise, finance, and strategic alliances.[86] Johnson ostensibly knew that the Congo was one of several ancestral homes of Black Americans and, as Africa's second-largest country, boasted unlimited natural resources and economic potential.

By 1960, it can be credibly argued that King was an expert on Africa, a Black American Africanist of sorts. He understood the complex histories of colonization on the continent and the accounts of the revolutionary and freedom movements that sought to liberate them. King likewise possessed a practical knowledge of Africa that, when combined with his in-depth understanding of racism and colonization, rivaled that of most commentators. Considering his well-publicized works on and travels to Africa and his growing relationships with leaders in the region, it is

---

[84] King regularly received copies of well-established journals such as *Africa Today* and frequent reports from ACOA.

[85] *Letter from Leslie G. Johnson, to Martin Luther King, Jr.* (July 29, 1960), MLKP-MBU (on file with Howard Gotlieb Archival Research Center, Boston University, Martin Luther King, Jr. Collection, Box 25, Folder 3).

[86] *Id.*

understandable why Johnson felt King would be interested in his "Back to Africa" proposal. In his formulation, Johnson argued that the void in Congo "must be filled from the ranks of colored Americans," and that King should exert his influence to facilitate the project.[87] He reasoned that Black Americans could help develop Congo in the wake of its independence.

This was not a novel proposal; however, it was one of few proposals on the subject made to King by an American, irrespective of race, and it was notable that Johnson's proposal was specific to the Congo. Millions of African Americans trace their ancestry to the Congo. Patrice Lumumba, the first prime minister, was very popular among Black Americans, and still today the Democratic Republic of the Congo is arguably the world's most resource-rich nation. Johnson argued that, based on the knowledge, training, and technical skills that Black Americans had obtained in America, it "seemed destined by divine providence and intervention to make educated, civilized, democratic colored people available in this great hour of democratic need," that is, to help develop and democratize the new nation.[88] Needless to say, Johnson presumed that King had Pan-African leanings and would be receptive to his proposal.

Johnson's correspondence to King was penned during Lumumba's short term as prime minister (seven months). Lumumba was an African nationalist and Pan-African leader. He was familiar with and thought well of King and "American Negroes," many of whom he rightly claimed originated in the Congo and were the "brothers" of the Congolese people.[89] As prime minister, Lumumba challenged American and Belgian control of Congo's natural resources and was a firm advocate for African unity, which on January 17, 1961, ultimately incited the two nations to conspire to divide the country and assassinate him using Congolese collaborators and Belgian security forces.[90] In fact, on August 27, 1960, a telegram from CIA Director Allen Dulles to the agency's station chief in the Congo directed the latter to kill Lumumba:

1. In high quarters here it is the clear-cut conclusion that if [garble – Lumumba?] continues to hold high office, the inevitable result will at best be chaos and at worst pave the way to Communist takeover of the Congo with disastrous consequences for the prestige of UN and for the interests of the free world generally. Consequently, we conclude that his removal must be an urgent and prime

---

[87] Id.
[88] Id.
[89] *Foreign Relations of US 1958–1960, Africa*, Vol. 14, 97, Brussels (February 25, 1960) (memorandum of a conversation between U.S. Ambassador to Belgium, William Burden and Patrice Lumumba, 265.
[90] U.S. Senate, Select Comm. to Study Governmental Operations with Respect to Intelligence Activities, Alleged Assassination Plots Involving Foreign Leaders: An Interim Report, Together with Additional, Supplemental, and Separate Views (1975), at 14. Telegram from the Central Intelligence Agency to the Station in the Congo, Dir 47587 (Out 62966), in Foreign Relations of the United States, 1964–1968, vol. XXIII, Congo, 1960–1968 (August 27, 1960), CIA Files, Job 79-00149A, DDO/IMS Files, Box 23, Folder 1, African Div., Senate Select Comm., vol. II (Secret; Rybat; Priority) (drafted by Allen W. Dulles) (available at https://history.state.gov/historicaldocuments/frus1964-68v23/d14#fn:1.5.4.4.42.16.4).

objective and that under existing conditions this should be a high priority of our covert action.

2. Hence we wish to give you wider authority along lines Leop 0772 and Leop 0785 and Dir 46115 including even more aggressive action if it can remain covert. We realize that targets of opportunity may present themselves to you and in addition to sums heretofore authorized, we further authorize expenditure up to a total of [dollar amount not declassified] to carry out any crash programs on which you do not have the opportunity to consult HQS. Advise your cash needs.

3. To the extent that Ambassador may desire to be consulted you should seek his concurrence. If in any particular case he does not wish to be consulted you can act on your own authority where time does not permit referral here.

4. This message has been seen and approved at competent level ODACID.[91]

Lumumba's assassination alarmed Black America. At the time, had King known about the heavy hand the US played in Lumumba's assassination, he would have likely made more strident public pronouncements condemning it. Instead, King only referred to student protests over Lumumba's assassination in a *New York Times* article titled "The Time for Freedom Has Come," published on September 10, 1961.[92] He later lamented the murders of Lumumba and Malcolm X in the *New York Amsterdam News*, noting:

> The America Negro cannot afford to destroy its leadership any more than the Congo can. Men of talent are too scarce to be destroyed by envy, greed, and tribal rivalry before they reach their full maturity. Like the murder of Lumumba, the murder of Malcolm X deprives the world of a potentially great leader. I could not agree with either of these men, but I could see in them a capacity for leadership which I could respect, and which was only beginning to mature in judgment and statesmanship.[93]

Beyond the above pronouncements, King remained largely silent about the killing of Lumumba because the truth surrounding his assassination was a secret cloaked in disinformation.

While King noted that he "could not agree" with Lumumba, he never expressly indicated potential areas of disagreement. American propaganda about Lumumba's

---

[91] Foreign Relations of the United States, 1964–1968, vol. XXIII, Congo, 1960–1968, at 15 (August 27, 1960) (telegram from Allen W. Dulles, Dir., CIA, to CIA Station Chief in the Congo) (CIA Files, Job 79–00149A, DDO/IMS Files, Box 23, Folder 1, African Div., Senate Select Comm., vol. II) (Secret; Rybat; Priority; "For COS from Ascham") (available at https://history.state.gov/historicaldocuments/frus1964-68v23/d14#fn:1.5.4.4.42.16.4). A typed notation on the telegram instructed the Cable Secretariat to "limit distribution to Mr. Helms."

[92] Martin Luther King Jr., *The Time for Freedom Has Come*, in Clayborne Carson, et al. (eds.), *King Papers, Vol. VII: To Save the Soul of America* (January 1961–August September 10, 1962, 1961), 270.

[93] Martin Luther King Jr., *The Nightmare of Violence*, NEW YORK AMSTERDAM NEWS (March 13, 1965).

shift toward the Soviet Union and socialism was false and suggestive of the US government's unwillingness to support Congo's total separation and independence from Belgium and other imperial controls over its natural resources and economy. Moreover, I am not familiar with any concrete evidence showing that King and Lumumba formally communicated, nor did King speak or read French, making it highly unlikely that he had easy access to information in real time, including press reports, official pronouncements, or other sources of information about the Congo. Nonetheless, Lumumba's perceived flirtation with the Soviet Union would have worried King, given the FBI's active efforts at branding him a communist. Notwithstanding, King would have supported Lumumba's African nationalist and anticolonialist positions aimed at freeing the Congolese people from the jaws of Belgium, America, and other Western imperialist control.

King's interest in and advocacy for the people of the Congo did not end with Lumumba's assassination. He understood the history of the Congo situation quite well, commenting:

> I've been very concerned about the problem in the Congo, and it is my conviction that we must see the Congo situation for what it is and deal with it in that light. What we have in the Congo is several wars, essentially civil strife, and I don't think that problem will be solved until there is a withdrawal of all foreign troops and mercenaries, and I think this needs to be done immediately and that the Congo situation be dealt with by the Organization of African States [Unity] under the auspices of the United Nations.[94]

What's interesting is King's understanding of the history of the Congolese conflict and the historical injustices cast upon her people by domestic and international forces. Employing biblical metaphors, King highlighted that the Congo was experiencing a "violent harvest, that came into being as a result of seeds of injustice, seeds of neglect and seeds of man's inhumanity to man planted across the years."[95] Not believing that a military solution to the situation in Congo was possible, he advocated for multilateral diplomacy and even peacekeeping through the OAU and UN. His understanding of the potential role of regional and international organizations like the OAU and UN, respectively, was rare in the US and indicative of his knowledge of international relations and international law and their intersections in Africa and beyond.

Ironically, Martin Luther King Jr. Day in the US is celebrated on the third Monday in January, which generally falls on the day Lumumba was assassinated. Although King and Lumumba did not have the opportunity to work together, King opined that the "liberation struggle in Africa has been the greatest single international influence on American Negro students."[96] For example, he noted that Black students firmly

---

[94] Martin Luther King Jr., *Radio Interview Regarding Nobel Peace Prize*, Oslo, Norway (December 9, 1964).
[95] Id.
[96] Martin Luther King Jr., *Speech Regarding the Influence of African Movements on U.S. Students* (on file with The King Center Archives [May 1962], p. 3, loose document on file with author).

believed that if Africans could break colonialism, the "American Negro can break Jim Crow" by drawing from Africa's variegated freedom movements. African Americans considered Africa's independence leaders to be "heroes" – especially at historically black universities and colleges (HBCUs) – which is why there was nationwide protest when Patrice Lumumba was assassinated.[97]

While it is not clear precisely what motivated Johnson to write King – whether it be Black American interests in the Congo or other economic, democracy, and human rights considerations – he seems to have firmly believed in his proposed project.[98] Johnson argued that Black Americans were the most qualified and capable group to drive Congolese development and democratization."[99] Despite the paternalistic wording ("civilized," for example, was commonplace during this period), his overall message aligned with King's. King boldly advocated for Black Americans to return to Africa to assist in its development. The spiritual conviction of Johnson's plea would, therefore, have resonated with King's religiosity and Afrocentricity. However, King may have objected to the hero-type thought in Johnson's reasoning. Interestingly, Johnson's call to action was racially exclusive. He argued: "[The] white man is not welcome – if the past 100 years of freedom that you have been granted by the white man's civil war means anything to your race and if the future of America means anything to the colored American you will exert your influence to fill the great vacuum left in the Belgian Congo by their departure from the Congo."[100]

Indeed, Johnson appears to have believed that Black American engagement in the Congo would "prove" to the American people that Black Americans were "worthy of classification as first-class citizens and prove to all the world that American democracy works."[101] Of course, with or without the Congo proposal, Black Americans were worthy of racial equality and equity. Although Johnson's thinking may appear condescendingly colonial in today's world, it was progressive for any white man in 1960. However, while Johnson argued that a "new army" of Black American democratic forces was needed to rebuild the Congo, he seems to have ignored the fact that Negroes in America were still fighting racial inequality, inequity, and injustice and, like the Congolese, had not experienced authentic democracy in America.

Black leadership and technical skills developed despite rather than because of America's illiberal democracy. Johnson acknowledged this reality in a position paper titled "The African Frontier," which he included in his letter to King. In it, Johnson candidly asks, "Will the American Negro lay down his cudgel of equality long enough to answer the call for leadership in Africa? Will the American Negro feel the call to service? Will the American Negro take his responsibility of leading the dark continent

[97] Id.
[98] Id.
[99] Id.
[100] Id.
[101] Id.

to Democracy?"[102] These exciting questions and his biased reference to the "dark continent" mistakenly imagined a one-way street in the relationship between Black Americans and Africa, something that King would have questioned since he viewed any "Back to Africa" enterprise as mutually beneficial. In King's universe, Africans had as much to share with Black Americans as the latter might share with Africa.

Finally, Johnson contended that Black Americans should take advantage of American law permitting American citizens to work on behalf of other nations. He argued that "[m]any of our laws are geared at allowing Americans to participate in governments of foreign countries."[103] One wonders whether he was specifically thinking about Jewish American support of Israel. These laws, he argues, "should be altered to allow our American colored to go to the countries of Africa and build that continent in the image of democracy."[104] Notwithstanding the colonial echoes in his thinking, Johnson and King agreed that Black Americans had a vital role in the socio-economic transformation of the African continent. Still, the truth remains that African democracy might have flourished if Western democracies ended their economic exploitation of her and stopped meddling in Africa's internal affairs.

Despite its paternal undertones, Johnson's proposal was timely and complemented King's antiracist, anticolonialist, and pro-Black American emigration to Africa ideals fortified during his pilgrimage to Ghana in 1957. Like Johnson, King believed that Black Americans should help develop Africa by moving to the continent and sharing knowledge, training, and technical skills. He based such beliefs on notions of Black unity, Pan-African unity, and spiritual ordination. Yet, while Johnson's proposal appealed to King's thinking on Africa, it lacked a nuanced understanding of the interethnic and geopolitics at play in the Congo. King had a greater understanding of the internal political dynamics of the Congo than Johnson, which may explain any reluctance on King's part to engage with Africa's second largest and most minerally prosperous nation.

Johnson wrote King again on August 29, 1960, and reiterated his argument for King to support an army of Negro technicians to help the Congo develop into a democracy. The tone and tenor of his second letter appeared to show vexation with King for not having responded to his first. Nevertheless, James R. Wood, a member of King's staff, replied to Johnson and confirmed King's belief that the "need for ambassadors of color from America to journey to Africa to assist with the development of this new frontier is self-evident and immediate."[105] Wood went on to share

---

[102] *Letter from Leslie G. Johnson, to Martin Luther King, Jr.* (July 29, 1960), MLKP-MBU (on file with Howard Gotlieb Archival Research Center, Boston University, Martin Luther King, Jr. Collection, Box 25, Folder 3).
[103] *Id.*
[104] *Id.*
[105] *Letter from James R. Wood to Mr. Leslie G. Johnson* (September 12, 1960), MLKP-MBU (on file with Howard Gotlieb Archival Research Center, Boston University, Martin Luther King, Jr. Collection, Box 25, Folder 3).

5.3 Pan-Africanism, Black Nationalism, and Black Zionism

that "every effort" to address the needs of the Congo would be taken by the Southern Christian Leadership Conference (SCLC), which was already engaged in activities in Algeria, Kenya, and South Africa. Of course, the presence of SCLC activities in Africa begs the question of whether the SCLC itself had become a Pan-African organization.[106]

5.3.2 Black Zionism?

The second noteworthy proposal received by King in 1960 came from Nathan Friedman, a prominent Jewish community member in New Haven, Connecticut. On May 7, 1960, Friedman penned a letter to King encouraging him to adopt a Black Zionist approach to empowering Black people in the US and Africa. He was appalled at the "denial of human dignity, the total repression of freedom" of Africans in South Africa, Kenya, Nyasaland, and the Congo.[107] He thought that the "white governments of Africa" were engaged in massive human rights violations and believed that the "American Negro" could play a vital role in freeing themselves as well as Africans in Africa.[108] To do so, Friedman wanted Black Americans to "look to the Jewish people and study what wonders their Zionist organization has accomplished for them."[109] In his letter, Friedman specifically encouraged King to study the Jewish world experience – namely, how the Zionist movement built "freedom in Israel against the active opposition" of most of the world, especially its neighboring states.[110] It's unclear whether Friedman suggested that King do the same in the US. Nonetheless, Jews are sorely outnumbered in the US and the Middle East. Despite their minority status, Friedman described how a small, organized faction – primarily American Jews – sought to create a free Jewish nation based on a "common ancestry and heritage, hope, faith, and dedication."[111] He argued that the "Zionist Organization allowed the American Jews to help build a free nation in Israel" as well as a "respected place for themselves as citizens of the United States."[112]

Friedman thus suggested that Black Americans form an organization modeled on the Zionist Organization that would enable them to represent the interests of Black Americans and Africans on the continent. He contended that, with such an organization, Black Americans "will be able to do for the Negro of Africa and America what the Zionist Organization has done for the Jewish people of Israel and the

---

[106] *Id.*
[107] *Letter from Leslie G. Johnson, to Martin Luther King, Jr.* (July 29, 1960), MLKP-MBU (on file with Howard Gotlieb Archival Research Center, Boston University, Martin Luther King, Jr. Collection, Box 25, Folder 3).
[108] *Id.*
[109] *Id.*
[110] *Id.*
[111] *Id.*
[112] *Id.*

world."¹¹³ He maintained that the "[c]onditions that made it possible for five million American Jews to build an organization as a weapon for freedom of Jewish people in other parts of the world exists for fifteen million American Negroes."¹¹⁴ Notably, however, Friedman's idea did not address the high-intensity violence employed to create the State of Israel nor differentiate the historical and modern divergencies and complexities of Black Zionism. In addition, his letter did not contemplate the political and economic complexities of establishing a sovereign Black nation in the US or abroad. No land was allocated or ceded to African Americans in the US or Africa to establish a Black homeland – land allocation, even if divisive, being a vital component of Jewish Zionism. Moreover, Friedman did not propose who might fund such an endeavor nor identify the myriad political obstacles that the US government would engineer to obstruct "Black Zionism." Although Blacks and Jews in the US experienced differentiated patterns of racial, ethnic, and religious discrimination inside and outside of the country, their histories were distinct and dissimilar, as were the social, economic, and political conditions that produced them.

Nonetheless, Friedman suggested that King create one organization that could operate nationally and internationally grounded in the history and tactics of other successful peoples and organizations while embracing the aspirations of Black Americans. He argued that the organization should embrace the "love of God" but be secular, positing that only one organization with broad aims could capture the "imagination of American Negroes," empower them, and direct their talents and aims in pursuit of a common agenda.¹¹⁵ According to Friedman, the primary goal of this Black Zionist organization should be to establish relations with the "free peoples of Africa, helping them with trained personnel, planning and carrying out projects to help them develop sound economies."¹¹⁶ His proposal strongly emphasized educating Blacks in the US and Africa in their "common heritage," especially Africans who remain enslaved in Africa. This, Friedman contended, was essential for Black people to enrich their "sense of identity" with the richness of African history – what he refers to as "historical beginnings" – while overcoming any "inferiority feelings."¹¹⁷

Friedman's Black Zionism proposal unwittingly bore a striking resemblance to Marcus Garvey's "Back to Africa" movement and the aims of his Universal Negro Improvement Association (UNIA) from nearly half a century earlier.¹¹⁸

---

¹¹³ Id.
¹¹⁴ Id.
¹¹⁵ Id.
¹¹⁶ Id.
¹¹⁷ Id.
¹¹⁸ In 1920, the Universal Negro Improvement Association (UNIA) held a meeting in Harlem's Liberty Hall and brought together 25,000 persons of African descent from around the world to adopt the "Declaration of the Rights of the Negro Peoples of the World," which became the principles of the UNIA. The delegates demanded and insisted on several rights, foremost among them Black

5.3 Pan-Africanism, Black Nationalism, and Black Zionism 135

It also aligned with King's SCLC activities and thinking in some ways, given the psychological impacts of centuries of racial subjugation by whites. There were certainly other points of intersection. Friedman argued that Africans needed a Zionist Organization for "administrative and educational economics," which was necessary for African development and the more significant aims of "equality among the nations of the world."[119] Further, he believed that oppressed Africans needed a Zionist Organization to fight for their freedom and "kill forever the lie that Negro slavery is an internal affair of South African white governments."[120] Friedman was opposed to Apartheid South Africa and its parastatal regimes in southern and central Africa. His goal was thus, in part, to mobilize international public opinion against Apartheid and colonization using diplomatic pressure and economic sanctions with the "united strength of the Negro peoples of the world."[121] Drawing from the Israeli experience, Friedman believed that Black Americans and continental Africans needed to work together "to supply arms and military help" to overthrow their oppressors and enslavers. Although his idea was not new, it was more militant than King's approach and, perhaps, more aligned with Garvey's thinking in that Friedman essentially advocated for transnational cooperation in the use of deadly force by nonstate actors to topple and supplant racist and colonial white regimes.

By suggesting that King embrace the Zionist approach taken by American Jews, Friedman promoted an approach that "allowed the American Jews to help build a free nation in Israel and at the same time build a respected place for themselves as citizens of the United States."[122] Interestingly, Friedman's proposal, like Johnson's, complemented the broader calls for Pan-Africanism embedded into the social conscience of many Black Americans. Simply put, Friedman's proposal was bold, arguing that the American Negro needed to mobilize around the world and unite for political, cultural, economic, and military assistance. The idea was aimed at 1) fighting injustice and overthrowing oppressive colonial and racist regimes and 2) guaranteeing fundamental freedoms to all Blacks so that, like Jews, Blacks could take their rightful place in shaping the destiny of humanity.[123] Like most Pan-Africanists,

---

self-determination. The declaration stated: "We declare that Negroes, wheresoever they form a community among themselves should be given the right to elect their own representatives to represent them in Legislatures, courts of law, or such institutions as may exercise control over that particular community." UNIA *Declaration of Rights of the Negro Peoples of the World*, New York, August 13, 1920. Reprinted in Robert Hill, ed., THE MARCUS GARVEY AND THE UNIVERSAL NEGRO IMPROVEMENT PAPERS, Vol. 2 (Berkeley: University of California Press, 1983), 571–580.

[119] *Letter from Leslie G. Johnson, to Martin Luther King, Jr.* (July 29, 1960), MLKP-MBU (on file with Howard Gotlieb Archival Research Center, Boston University, Martin Luther King, Jr. Collection, Box 25, Folder 3).

[120] Id.
[121] Id.
[122] Id.
[123] Id.

Friedman argued for a Pan-African army comprised of Black Americans who would overthrow, violently if necessary, racist and oppressive regimes, particularly those dominated by white colonists in central and southern Africa. He also believed in an African American manifest destiny where Black Americans would be the saviors or redeemers of Africans and the Black race. Although Friedman's thinking may also have embraced biased "Dark Continent" preconceptions, not enough white Americans shared his understanding of the critical role that Black Americans play and have played in Africa's development and in combatting white supremacy at home and abroad.

King was already deeply engaged in providing moral, political, and financial assistance to Black African liberation movements seeking to end foreign domination. But he would have rejected Friedman's savior thinking as grandiose and ill-informed because he believed that Black Americans must actively support African solutions to African problems. Notwithstanding, Friedman's proposal was intriguing given King's views on Zionism and the Middle East, which were complex, sophisticated, and expanding, particularly after the Six-Day War, also known as the 1967 Arab–Israeli War between Israel and Egypt, Syria, and Jordan from June 5 to June 10, 1967. King was not a novice, having traveled to Israel in March 1959, eight years before the Six-Day War when the territory was still divided between Israel (western part) and Jordan (eastern part). He visited the eastern part of Jerusalem, Hebron, Bethlehem, Jericho, Nablus, Mount Gerizim, the West Bank (Palestine), and the Samaria region, which were all under the control of Jordan at the time. In the wake of the Six-Day War, according to one scholar, King "supported Israeli actions to assure its 'survival,' but did not favor Israel's continued hold on the territories it had conquered."[124] He believed Israel's continued possession of Palestinian land would lead to further armed conflict.[125] In fact, before the war, he had been planning to bring a large delegation of Black Americans to Israel at the invitation of the prime ministers of Israel and Jordan; however, the "Six-Day War threw a wrench into the plan" because, in his words: "I just think that if I go, the Arab world, and of course Africa and Asia for that matter, would interpret this as endorsing everything that Israel has done, and I do have questions of doubt."[126] In the early 1960s, King supported Israel's sovereignty and right to exist, stating that "Israel's right to exist as a state in security is

---

[124] Martin Kramer, THE WAR ON ERROR, supra note 73 at 257.

[125] King interviewed by Tom Jerriel and John Casserly, ABC "Issues and Answers," June 18, 1967, The King Center Digital Archive, transcript archived at http://web.archive.org/web/20150304113151/. See also, DeNeed L. Brown, Retropolis, *The Sermon Where MLK Spoke Candidly on the Arab-Israeli Conflict*, THE WASHINGTON POST, available at www.washingtonpost.com/history/2024/01/15/martin-luther-king-israel-palestinians/

[126] Transcript of conference call, July 24, 1967, in The Martin Luther King, Jr., FBI File, Part II: The King-Levison File (microfilm), ed. David J. Garrow (Frederick, MD: University Publications of America, 1987), reel 8 (hereafter: King-Levison File).

incontestable."¹²⁷ He believed the "whole world must see that Israel must exist and has the right to exist and is one of the great outposts of democracy in the world,"¹²⁸ despite being deeply troubled by Israel's preemptive military action against Egypt in 1967, the ensuing wars with Syria and Jordan, and the massive and disproportionate killing that resulted. King's position was synonymous with many Pan-Africanists who were concerned about the plight of Palestinians. It reflected Africa and Asia's influence on his thinking during this period, his understanding of geopolitics, and the volatility of the post- Arab–Israeli War environment.

Whether or not King would have supported a Black American Zionist state inside or outside of the US is unclear, but likely doubtful within the territory of the US because he believed that America should be a multiracial democracy – though it had yet to live up to its creed and purported values. In a September 1967 speech to the American Psychological Association (APA) Annual Convention in Washington, DC, King patently rejected arguments made by some white scholars, including Henry Loomis, the president of the APA, who argued for the establishment of an "all Negro" homeland in South America. According to King, Loomis suggested "'that the valleys of the Andes Mountains would be an ideal place for American Negroes to build a second Israel" and declared that "[t]he United States Government should negotiate for a remote but fertile land in Ecuador, Peru or Bolivia for this relocation."¹²⁹ King pointedly responded to Loomis's assertion:

> I feel that it is rather absurd and appalling that a leading social scientist today would suggest to black people, that after all these years of suffering and exploitation as well as investment in the American dream, that we should turn around and run at this point in history. I say that we will not run! Professor Loomis even compared the relocation task of the Negro to the relocation task of the Jews in Israel. The Jews were made exiles. They did not choose to abandon Europe, they were driven out. Furthermore, Israel has a deep tradition, and Biblical roots for Jews. The Wailing Wall is a good example of these roots. They also had significant financial aid from the United States for the relocation and rebuilding effort. What tradition does the Andes, especially the valley of the Andes Mountains, have for Negroes?¹³⁰

---

[127] Jewish Telegraphic Agency, *Dr. King Repudiates Anti-Semitic, Anti-Israel Black Power Stand*, October 10, 1967, archived at http://web.archive.org/web/20160229154145/ www.jta.org/1967/10/11/archive/dr-king-repudiates-anti-semitic-anti-israel-black-power-stand. See also, "Martin Luther King Jr: 'Israel … is one of the great outposts of democracy in the world'" (video excerpt from interview), posted at www.youtube.com/watch?v=kvr2Cxuh2Wk

[128] "Martin Luther King Jr: 'Israel … is one of the great outposts of democracy in the world'" (video excerpt from interview), posted at www.youtube.com/watch?v=kvr2Cxuh2Wk *Martin Luther King, Jr., Other Prominent U.S. Christian Clergymen Urge Support for Israel*, Jewish Telegraphic Agency (May 29, 1967), archived at http://web.archive.org/web/20160109103941/ www.jta.org/1967/05/29/archive/dr-king-other-prominent-u-s-christian-clergymen-urge-support-for-israel. New York Times (May 28, 1967).

[129] Martin Luther King Jr., King's Challenge to the Nations's Social Scientists, supra note 75; print version appeared in the APA Monitor, Vol. 30, No. 1 (January 1999).

[130] *Id.*

King's answer to this final question was simple: None! King would likely have agreed if Loomis's ideas were centered around emigration to Africa (like Johnson's had been), given that he generally encouraged Black American emigration to the continent. However, emigration to Africa, in many ways, would alleviate the need for a new Negro homeland altogether. Knowing the historical failures of the Liberia experiment well, King believed in Black American integration into African societies as part of any emigration project, not the establishment of a distinct or exclusive African American homeland in Africa or elsewhere. King's version of Pan-Africanism did not contemplate abandoning the 400-year reverie for racial equality and justice in the US. Moreover, he believed that, like Jews in Israel, African Americans had "deep traditions" and biblical roots in Africa – ancestrally derived racial, ethnic, social, cultural, political, and economic connections, interests, and histories in the continent. These did not exist for African Americans in Peru.

Ironically, however, these roots and ties presumably did extend to and saturate ancient and modern Israel, Judaism, and Christianity, given the strong presence of Africa and Africans in biblical history.[131] The African seed in biblical history is something that King forthrightly embraced and understood. Black peoples represented by African nations, particularly Egypt, Ethiopia, Kush or Cush (northern Sudan and southern Egypt),[132] Nubia,[133] Put (Cyrene or Libya), Punt (Eritrea, Somali and Djibouti) appear throughout the Bible: The Old Testament refers to Africa, African nations, and African persons well over 1000 times, with 740 references to Egypt alone. Yet, in their letters to King, Friedman and Johnson discounted the foundational dimension or organizing principle of Jewish Zionism – religion – and overlooked the fact that African Americans are rooted in – as founders, descendants, and subscribers – all three Abrahamic traditions: Judaism, Christianity, and Islam. Notably, Black Americans comprise 20 percent of Muslims in the US, so any unity principle could not be anchored in any one religion. So, to the extent that Jewish Americans identify themselves as a religious group rather than a racial or ethnic grouping, there was and is no religious basis from which to organize or replicate the Zionist movement concretely.[134]

---

[131] Walter Arthur McCray, THE BLACK PRESENCE IN THE BIBLE: DISCOVERING THE BLACK AND AFRICAN IDENTITY OF BIBLICAL PERSONS AND NATIONS, TEACHERS EDITION (Chicago: Black Light Fellowship, 1995); Walter Arthur McCray, THE BLACK PRESENCE IN THE BIBLE AND THE TABLE OF NATIONS: GENESIS 10: 1–32 (Chicago: Black Light Fellowship, 1995); Dr. Cain Hope Felder (excerpt), BLACKS IN BIBLICAL ANTIQUITY, published in AMERICAN BIBLE SOCIETY, available at https://bibleresources.americanbible.org/resource/blacks-in-biblical-antiquity; and see generally, Tony Evans, *Black Heritage throughout Biblical History*, BIBLE TO LIFE, available at https://bibletolife.com/resources/articles/black-heritage-throughout-biblical-history/.

[132] Historically, the terms Kush and Nubia were used interchangeably, but Kush or Cush represented the southern region of Nubia and the location of the Kingdom of Kush or Kushite empire. It was a region of Nubia for two millennia.

[133] Nubia was in northeastern Africa stretching from the Nile River Valley to the Red Sea, Libyan Desert, and into the heart of Sudan.

[134] Notwithstanding, any notion of a Jewish people seems to transcend religion and speak to the ethnic and cultural origins of Jewishness that derive from the Laws of Jewish Life codified in the Halacha,

Indeed, Black Americans are defined as a racial group despite their foundational connection to Judaism, Christianity, and Islam. About 80 percent of African Americans identify as Christian, however, raising the question about the potential of a Black Christian Zionistic movement – something that Friedman seems to have had in mind.[135] It is unlikely that King would have seriously entertained such a proposal during this period; however, he may have been intrigued by it. As noted just above, the New Testament is replete with references to Africa and Africans. King's foundational training under the liberating tutelage of Daddy King at Ebenezer Baptist Church, as well as the core theological studies at Morehouse University, Crozer Theological Seminary, and Boston College, provided him with a thorough understanding of biblical geography, including Africa's foundational role in biblical history. His education further included a firm awareness that many key leaders and theologians in the early church were Africans. For example, Cyprian and Tertullian were from Carthage, or modern-day Tunisia; Saint Augustine of Hippo originated from Algeria; Clement, Origen, Athanasius, and Cyril all came from Egypt; and several early popes were born in Africa, including Victor I, Melchaides, and Gelasius I.

Friedman's letter to King was written with a firm understanding of the symmetry between the histories of persecution of the two groups, Jews and Blacks. Before the establishment of the State of Israel in May 1948, and given their history of oppression and genocide, Jews and/or Hebrews, broadly defined, arguably had no homeland. By contrast, however, African Americans had Africa (real or imagined) and the US despite being kidnapped, enslaved, and systemically brutalized and disadvantaged. Jews had religion, culture, ethnicity, ethno-religious discrimination, and a legacy of violence, genocide, and the Holocaust to bind them. African Americans had race, culture, religion, the slave trade, enslavement, racial discrimination, and a heritage of brutal violence and genocide. Yet Black progressives and radicals – whether Black nationalists or Pan-Africanists – have rarely called for the establishment of an African American nation-state solely for Americans of African descent. Even in ethnically specific or exclusive iterations of Black nationalism, Black people on the continent and in the diaspora shared in the cognitive design and theories of Black liberation.

King was an Africanist and presumably, a Pan-Africanist. Consequently, he rejected Loomis's idea of Black Zionism in Central America as well as the comparison of Black Americans and Ashkenazi Jews – not only for the reasons stated above,

which defines a Jew as anyone who was or is born of a Jewish mother or lawful conversion, with the former being more authoritative.
[135] The ancient or historical basis for a Black Christian Zionist-like movement has some foundation. For example, early Christianity has its origins in Africa, from Nubia and Egypt (including the ancient history of Pharoah Silko's Nubian Christian Kingdom) to Coptic Christianity in Egypt and Sudan, as well as Orthodox Christianity in Ethiopia. See generally, Salim Faraji, THE ROOTS OF NUBIA CHRISTIANITY UNCOVERED: THE TRIUMPH OF THE LAST PHARAOH (Trenton, NJ: Africa World Press, 2012). Finally, the Antonian movement led by the early eighteeth-century prophetess Dona Beatriz Kimpa Vita in the Kingdom of Kongo radically contested the theological and cultural hegemony of European Christianity by advancing a decolonizing hermeneutic that relocated Christian sacred history within Kongo's own historical, cultural, and geographical landscape.

but because the latter was provided substantial political and financial support by the US and other nations to establish, relocate, develop, and defend Israel, including heavy investment in its military-industrial complex. King did not consider Black Zionism an attractive option for Black Americans because he believed that Negroes had too greatly invested in America's success and suffered too prominently to give up. Yet King recognized that, like Jewish Americans, Black Americans and other diasporic groups can have more than one homeland. King was aware that, beyond Liberia and Sierra Leone, African Americans had been emmigrating and integrating into African communities throughout Africa for 100 years (e.g., in Ethiopia, Nigeria, Senegal, Ghana, and South Africa).

Unfortunately, King could not constructively respond to Johnson and Friedman's self-empowering propositions. In February 1960, a few months before receiving their proposals, King became immersed in a monumental legal fight for his life after being wrongly prosecuted by the State of Alabama for two counts of felony perjury related to income tax evasion. Four years prior, in 1956, Alabama had already prosecuted him for his boycott of the Montgomery City Lines, Inc.[136] State officials sought to destroy King. The retaliatory and vengeful targeting of King by southern polities – a form of lawfare against the civil rights movement – combined with the FBI's counterintelligence activities, which aimed to discredit him and dismantle civil rights leaders and groups. These forces, however, inspired King to double down on his efforts in the US. The same month that the two proposals were received, King moved from Montgomery back to Atlanta to enhance the operational capacity of the SCLC to fight Jim Crowism and co-pastor Ebenezer Baptist Church with his father. Still, I suppose both proposals would have intrigued King had he been able to devote his full attention to them. They were Africa-centered, complemented one another, and added to his thinking about Black American emigration to Africa and the need for new organizational structures to combat war, racism, and poverty in the US and abroad.

Luckily, in May 1960, a white jury in Montgomery found King not guilty of tax fraud.[137] This episode seems to have reignited his human rights advocacy domestically and internationally, including a June 1960 private meeting about racial equality in New York with John F. Kennedy while he was running for

---

[136] Edgar Dyer, A *"Triumph of Justice" in Alabama: The 1960 Perjury Trial of Martin Luther King, Jr.*, JOURNAL OF AFRICAN AMERICAN HISTORY, Vol. 88, No. 3 (Summer 2003), 245, *Gale Literature Resource Center*, link.gale.com/apps/doc/A108788089/LitRC?u=anon~7f1ff7ff&sid=googleScholar&xid=78aefeb2.

[137] The acquittal shocked King, and he commented: "This represents, to my mind, great hope and it reveals that as I have said on many occasions, that there are hundreds of thousands of people, white people, of goodwill in the South. And even though they may not agree with one's views on the question of integration, they are honest people and people who will follow the just and righteous path. And so, this reaffirms my faith in the ultimate decency of man." Transcript of Television Interview of Martin Luther King, Jr. (May 28, 1960) (MLKPP, Accession No. 600528–002) (orig. in WSB Television News Video Archive, University of Georgia., Athens, Georgia.).

the American presidency, sit-in demonstrations in Atlanta, and a November visit to attend the inauguration celebration of Nnamdi Azikiwe, Nigeria's Governor-General and Commander-in-Chief. Between 1960 and his untimely assassination, he continued to dedicate considerable time and resources to supporting anticolonial and antiracist freedom movements in Africa. On the one hand, he petitioned the US government for more development assistance and to affirm relations with African states and peoples; on the other hand, he worked directly with African leaders – often to the consternation of US officials – to support liberation and independence movements and dismantle colonialism. Though he did not have a chance to respond to them, the "Back to Africa" and "Black Zionism" proposals fit into the universe of King's thinking and global ministry. They complimented his magnanimous and globally centered stream of consciousness, Beloved Pan-Africanism.

5.4 GLOBAL BLACKNESS AND RECIPROCITY

King's Beloved Pan-Africanism, I argue, includes an enduring quality found among most Pan-Africanists: global Blackness and empathy for poor and oppressed people and peoples. As already noted, King's compassion for Black people and other persons of color,[138] irrespective of their ethnicity or national origin, is an inherent aspect of Pan-African discourses and activism – and it is a quality more sacred than any subjective "African roots" test. King's Beloved Pan-Africanism also fits squarely within the BIT, bolstering his rightful designation as a human rights leader and fortifying the notion that King was a legitimate Pan-Africanist leader. One could rightly argue that it is not possible to understand the depth and breadth of King's human rights-oriented ministry without first recognizing his Pan-African inclinations, activism, and philosophy.

King's Beloved Pan-Africanism is exceptional for what it proposes and disregards. It nicely outfits Pan-Africanism – traditionally dressed in socialist-atheist garb – with a Black liberation theology embroidered robe. It illuminates the spiritual and human dimensions of Pan-Africanism, arguing for intra-racial solidarity over disharmony, nonviolent direct action over militaristic confrontation, love over hate, divine justice over worldly chaos, courage over fear, and activism over passivity. It also boldly recognizes the need of the Black diaspora, particularly African Americans, to move back to Africa to assist in the continent's economic, technical, industrial, social, cultural, and political development and security, a cornerstone of Pan-Africanist ideology. In "Birth of a New Nation," for example, King emphasized his hope that Blacks would "go to Africa [Ghana]

---

[138] Martin Luther King Jr., *Beyond Vietnam: A Time to Break Silence*, April 4, 1967, Riverside Church, New York City. *Dr. Martin Luther King: Beyond Vietnam and Remaining Awake through a Great Revolution*, 90th Cong., 2d sess., Congressional Record 114 (April 9, 1968): 9391–9397.

as immigrants" to offer their technical assistance.[139] However, I believe that King specifically intended for African/African American relations to be mutually beneficial in the form of dual citizenship initiatives; diaspora investment programs in Africa; and African advocacy for and investment in predominantly Black American urban communities, consul-general appointments, global positions (positioning African Americans in international organizations), and support for nonprofit agencies engaged in civil rights activities. Knowing that Nkrumah was a Pan-Africanist, King shared Nkrumah's encouragement and enthusiasm for Black Americans to emigrate to Ghana, believing that "hundreds and thousands" would ultimately follow the examples of dentists Robert and Sarah Lee and businessman David Jones (see Chapter 3).

Indeed, King's global ministry, leadership, human rights activism, and persona are more appropriately viewed through the prism of Beloved Pan-Africanism, his unique version of Pan-Africanism.[140] Over time, King's human rights ministry and doctrine, which was largely focused on African liberation, progressed into Beloved Pan-Africanism, birthing a formidable global human rights ministry that expanded into Africa and Asia. Thus, Beloved Pan-Africanism arguably was conceived alongside King's notion of the Beloved Community, which was his global vision that the earths wealth must be shared with all people to eliminate poverty and homelessness in accordance with global standards that aim to safeguard the human dignity of mankind.[141] Here, King's reference to international standards while contemplating racial segregation in the US is yet another claim to outside law, that is, UN standards of humaneness enshrined in the UN Charter and prevailing human rights law. King's Beloved Community seems to universalize and cross-fertilize Beloved Pan-Africanism with experiential insights from the Montgomery Bus Boycott and his sojourner to Ghana. King observed:

> Racism and all forms of discrimination, bigotry and prejudice will be replaced by an all-inclusive spirit of sisterhood and brotherhood. In the Beloved Community, international disputes will be resolved by peaceful conflict-resolution and reconciliation of adversaries, instead of military power. Love and trust will triumph over fear and hatred. Peace with justice will prevail over war and military conflict.[142]

King believed that "there is something in the soul that cries out for freedom. There is something deep down within the very soul of man that reaches out for Canaan."[143] King believed that African Americans should fight against racist oppression in the

---

[139] Martin Luther King Jr, *The Birth of a New Nation*, supra note 64 at 156.
[140] See generally, Jeremy I. Levitt, *Beyond Borders*, supra note 3.
[141] *The King Philosophy-Nonviolnce365*, The King Center, available at www.thekingcenter.org/king-philosophy (last visited March 11, 2017).
[142] *Id.*
[143] Martin Luther King Jr, *The Birth of a New Nation*, supra note 64 at 161.

US and Africa, which is consistent with conventional Pan-Africanist philosophy. He believed that "[f]reedom only comes through persistent revolt, through persistent agitation, through persistently rising up against the system of evil" because "[p]rivileged classes never give up their privileges without strong resistance."[144]

Consequently, King's Beloved Pan-Africanism rests on five pillars: 1) global Blackness; 2) radical nonviolent resistance; 3) empathy; 4) grave personal sacrifice; and 5) divine justice. It thus resembles ancient Egypt's MA'AT, encompassing harmony, balance, reciprocity, justice, truth, and righteousness precepts. And like MA'AT, Beloved Pan-Africanism was King's spiritual algorithm and framework for contributing to an ideal state of the universe, a World House. It guided his spiritual frequency, directing his approach, behavior, and tactics from which his notion of morality, justice, and Black liberation emanated. King's Beloved Pan-Africanism was inspired by radical resistance, i.e., the anti-Black racist, anti-colonial, decolonization, and anti-Apartheid movements in the US as well as Algeria, Ghana, Kenya, Nigeria, and South Africa, as well as Ethiopia's victory over Italy at the 1896 Battle of Adwa. Along with the Haitian Revolution, these examples became influential symbols of Pan-Africanism in the Black world. Despite the violence inherent in several of these liberation struggles, however, Beloved Pan-Africanism was underwritten by nonviolent direct action, cemented by King's dedication to "racial justice and equality at the domestic and international levels, and lastly, his empathy for oppressed people of color fighting colonialism and neo-colonialism from Hanoi to Harare and Havana to Honiara."[145]

Framing King's Pan-Africanist ideals is important given that his Pan-African persona preceded his October 14, 1964, crowning as a Nobel Laureate and global human rights leader by at least a decade – a timeline that supports the idea that King's Pan-African ideals and activism significantly influenced his nobel ministry. Cone argues that "King's focus on the global implications of racism in relation to poverty and war led him to conclude that the slums in American cities were a 'system of internal colonialism' not unlike the exploitation of the Third World by European nations."[146] Moreover, Cone contended that King "did not believe that one could participate with God in the creation of the beloved community and at the same time use violent methods."[147] Cone suggests that King firmly believed that, "people who use violence have lost faith in the God of love and thus, have lost hope that a beloved community can be created."[148]

---

[144] Id.
[145] Jeremy I. Levitt, *Beyond Borders: Martin Luther King, Jr., Africa and Pan-Africanism*, supra note 3 at 307.
[146] James H. Cone, *Martin Luther King Jr., and the Third World*, JOURNAL OF AMERICAN HISTORY, Vol. 74 (1987), 462.
[147] Id.
[148] James H. Cone, *Martin Luther King Jr., and the Third World*, in WORLD ORDER AND RELIGION 119 (Wade Clark Roof eds., 1991), 119.

Meanwhile, Richardson highlighted several important normative arguments forwarded by King in his "Riverside Church" speech and the "Letter." For example, in the former address, Richardson comments that King "projected an African American alternative approach to international relations and international law" based on "non-violence and profound love of humans and humanity."[149] In the Letter, he argues that King identified the "intertwining of black freedom and inspirational struggle between the civil rights movement, the global decolonization movement, the Pan-African freedom struggle for independence, including against South African apartheid."[150] According to Richardson, King defined the necessity of enforcing both "international political and civil rights, and economic, social and cultural rights as a matter of law for poor people and people of color,"[151] and he "defined and upheld the general right of Black people to take international positions on major issues, here following W. E. B. Du Bois and his own recent examples."[152]

In the "Riverside Church" speech, King specifically injected the global human rights movement with a new vision linking African American civil rights with the Vietnam War.[153] King's opposition to the Vietnam War was underwritten by his antiwar philosophy and emboldened by the UN Charter's prohibition on the use of force, which is why, on April 15, 1967, he led a 125,000-person demonstration from Central Park to the UN in "New York's biggest anti-war march."[154] King boldly condemned American brutality against the Vietnamese people during the war. As a Nobel Laureate, King's internationalization of the American civil rights movement was monumental; Blacks disproportionately fought and died in Vietnam and faced racial tyranny and Jim Crowism upon returning home. His appeal to outside law (international law), African nations (e.g., Ghana and Nigeria), and global institutions like the UN for moral backing was forged by his belief in natural law and justice and informed by a deep spiritual conviction in the nonviolent disruption and dismantling of unjust systems.

As Richardson wisely noted, King's activism was powered by his ardent belief in the international rule of law through the "United Nations binding powerful states, the unity of love including for opponents and enemies, and a worldwide fellowship as a supreme unifying principle of life which unlocks the door to ultimate reality

---

[149] Henry J. Richardson III, *Dr. Martin Luther King, Jr. as an International Human Rights Leader*, supra note 7 at 473.

[150] Henry J. Richardson III, *From Birmingham's Jail to beyond the Riverside Church: Martin Luther King's Global Authority*, TEMPLE UNIVERSITY LEGAL STUDIES Research Paper No. 2015–08 (2015), https://ssrn.com/abstract=2554549.

[151] *Id.*

[152] *Id.*

[153] *Id.*

[154] *Vietnam War Protests with Martin Luther King and the FBI*, Universal Newsreel, April 15, 1967, NBC Learn, available at https://media.un.org/avlibrary/en/asset/d316/d3164748.

and is necessary for the survival of mankind."[155] King's Pan-African advocacy created a needed intersection between American civil rights and global human rights while projecting an African-American alternative approach to international relations, particularly with Africa and international law. His was a radical approach based on fervent peaceful advocacy, protest, and a profound love of humanity, on the one hand, and, on the other, fierce insistence that the US was obligated to adhere to international legal norms protecting the rights and well-being of African Americans and Africans. King's stalwart advocacy was a significant influence in the United Nations General Assembly's adoption of Resolution 2106 (XX), establishing the International Convention on the Elimination of All Forms of Racial Discrimination (CERD).[156] His tireless advocacy for racial justice, civil rights, and human rights in the US, Africa, and beyond, and his international prominence, particularly his influence on African leaders, contributed mightily to US support of CERD and the global climate for its landmark adoption.[157] Despite the views of some commentators such as Roger Alford, King intended to influence the international law prohibition against racism, colonialism, and Apartheid.[158] This was his life's work.

King understood that Black Americans were determined in their pursuit of racial justice, and the transnational winds of change eventually hit Plymouth Rock. King reasoned, "something within has reminded the Negro of his birthright of freedom, and something without has reminded him that it can be gained. Consciously or unconsciously, he has been caught up by the Zeitgeist, and with his black brothers of Africa and his brown and yellow brothers in Asia, South America, and the Caribbean, the United States Negro is moving with a sense of great urgency toward the promised land of racial justice."[159]

---

[155] Henry J. Richardson III, *From Birmingham's Jail to beyond the Riverside Church: Martin Luther King's Global Authority*, supra note 150 at 189.

[156] CERD was adopted on December 21, 1965, and formally entered into force on January 4, 1969, one year after King was assassinated. It represented the UN's first racial justice orientated international human rights treaty.

[157] *Goldberg Says U.S. Will Sign U.N. Pact for Racial Equality*, NEW YORK TIMES, Thursday July 7, 1966, p. 22. See also, Henry J. Richardson, III, *Dr. Martin Luther King, Jr. as an International Human Rights Leader*, supra note 7 at 476; and Roger Alford, *The Impact of Martin Luther King on International Law*, OpinioJuris, January 1, 2008, available at https://opiniojuris.org/2008/01/21/the-impact-of-martin-luther-king-on-international-law/

[158] Roger Alford, *The Impact of Martin Luther King on International Law*, OpinioJuris, January 1, 2008, available at https://opiniojuris.org/2008/01/21/the-impact-of-martin-luther-king-on-international-law/

[159] Martin Luther King Jr., *Letter from Birmingham Jail* (London: Penguin Classics, 2018).

6

Conclusion

The Relevance and Impact of Martin Luther King Jr. on Black Liberation

FIGURE 6.1 April 15, 1967: Martin Luther King Jr. and anti-Vietnam leaders meet in the office of UN Under-Secretary Ralph J. Bunche in New York. From left: David Dellinger, editor of *Liberation Magazine*; Rev. James Bevel, aide to Dr. Martin Luther King Jr.; noted pediatrician Dr. Benjamin Spock; Cleveland Robinson, Negro labor leader; Dr. Martin Luther King Jr.; Dagmar Wilson of Women Strike for Peace; and Dr. Bunche.

6.1 MY ANCESTRAL HOMELAND

America is enamored with placing Martin Luther King Jr. in a dreamer's box while disregarding his radical conviction, Pan-African consciousness, and Great World House thesis demanding an end to the three evils of racism, poverty, and war (the foundational facets of white supremacy). King dedicated his life to a "pro-Black," anti-white supremacy, liberation-oriented mission to "transform this worldwide neighborhood into a worldwide brotherhood," always seeking to "bridge the gulf between our scientific progress and our moral progress."[1] Far from being an idealist, he was a cutting-edge thinker who thought outside the box to confront Jim Crow paradoxes. He argued that Black people must declare:

> "I am somebody. (Oh yeah) I am a person. I am a man with dignity and honor. (Go ahead) I have a rich and noble history, however painful and exploited that history has been. Yes, I was a slave through my foreparents (That's right), and now I'm not ashamed of that. I'm ashamed of the people who were so sinful to make me a slave." (Yes sir) Yes [applause], yes, we must stand up and say, "I'm black (Yes sir), but I'm black and beautiful." (Yes) This [applause], this self-affirmation is the black man's need, made compelling (All right) by the white man's crimes against him. (Yes) Whether the dream propaganda paradigm has hurt us?[2]

To confine King's contribution to the Black world to an integrationist-dreamer framework is folly and a deceptively dangerous mis-characterization. To discount his revolutionary genius, transnational ethos, and Pan-African inclinations is to steal from the Black world his antidote against the persistent forces of violent white supremacy and their antecedents.

King's human rights leadership was theoretically and physically militant and aggressive. It was nonviolent but simultaneously passionate, sacrificial, and transformative. He understood that "through violence, you may murder a murderer, but you cannot murder murder. (Yes) Through violence, you may murder a liar, but you can't establish the truth. (That's right) Through violence, you may murder a hater, but you can't murder hate through violence. (All right, that's right) Darkness cannot put out darkness; only light can do that."[3] From 1956 until his assassination in 1968, King directed his light on Africa and her struggle for freedom, and she reciprocated. He claimed Africa as his ancestral homeland and Africans as his kin. He argued that systems of racial oppression are transnational and mutually reinforcing in the exploitation of Black people.[4] His commitment to ending them on both sides of the Atlantic was unwavering, as was his pursuit of a common humanity among all peoples.

---

[1] Martin Luther King Jr., WHERE DO WE GO FROM HERE: CHAOS OR COMMUNITY? (Boston: Beacon Press, 1967), 181.

[2] Martin Luther King, Jr., *Where Do We Go from Here*, Atlanta, Georgia (August 16, 1967), (on file with Martin Luther King, Jr. Research and Education Institute, Stanford University), (available at https://kinginstitute.stanford.edu/where-do-we-go-here).

[3] Id.

[4] Press release, *Martin Luther King, Jr.'s Statement at American Negro Leadership Conference on Africa*, November 28, 1962, in *Southern Christian Leadership Conference Records, 1954–1970*, (on file with Martin Luther King, Jr., Center for Nonviolent Social Change, Inc., Atlanta, GA, loose document on file with author).

Beyond Borders locates Martin Luther King Jr.'s relationship with, and contribution to, Africa and African liberation and examines how he merged the Black American civil rights movement with Africa's decolonization and liberation struggles. It examines King's ideals, ministry, advocacy, activities, initiatives, influence on Africa and African leaders, and, referentially, US foreign policy on Africa. His anti-white supremacy ministry focused on Black America and Africa, forming a part of the Black International Tradition (BIT) and today's global peace historiography and architecture. *Beyond Borders* sheds a radiant light on Martin Luther King Jr.'s close relationship with African leaders and how he influenced and supported African freedom struggles. Equally important, it highlights the intersections that King fashioned – ideological, political, material, spiritual, and otherwise – between the anticolonial, antiracist, antipoverty, and antiwar movements beyond borders. *Beyond Borders* forwards the thesis that King was a human rights-orientated Pan-Africanist, not simply a civil rights leader focused on the plight of Blacks in the US.

Beyond Borders has documented the circumstances, experiences, and phenomena that influenced King's Pan-African consciousness and actions – actions that forced him to invoke the binding authority of law, domestic and international, for Black liberation. In the process, it has provided keen insight into how King's African ministry and nonviolent direct-action philosophy and approach, that is, "Beloved Pan-Africanism," may reposition him in scholarly literature as a spiritual leader who informed and transformed racial justice, human rights, and peace processes in Africa and the Black Diaspora. In this study and elsewhere, I have argued that "King's Pan-African advocacy helped recast and globalized African American uniqueness, repression, and appeals to outside law, namely by reclassifying civil rights claims as international human rights law violations through the prism of Pan-Africanism."[5] While the US government sought to control and limit the transnational dimensions of the civil rights movement, discourage African Americans from influencing US policy toward Africa, and undermine Africa's new and progressive leadership, King unified them America's anti-Black racism movements. Apart from W. E. B. Du Bois, perhaps no other leader of national prominence can effectively claim to have openly and effectively contested racial oppression in Africa and the US simultaneously and decisively.

While King was, debatably, one of the most effective Black American advocates for Africa, he did not identify himself as a Pan-Africanist, given the infrequent use of the term in the 1950s and its eventual use by Black nationalist separatist movements. Ironically, this reality did not stop W. E. B. Du Bois, one of Pan-Africanism's pioneering and most forthright leaders, from openly identifying as one. One reason for this dichotomy was that, unlike Du Bois, King was not a socialist (despite supporting

---

[5] Jeremy I. Levitt, *Beyond Borders: Martin Luther King, Jr., Africa and Pan-Africanism*, TEMPLE JOURNAL OF INTERNATIONAL AND COMPARATIVE LAW, Vol. 31, No. 1 (Spring 2017), 303.

several socialist-inspired independence movements in places such as Algeria, Ghana, Guinea, Kenya, Angola, South Africa, and Zambia). Another reason was that as a radical theologian and pastor, King's starting point was spiritual – a mixture of Black liberation theology, neoorthodoxy, and personalism – which sought to free Black people and other oppressed groups from social, economic, political, militaristic, and religious subjugation. His cosmogony interconnected and transcended the political secularity of traditional Pan-Africanism, leading to Beloved Pan-Africanism, which embraces the concept of divine justice.

In the Introduction to this book, Pan-Africanism was defined as a campaign for the globalization of African liberation and unification. Consequently, a Pan-Africanist is liberation-oriented and actively struggles – spiritually, socially, culturally, politically, and economically – to combat the evil impacts of colonialism and white supremacy on Black people all around the world. Pan-Africanism seeks to maximize the full potential of persons of African descent by creating just and equal societies. King embraced all these currents. Beloved Pan Pan-Africanism is rooted in them. Notwithstanding, George Houser, one of few to offer any thought into whether King was a Pan-Africanist, undervalued King's place within the pantheon of Pan-Africanist leaders. While he rightly noted that liberation struggles in Africa and the civil rights movement in the US were mutually reinforcing and inspiring, he distinguishes them from each other and ignores the fact that King consciously interwove them. Houser contends that "one was organized to resist domination by a foreign occupying power; the objective was revolution. The other aimed at protesting inequalities and racial injustices within the system; its purpose was reformation."[6] Notably, Houser did not define what he meant by revolution or its modality – peaceful or forceful – but conceivably understood there were variants. Indeed, Houser, who often depended on King to raise funds and legitimize the American Committee on Africa's (ACOA) activities in support of forceful African liberation movements, claimed that even though the freedom struggles in Africa and the US "were influenced by the same forces of history," their tactical differences meant that "they could not effectively embark on coordinated, joint tactics in a fundamental way. They could maintain at best fraternal relationship and could influence each other only at a distance."[7] King proved Houser wrong. His strategy for coordinating a united front to challenge and dismantle white supremacist systems in Africa and the US predominated tactical variances.

This is the same stream of disassociated reasoning Houser used to claim that King "was not essentially a Pan-Africanist" when attempting to differentiate him from Du Bois,[8] whose Pan-African credentials were beyond reproach. He even stated that in

---

[6] George Houser, *Martin Luther King, Jr., and International Movements of Liberation*, in Peter J. Albert and Ronald Hoffman (eds.), WE SHALL OVERCOME: MARTIN LUTHER KING, JR., AND THE BLACK FREEDOM STRUGGLE (Panthron Books and United States Capitol Historical Society, 1941), 188.
[7] *Id.*
[8] *Id.* at 183.

King's "psychological emphasis: the understanding of self is different," whatever that means.⁹ While Houser acknowledged that Du Bois's and King's approaches were "almost indistinguishable" and that both leaders believed in the internationalization of the "struggle against colonialism, inequality, and racism," he claimed that one was a Pan-Africanist and the other not despite acknowledging that there was "is no basic contradiction between Du Bois's Pan-Africanism and King's belief in the universality of the struggle for racial justice."¹⁰ In this respect, Houser's analysis was divergent and counterintuitive.

King, meanwhile, understood that resisting domination and combatting racial injustice were the *sine qua nons* of the Black experience in America. He knew that Native Americans, enslaved Africans, and Black Americans had long resisted white domination, engaging in strikes, sabotage, flight to runaway communities, enlistment in federal forces, violent rebellions and wars,¹¹ including the Stono River Rebellion of 1739, and repatriation to West Africa. King unified both ways of thought (African and African American) into one revolutionary and reformatory movement. Consequently, Houser's typology of King was the very in-the-box reasoning that is partly responsible for the widespread mischaracterization of King in the public realm. Again, Houser argued that King was too much of a universalist to embrace his Africanness and the plight of Africans and Africa, positing that, by contrast, "Pan-Africanism universalizes the concept of one's Africaness."¹² He thereby discounted King's Pan-African credentials because, as a white man, Houser believed that King did not firmly embrace his African roots. I strongly disagree. Houser misjudged the depth of King's connection to Africa and the internalization of his African heritage.

One of the problems with Houser's Pan-African litmus test and analysis appears to be his misunderstanding of Pan-Africanism as a universal approach to liberation dependent on universal freedom. King believed that colonialism and segregation were the same. Consequently, Houser and perhaps others have too often applied a blanket lens to Africa's variegated movement typologies and the historical role that Black Americans such as King played in physically and materially supporting peaceful and forceful movements against colonization and white domination in Africa.¹³ One observer noted:

> As early as the 1850s, when Martin Delaney and Robert Campbell argued that a strong free black African could contribute to the liberation of Negro slaves in America, some black Americans have sought to organize and emancipate the entire black world. Various Negro religious sects, Back-to-Africa movements, philanthropic foundations,

---

9 *Id.*
10 *Id.* at 182.
11 See generally, Herbert Aptheker, American Negro Slave Revolts, SCIENCE & SOCIETY, Vol. 1, No. 4 (Summer 1937), 512–538.
12 George Houser, *Martin Luther King, Jr., and International Movements of Liberation*, supra note 6, 182–183.
13 See generally, James L. Roark, *American Black Leaders: The Response to Colonialism and the Cold War, 1943–1953*, AFRICAN HISTORICAL STUDIES, Vol. 4, No. 2 (1971), 253.

and black writers and scholars have rejected the domestic perspective on race. American Negroes protested the Spanish-American War and the Philippine campaign, the Congo atrocities, the Haitian occupation, and the Ethiopian invasion.[14]

Several Black Americans became "devoted advocates of Pan-Africanism and played significant roles in the awakening of nationalism in Africa."[15] Referring to early New World Pan-Africanists such as W. E. B. DuBois, Kwame Nkrumah reasoned, "[l]ong before many of us were even conscious of our degradation, these men fought for African national and racial equality."[16] King's Beloved Pan-Africanism continued and fortified the legacy of these early twentieth-century New World Pan-Africanists,[17] which, using Julius Nyerere's measure, demands one's African consciousness, loyalty, and dedication to the freedom and development of African states. King's life and works embraced all three principles.

Martin Luther King Jr.'s relevance to and impact on Africa was remarkable. His support of nonviolent and forceful freedom movements was exceptional. He should be repositioned in the scholarly literature as a prince of liberation, self-determination, and peace. Beloved Pan-Africanism's core principles, global Blackness, radical nonviolent resistance, empathy, grave personal sacrifice, and divine justice, provide a pathway to societal transformation away from racism, repression, and war. King's belief in and adherence to these principles catapulted him into international repute.

6.2 LIFE ACHIEVEMENTS, AWARDS, AND LEGACY

King is one of the world's most respected, celebrated, and honored human rights leaders, let alone the most internationally renowned African American. He may be more revered outside of the US than within it, a fact that reveals more about the troubling state of race relations in the US than anything else. His global footprint was etched in his Pro-Black advocacy. The countless memorial sites, parks, buildings, churches, statues, sculptures, libraries, centers, schools, and awards named after King dwarf all civil rights and human rights leaders apart from Nelson Mandela. Interestingly, the US only honored King with two stamps, in 1979 and 1999. In contrast, African nations

---

[14] Id. See generally M. R. Delany and Robert Campbell, SEARCH FOR A PLACE: BLACK SEPARATISM AND AFRICA (Ann Arbor: University of Michigan Press, 1969); Adelaide C. Hill and Martin Kilson, eds., APROPOS OF AFRICA: SENTIMENTS OF NEGRO AMERICAN LEADERS ON AFRICA FROM THE 1800S TO THE 1950S (London: Routledge, 1969); Lawrence P. Neal, "Black Power in the International Context," in Floyd B. Barbour, eds., THE BLACK POWER REVOLT (Boston: Porter Sargent Publishers, 1968), 136–137.

[15] James L. Roark, *American Black Leaders: The Response to Colonialism and the Cold War*, supra note 13, at 254.

[16] Id.

[17] Quoted in E. U. Essien-Udom, *The Relationship of Afro-Americans to African Nationalism*, FREEDOMWAYS, Vol. 2, No. 4 (Fall 1962). See also, George Shepperson, *Notes on Negro American Influence on the Emergence of African Nationalism*, JOURNAL OF AFRICAN HISTORY, Vol. 1, No. 2 (1960), 299–312.

(e.g., Congo, Dahomey, Djibouti, Gabon, Liberia, Mali, Rwanda, and Togo) began honoring him with stamps immediately after his assassination in 1968. Cameroon and Rwanda were the first to feature him on stamps in 1968, followed by Gabon and Mali. Memorial or commemorative stamps of deceased persons signify a nation's recognition of their monumental contribution to advancing humanity at home and abroad. In this context, African nations honored King's contribution and influence on the world stage before and more formidably than did his own (Figure 6.2).

Africa also leads the world in honoring King with, for example, statues in the Imo State in Nigeria, centers of learning in Johannesburg, South Africa, and Ongwediva, Namibia, as well as at schools in Accra, Ghana. Outside of Africa and the US, his legacy is honored with statues in Mexico City, Mexico; Newcastle University in northeast England; and Westminster Abbey, in London, UK. There is a memorial garden in New Delhi, India; a forest in Israel's Southern Galilee region; a church in Debrecen, Hungary; a park in Uppsala, Sweden; and a civic center in Havana, Cuba. The world loved King whereas America's appreciation of him was unresolved until thirty-two years after his murder when in 2000 all fifty states finally recognized his birthday as a national holiday.

While independence in Liberia (1847), Egypt (1922), Ethiopia (1941), Libya (1951), Sudan (1956), Morocco (1956), and Tunisia (1956) all preceded King's ascendancy as a global human rights icon in the wake of the Montgomery Bus Boycott, Ghana's liberation (1957) established a pathway for Black Africa's and Black America's liberation leaders and movements. Ghana's example emboldened nationalist movements in West Africa, particularly in the former French colonies (e.g., Guinea, Cameroon, Senegal, Togo, Mali, Benin, Niger, Burkina Faso, Côte d'Ivoire, Chad, Central African Republic, Congo-Brazzaville, and Gabon). Except Guinea, all the above-referenced states became independent in 1960, when seventeen African states in total achieved their independence. Through ACOA, the American Negro Leadership Conference on Africa (ANLCA), and the Southern Christian Leadership Conference (SCLC), King actively supported all these African independence and freedom movements. For example, he fundraised for liberation leaders, organizations, and movements such as South Africa's African National Congress (ANC); attended independence celebrations in Ghana and Nigeria; supported conflict resolution efforts in Nigeria; organized protests and lobbied the US government for development assistance for African states and governments; mobilized university scholarships for African students; and openly criticized European and American colonialism and racism through hundreds of speeches, lectures, and media interviews.

Notably, along with Houser, who was also an ordained Christian minister, King openly supported African independence even when it was not achieved peacefully. He embraced potent anticolonial movements in Algeria, Angola, Belgian Congo, Guinea-Bissau, Kenya, South Africa, Malawi, Mozambique, and Zambia. All these movements either began or transformed into full-fledged guerilla wars. For example, Nelson Mandela established the Umkhonto we Sizwe (Spear of the

FIGURE 6.2 African stamps showing Dr. Martin Luther King Jr.

Nation) paramilitary or guerilla wing of the ANC in the wake of the March 21, 1960, Sharpeville Massacre, which resulted in the murder of sixty-nine innocent and nonviolent protestors at the hands of Apartheid police and soldiers in South Africa.[18] It proved to be a watershed moment in Africa's beleaguered nonviolent movements. It intensified opposition to white-minority, settler-controlled regimes and buttressed protracted armed conflicts against Afrikaner, British, French, and Portuguese colonialism. King, too, decried the Sharpeville killings. Reflecting on King's legacy of nonviolence, Andrew Young, King's close advisor and acolyte, argued:

> Non-Violence came to us from Africa. It was Mahatma Gandhi who his early protest used non-violence against apartheid. It moved on to India. It was reborn again under the leadership of Chief Albert Luthuli whose daughter happens to now reside in Atlanta. We have seen it develop in such a way in the US of America that is quite different from the experiences which occurred in other parts of the world. That is as it should be. But one of the things that concerns me is that we in the United Nations and those of us who come out of this non-violent tradition have always tended to think of non-violence as it was last demonstrated in our town. I would like to contend that what we see happening across the world today is very much influenced by a non-violent understanding of how change can occur.[19]

King's advocacy for persons of African descent was formidable, from Compton to Cairo and Atlanta to Algiers. His effectiveness was partly due to his acute understanding of the social psychology and transnational impacts of racism. He opined:

> Ever since the birth of our nation, White America has had a Schizophrenic personality on the question of race, she has been torn between selves. A self in which she proudly professes the great principle of democracy and a self in which she madly practices the antithesis of democracy. This tragic duality has produced a strange indecisiveness and ambivalence toward the Negro, causing America to take a step backwards simultaneously with every step forward on the question of Racial Justice; to be at once attracted to the Negro and repelled by him, to love and to hate him. There has never been a solid, unified, and determined thrust to make justice a reality for Afro-Americans.[20]

Beyond Borders recognizes King's thesis that African Americans are of two cultures, one African and the other American, yet they are neither "totally African nor totally

---

[18] United Nations Secretary-General Kofi Annan, *Forty Years after Sharpeville Massacre, Fight against Racism Not Yet Won, Says Secretary-General in Message on International Day* (March 21, 2003); S.C. Res. 134, U.N. Doc. S/RES/134 (April 1, 1960); see also Boutros Boutros-Ghali, *The United Nations and Apartheid, 1948–1994*, U.N. Blue Book Series, at 244–45 (U.N. Dep't of Pub. Info. 1994) (document 15).

[19] Andrew Young, Permanent Representative of the U.S. to the U.N., Martin Luther King, Jr. and the Tradition of Non-Violence, Statement at the Special Session of the Special Committee Against Apartheid, Atlanta, Ga. (January 16, 1979), in International Tribute to Martin Luther King, Jr. (U.N. Ctr. Against Apartheid, Dep't of Political & Sec. Council Affs. 1979). Young's statement was made to pay tribute to the late Reverend Dr. Martin Luther King, Jr. on occasion of his 50th birthday.

[20] Martin Luther King Jr., *The Three Evils of Society*, Address Delivered at the National Conference on New Politics (August 31, 1967), transcribed from an Internet recording (loose document on file with author).

Western"; instead, Black Americans are "a true hybrid, a combination of two cultures" in the same way that King was a dual activist.[21] With this recognition, this book has demonstrated how King identified and fought against the lethal intersectionality between racism, poverty, and war through the lens of Beloved Pan-Africanism. He grasped the parallels between anticolonial and anti-Apartheid movements, among others, and America's civil rights movements. In the US, the winds of change were also blowing. Non-violent sit-ins at lunch counters across the nation became popular, and with them, the demise of segregated eateries and, after the freedom rides of 1961, the dismantling of segregation in interstate travel.[22]

King and his team of writers and advisors were brilliant. Between 1957 and 1967, he was awarded at least eighteen honorary degrees from American and foreign universities, half of which were doctorates of law, perhaps signaling the legal community's appreciation of his brand of human rights lawfare. Together, these offer yet another perspective on the global respect he garnered while litigating the liberation cases of Black Americans and Africans.

Martin Luther King Jr.'s honorary degrees

- 1957 Doctor of Humane Letters, Morehouse College (Atlanta, Georgia)
  Doctor of Laws, Howard University (Washington, DC)
  Doctor of Divinity, Chicago Theological Seminary (Chicago, Illinois)
- 1958 Doctor of Laws, Morgan State College (Baltimore, Maryland)
  Doctor of Humanities, Central State College (Wilberforce, Ohio)
- 1959 Doctor of Divinity, Boston University (Boston, Massachusetts)
- 1961 Doctor of Laws, Lincoln University (Lincoln, Pennsylvania)
  Doctor of Laws, University of Bridgeport (Bridgeport, Connecticut)
- 1962 Doctor of Civil Laws, Bard College (Annandale-On-Hudson, New York)
- 1963 Doctor of Letters, Keuka College (Keuka Park, New York)
- 1964 Doctor of Divinity, Wesleyan College (Middletown, Connecticut)
  Doctor of Laws, Jewish Theological Seminary (Boca Raton, Florida)
  Doctor of Laws, Yale University (New Haven, Connecticut)
  Doctor of Divinity, Springfield College (Springfield, Massachusetts)
- 1965 Doctor of Laws, Hofstra University (Long Island, New York)
  Doctor of Human Letters, Oberlin College (Oberlin, Ohio)
  Doctor of Social Science, Amsterdam Free University (Amsterdam, Netherlands)
  Doctor of Divinity, St. Peter's College (Jersey City, New Jersey)
- 1967 Doctor of Civil Law, University of New Castle (Newcastle upon Tyne, UK)
  Doctor of Laws, Grinnell College (Grinnell, Iowa)

---

[21] George Houser, *Martin Luther King, Jr., and International Movements of Liberation*, supra note 6, 184.
[22] *Id.* at 170.

King's honorary degrees were complemented with various awards during his life, including the Spingarn Medal from the National Association for the Advancement of Colored People (NAACP) (1957), being named Man of the Year by *Time Magazine* (1963), the Nobel Peace Prize (1964), the American Liberties Medallion from the American Jewish Committee (1965), and the Marcus Garvey Prize for Human Rights conferred by the Jamaican Government (1968). Posthumous honors include the US Presidential Medal of Freedom (1977) and the Congressional Gold Medal (1994).

As discussed in earlier chapters, King's leadership roles in ACOA, ANLCA, and SCLC, along with his various trips and invitations to travel to Africa, kept King well apprised of African Affairs and US foreign policy toward Africa. He helped found the SCLC in 1957, joined ACOA's executive leadership the same year, and created ANLCA with others in 1962. For its part, the SCLC was far more than a civil rights organization dedicated to nonviolently dismantling Jim Crow and achieving social, economic, and political justice in the South for Black Americans; it was a Black Southern Christian civil rights organization helping the Global South combat colonialism and prepare for independence. For example, the SCLC raised significant funds to support ACOA's Africa Defense and Aid Fund, created in 1958 to help address emergencies in South Africa and Central Africa.[23] The SCLC likewise raised funds to address the needs of the Congo amid its post-independence civil war. It also gave financial support for educational and political initiatives in Algeria, Kenya, and South Africa. In this vein, under King, it had strong African currents.[24] ACOA was an interracial group of community leaders, scholars, and policy experts dedicated to influencing US-Africa policy, mainly in support of anticolonial movements and newly independent African nations. ANLCA was founded and led by African Americans to mobilize the Black community to influence American foreign policy on Africa to eliminate colonialism and Apartheid and help repatriate Black Americans to the continent. King used ANLCA to anchor his racial bonds of connection to African nations. The organization openly acknowledged and embraced African Americans' "special responsibility" to lobby for African liberation.[25] Black Americans cannot, it argued, "separate this struggle at home from that abroad."[26] ANLCA organized vital meetings and conferences to consider the situation in southern Africa, central Africa, and beyond, always unabashed in challenging white supremacist regimes and norms. This stance frustrated American foreign policy in

---

[23] Id. See also, *A Letter from Martin Luther King, Jr., to Potential Contributors to the Africa Defense and Aid Fund*, Martin Luther King, Jr. Archive, Howard Gottlieb Archival Research Center, Boston University, November 12, 1959 (loose document on file with author).

[24] Id.

[25] Preamble, The American Negro Leadership Conference on Africa: Resolutions, Arden House Campus of Columbia University, Harriman, New York (November 23–25, 1962), (on file with African Activist Archivist), (available at https://africanactivist.msu.edu/recordFiles/210-849-28596/african_activist_archive-a0a0l4-a_12419.pdf.)

[26] Id.

the region in support of Apartheid and white rule. King's support of African liberation had a reciprocal benefit in the US. Africa's anti-colonial movements through organizations (such as SLCL, ANLCA, ACOA, and Black churches) galvanized Black American youth and encouraged a new generation of civil rights activists. As the above analysis demonstrates, King's dedication to Africa's varied freedom movements was unswerving – and the impact of this support galvanized youth in the US.

King's Beloved Pan-Africanism complemented the Pan-African philosophies of early Black Christian leaders. He supported the establishment of a "permanent liaison between American Negro leadership and the new African nations" aimed at evolving "a permanent national organization with the mission of identifying the American Negro's consciousness with Black Africa" and to "discuss problems of mutual interest and to support each group's aspiration."[27] The areas of mutual interest were broad, from fighting anti-Black racism, colonialism, poverty, war, and nuclear proliferation. His ideas were practical and effective in a new age of decolonization. Yet he remained committed to the idea that "violence as a way of achieving racial justice is both impractical and immoral."[28] To him, racism was "no mere American phenomenon. Its vicious grasp knows no geographical boundaries. In fact, racism and its perennial ally – economic exploitation – provide the key to understanding most of the international complications of this generation."[29] He was never deterred from advocating for the freedom and justice of Black people and other colored nations and persons (including Vietnam), irrespective of the ferocious nature of the colonial metropoles holding power and arming themselves with ever-more devastating modern weapons.

King was a scholar, and his Pan-African inclinations developed after rigorous study, advocacy, and thinking derived from meaningful theoretical and experiential understandings and experiences. He was a vociferous reader, an intellectual, and an interdisciplinary thinker long before it was a term of art. His massive personal library of books was littered with copious notes in the margins. It included various volumes on Africa, the Caribbean, Black America, race relations, civil rights, world politics, law, international law, philosophy, ethics, morality, economics, and world religions. Indeed, King's accomplishments as an activist, thinker, scholar, and pastor derive in no insignificant part from his prolific literacy, his intersectional and multidisciplinary understandings of the major branches of social sciences (anthropology, archaeology, economics, geography, history, law, linguistics, politics, psychology, and sociology) and humanities (law, languages, philosophy, religion and mythology, international

---

[27] M.S. Handler, *U.S. Negroes Plan Active Link with Peoples of African Nations*, NEW YORK TIMES, Thursday (April 4, 1963).

[28] Martin Luther King, Jr., Acceptance speech in the auditorium of the University of Oslo, on the occasion of the award of the Nobel Peace Prize, December 10, 1964, The Nobel Prize, available at www.nobelprize.org/prizes/peace/1964/king/acceptance-speech/

[29] Martin Luther King Jr., WHERE DO WE GO FROM HERE: CHAOS OR COMMUNITY? (Boston: Beacon Press, 1968), at 183.

relations, gender and women's studies, multicultural and regional studies, popular culture, and art and music) concerning the Black race. King constantly studied the dynamics of the human world, including its diverse religions, cultures, social mores, and communities. He was interested in how these dynamics function influence, and interact with institutions, structures, and other norms at the individual and societal levels. Arguably, his deep understanding of the intricacies of the African world in and outside of Africa was superior to that of many scholars of his time. His literary architecture was built upon a long line of progressive, even radical, influences from his grandparents, parents, family friends, Sweet Auburn, universities, and a host of mentors and confidantes who collectively poured into the making of his radical mind.

Notwithstanding, King faced an often-unbearable crisis of tactical theory. On the one hand, he sought to free Black people in the US and Africa facing violent structural racism, including Jim Crowism, Apartheid, colonial oppression, and repressive norms based on competition for geopolitical terrain, natural resources, and ideological space. King understood these transnational complexities and cognitive disparities. On the other hand, he had to navigate domestic swamps – to build and sustain a movement while competing against alternative theories of liberation (accommodationism, progressive reformism, and Black nationalism), all seeking to influence the hearts and minds of African Americans. Still, he was a student of Black liberation and empowerment and the various movements that sought to effectuate Black freedom in the US. This included Booker T. Washington's racial accommodationist economic and vocational approach represented by the adage, "[l]et down your buckets where you are"; W. E. B. Du Bois's "Talented Tenth" educational elitism and Pan-Africanism models; Marcus Garvey's Black nationalist and Back-to-Africa plans; and the NAACP's lawfare against Jim Crow. All these approaches held merit, but none of them solved the existential crises of the Negro. As he put it:

> No discussion of the influences that bore on the thinking of the Negro in 1963 would be complete without some attention to the relationship of this revolution to international events. Throughout the upheavals of Cold War politics, Negroes had seen their government go to the brink of nuclear conflict more than once. The justification for risking the annihilation of the human race was always expressed in terms of America's willingness to go to any lengths to preserve freedom. To the Negro, that readiness for heroic measures in defense of liberty disappeared or became tragically weak when the threat was within our own borders and was concerned with the Negro's liberty. While the Negro is not so selfish as to stand isolated in concern for his own dilemma, ignoring the ebb and flow of events around the world, there is a certain bitter irony in the picture of his country championing freedom in foreign lands and failing to ensure that freedom to twenty million of its own.[30]

---

[30] Dr. Martin Luther King, Jr. speaking at The New School (February 6, 1964), re-broadcast on WAMF on December 8, 1964, available at www.amherst.edu/library/archives/holdings/mlk/transcript.

King encouraged his position on the impacts of African liberation on Black Americans by highlighting their first-hand witness of the transformation of Africans from colonized peasants to liberated landlords with the power to positively effectuate change domestically and on the world stage through institutions like the UN, where human rights and the concept of the sovereign equality of nations predominates (Figure 6.1). Although he recognized Africa as the familial home of Black Americans, he knew that for most Black Americans, escaping to one's ancestral homeland was impracticable, especially given the oppressive impacts of Jim Crowism on the daily lives of Black folk living in the US. Therefore, the liberating force of decolonization inspired King and Black Americans to intensify freedom movements in the US. In this vein, King noted:

> From beyond the borders of his own land, the Negro had been inspired by another powerful force. He had watched the decolonization and liberation of nations in Africa and Asia since World War II. He knew that yellow, black, and brown people had felt for years that the American Negro was too passive, unwilling to take strong measures to gain his freedom. The American Negro saw, in the land from which he had been snatched and thrown into slavery, a great pageant of political progress.[31]

King further opined that no theory of social change can manifest effectively without considering the period for which change is needed: "It is an axiom of social change that no revolution can take place without a methodology suited to the circumstances of the period."[32] King's Beloved Pan-Africanism offers a theory, method, and remedy to a centuries-old problem for Black Americans, other Diasporians, and Africans, but it is largely dependent on Africa's readiness to embrace Pan-Africanism as a solution to neocolonialism, global indebtedness, chronic underdevelopment, acute poverty, perpetual warfare, rapid disease progression, and the new Jim Crow in America.

In his last scholarly work, King asked the pertinent question: Where do we go from here? Is it chaos or community?" He added: "Why is equality so assiduously avoided? Why does white America delude itself, and how does it rationalize the evil it retains?"[33] For King, the answer was simple. White civilization will always resist changes to the status quo that may lead to the numerical, social, cultural, political, and economic decline of white people. He knew progress is defined and measured against their comfort nexus, knowing elite classes hoard power.

King's profound understanding of the linkages and interdependence of white supremacist systems and their coarse impacts on persons of African descent all over the world – including what he referred to as the Asian-Africa bloc – shows the rich

---

[31] Speech from Dr. Martin Luther King, Jr. at The New School (February 6, 1964), re-broadcast on WAMF on December 8, 1964, available at www.amherst.edu/library/archives/holdings/mlk/transcript (on file with author).
[32] Id.
[33] Martin Luther King Jr., WHERE DO WE GO FROM HERE, supra note 29, at 4.

depths of his Pan-African intellect. Connecting in common cause and identifying with the challenges of the colored peoples of the Caribbean, Africa, Asia, and related diasporas comprised an essential dimension of Pan-Africanism that King embraced well before the mid 1950s Montgomery Bus Boycott and the rise of the 1960s Black Power movements. He was a militant, a defender of Black liberation in the BIT of African American pursuits of outside norms, doctrine, and law to achieve freedom, justice, and equality for persons of African descent. He was a much-admired son of Africa devoted to her freedom – an unrecognized Pan-Africanist morally convicted in his commitment to dismantling the structures, systems, and nations oppressing Black people globally. King led the most successful nonviolent movement against poverty, racism, and war in the history of the Western world.

King's Beloved Pan-Africanism is rooted in self-determining identity values deeply embedded in African customary law – the law that governed all Africans captured during the Transatlantic Slave Trade, African American and West Indian resistance norms, and Black Christian ethical values. These norms and values predated and influenced the development of continental Pan-Africanism and, eventually, the public law of Africa.[34] Said norms, customs, and ethics are deeply embedded into African American culture and, according to King, compel appeals to outside law, norms, doctrine, and jurisprudence, that is, the civil rights, human rights, self-determination, and independence standards that, in turn, inform them. King's ideals, calling, advocacy, activities, initiatives, and influence on Africa can no longer be ignored in scholarly literature, nor can Africa's considerable effect on him.

6.3 OUR HERITAGE IS AFRICA

When the eminent Black writer and author Alex Hailey asked if King believed whether Black nationalism's emphasis on building unity between the "American Negro and his African 'brother,' a sense of identity between the emergence of black Africa and the Negro's struggle for freedom in America," was positive, King replied, "Yes, I do, in many ways."[35] He explained that there was a "distinct, significant and inevitable correlation" between Black Americans and African freedom, and the advances made in Africa reminded Negroes of his inferior position.[36] Black diplomats were voting at the UN on pressing world issues, and Black kings lived in palaces, while Negroes could not vote and were forced to live in slums. King referred to this anticipation as the "black Zeitgeist" because Black Americans had a profound sense of identification and connection to their Black African brothers

---

[34] Abdulqawi A. Yusuf, PAN-AFRICANISM AND INTERNATIONAL LAW (Leiden: Brill, 2014), 18.
[35] Alex Haley, *The Playboy Interview: Martin Luther King Jr.*, PLAYBOY MAGAZINE, January 1965, available at www.playboy.com/read/playboy-interview-martin-luther-king/?srsltid=AfmBOor-MMNpjjsmgdIxrr4g-CAwOs2ObJEEbhvEsWlhg9aL5gNMgjz5.
[36] *Id.*

and with "brown and yellow brothers of Asia, South America and the Caribbean."[37] He noted that the success of freedom movements in Africa, Asia, the Caribbean, and South America intensified the call for racial justice in America.[38] When Hailey asked King whether newly independent African nations should involve themselves in Black Americans' freedom struggles and affairs, King firmly said, "I do indeed."[39] In 1965, King argued that the world was so interconnected that "no nation should stand idly by and watch another's plight," which showed his deep understanding of the universality of human rights. He recognized that human rights law obligates governments to refrain from certain acts (e.g., arbitrary arrests and summary executions) and to promote and protect individual and group rights and fundamental freedoms. Human rights law disregards nationality because it directly confers rights to all individuals subject to a state's jurisdiction. The moral values and ethics inherent in human rights law – that there is a moral authority above man and the state – complemented King's belief in a personal God or personalism,[40] and informed his confidence in the reciprocal responsibility of Black people to fight against white supremacy and other forms of repression in the US, Africa, and beyond.

King believed that Africans had a moral and ancestral responsibility to "use the influence of their governments to make it clear that the struggle of their brothers in the US is part of a worldwide struggle,"[41] suggesting an affirmative duty or responsibility of African states and leaders to safeguard the rights of Black Americans. To highlight his position on Africa's responsibility to assist Black American freedom struggles, as noted in earlier chapters, King argued that an "injustice anywhere is a threat to justice everywhere, for we are tied together in a garment of mutuality. What happens in Johannesburg affects Birmingham, however indirectly."[42] King strongly believed that African Americans are African descendants with a collective African heritage and that Black Americans "should never seek to break the ties, nor should the Africans."[43] The question remains, do Africans share the same conviction? King's thinking was rare because it imposed the principle of reciprocity on Africans to help Black Americans in the same way that African Americans have and continue to embrace and support Africans. King leaned on reciprocity over romanticism. In this context, reciprocity is the activating principle that completes Beloved Pan-Africanism. He knew that even though formerly enslaved and free

---

[37] *Id.* at 9. See also, Martin Luther King Jr., LETTER FROM BIRMINGHAM JAIL (London: Penguin Classics, 2018).
[38] Alex Haley, *The Playboy Interview: Martin Luther King Jr.*, supra note 35.
[39] *Id.*
[40] Personalism supports the view of a personal God with a personality concerned with people and with whom people have a personal relationship where God is forever loving, righteous, just, and a sustainer of life.
[41] Alex Haley, *The Playboy Interview: Martin Luther King Jr.*, supra note 35.
[42] *Id.*
[43] *Id.*

Black Americans helped establish a nation in Africa (e.g., in Liberia), supported freedom struggles (e.g., in Angola, Algeria, Kenya, and South Africa), fought with African armies against colonialism (e.g., in Ethiopia), trained African leaders at Historically Black Colleges and Universities beginning in 1896 (e.g., at Lincoln University),[44] financed anticolonial movements, conducted peace missions, organized demonstrations, lobbied for progressive economic and trade policies, boycotted racist regimes, and educated the public about vital issues facing Africa for over 150 years,[45] Black American African relations must be mutually beneficial and reinforcing. While Black Americans have supported African liberation and freedom, King's notion of reciprocity sheds a soulful light on the arguably brazen isolation and growing gaps between Africans and Americans of African origin. Have African nations and leaders supported Black America's racial justice and freedom struggles? This is a pertinent question because Pan-Africanism demands reciprocity and mutuality. And, while King encouraged Black Americans to emigrate to Africa to assist in its development, an appeal that African Americans are unilaterally answering affirmatively today more than ever, not even one of Africa's fifty-four nations has adopted and instituted an unadulterated Law of Return for Foundational Black Americans.

---

[44] James H. Meriwether, PROUDLY WE CAN BE AFRICANS: BLACK AMERICANS AND AFRICA, 1935–1961 (Chapel Hill: The University of North Carolina Press), 152–153.

[45] See generally, Heywood, Linda M. (Linda Marinda), ed., AFRICAN AMERICANS IN U.S. FOREIGN POLICY: FROM THE ERA OF FREDERICK DOUGLASS TO THE AGE OF OBAMA (Urbana: University of Illinois Press, 2015). See also, Mina Yakuba, *The Interconnectedness of Black Liberation: The Cross-Political Relationship of African and African American Leaders in the Struggle for Independence and the Civil Rights Movement (1950–1960)*, GLOBAL AFRICANA REVIEW, Vol. 6 (Spring 2022).

Bibliography

PRIMARY SOURCES

Archives

Act of April 3, 1948, European Recovery Act [Marshall Plan]; Enrolled Acts and Resolutions of Congress, 1789–1996; General Records of the United States Government; Record Group 11; National Archives. www.archives.gov/milestone-documents/marshall-plan.
African Studies Center, University of Pennsylvania, www.africa.upenn.edu/Articles_Gen/Letter_Birmingham.html.
Alleged Assassination Plots Involving Foreign Leaders, An Interim Report of the Select Committee to Study Governmental Operations with Respect to Intelligence Activities United States Senate Together with Additional, Supplemental, and Separate Views. U.S. Senate. Select Comm. to Study Governmental Operations (1975). Office of the Historian, 14. Telegram from the Central Intelligence Agency to the Station in the Congo, Dir 47587 (Out 62966), Foreign Relations of the United States, 1964–1968, Volume XXIII, Congo, 1960–1968, Washington, August 27, 1960. Central Intelligence Agency Files, Job 79–00149A, DDO/IMS Files, Box 23, Folder 1, African Division, Senate Select Committee, Volume II. Secret; Rybat; Priority. For COS from Ascham. Drafted by Director of Central Intelligence Allen W. Dulles. A typed notation on the telegram instructed the Cable Secretariat to "limit distribution to Mr. Helms," https://history.state.gov/historicaldocuments/frus1964-68v23/d14#fn:1.5.4.4.42.16.4.
Archives Research Center, Atlanta University Center, Robert W. Woodruff Library, www.auctr.edu/archives-and-collections/archives/.
Asa G. Hilliard, III Papers, Atlanta University Center, Robert W. Woodruff Library, https://radar.auctr.edu/islandora/object/auc.092:9999.
Brown, Theodore E. "Memorandum to Dorothy Height, Martin Luther King, A. Philip Randolph, Roy Wilkins, and Whitney Young." March 21, 1967. Box A42, File 'NAACP Administration 1966- General Office File American Negro Leadership Conference on Africa 1966–69.' The Records of the National Association for the Advancement of Colored People (TRNAACP). Library of Congress (LOC), Washington, DC.
Christine King Farris Collection, The Martin Luther King, Jr. Research and Education Institute, Stanford University. https://kinginstitute.stanford.edu/king-papers/documents/martin-luther-king-sr-1.
Dr. Martin Luther King, Jr. Archive, Howard Gotlieb Archival Research Center, Boston University, www.bu.edu/library/gotlieb-center/collections/dr-martin-luther-king-jr-archive/.

Foreign Relations of U.S 1964–1968, Volume XXIII, Congo, 1960–1968, Interim Report. 15 (1960) (Allen W. Dulles, Dir. CIA sent a telegram to the CIA station chief in the Congo).

Homer A. Jack Papers from 1984 to 1986, Swarthmore College Peace Collection, TriCollege Libraries, https://archives.tricolib.brynmawr.edu//repositories/8/archival_objects/507835.

King Papers, Volume I: Called to Serve from January 1929 to June 1951, The Martin Luther King, Jr. Research and Education Institute, Stanford University, https://kinginstitute.stanford.edu/publications/papers-martin-luther-king-jr-volume-i.

King Papers, Volume II: Rediscovering Precious Values July 1951–November 1955, The Martin Luther King, Jr. Research and Education Institute, Stanford University, https://kinginstitute.stanford.edu/publications/papers-martin-luther-king-jr-volume-ii.

King Papers, Volume III: Birth of a New Age from December 1955 to December 1956, The Martin Luther King, Jr. Research and Education Institute, Stanford University, https://kinginstitute.stanford.edu/publications/papers-martin-luther-king-jr-volume-iii#:~:text=His%20impromptu%20remarks%20to%20the,was%20unexpectedly%20thrust%20upon%20him.

King Papers, Volume IV: Symbol of the Movement, January 1957–December 1958, The Martin Luther King, Jr. Research and Education Institute, Stanford University, https://kinginstitute.stanford.edu/publications/papers-martin-luther-king-jr-volume-iv.

King Papers, Volume V: Threshold of a New Decade from January 1959 to December 1960, The Martin Luther King, Jr. Research and Education Institute, Stanford University, https://kinginstitute.stanford.edu/publications/papers-martin-luther-king-jr-volume-v#:~:text=Threshold%20of%20a%20New%20Decade,at%20the%20beginning%20of%201960.

King Papers, Volume VI: Advocate of the Social Gospel, September 1948–March 1963, The Martin Luther King, Jr. Research and Education Institute, Stanford University, https://kinginstitute.stanford.edu/publications/papers-martin-luther-king-jr-volume-vi.

King Papers, Volume VII: To Save the Soul of America, January 1961–August 1962, The Martin Luther King, Jr. Research and Education Institute, Stanford University, https://kinginstitute.stanford.edu/publications/papers-martin-luther-king-jr-volume-vii.

Larry Neal Papers, The New York Public Library Archives and Manuscripts, https://archives.nypl.org/scm/20745.

Martin and Jessie Glaberman Collection Papers from 1942 to 1965, Walter P. Reuther Library, Archives of Labor and Urban Affairs, Wayne State University, https://reuther.wayne.edu/files/LP000621.pdf.

Martin Luther King, Jr. Papers from 1950 to 1968, The King Center, The Center for Nonviolent Social Change, The King Center.

Minutes of the Executive Board Meeting of the American Committee on Africa, September 9, 1957 (on file with African Activist Archive, PETER WEISS PAPERS, Michigan State University Libraries Special Collection), https://projects.kora.matrix.msu.edu/files/210-849-24904/PWACOAEB9-9-57opt.pdf

National Archives, General Records of the United States Government.

Peter Weiss, African Activist Archive, Michigan State University. https://africanactivist.msu.edu/.

Statement by H.E. Mr. Andrew Young, Permanent Representative of the United States of America to the United Nations, *Martin Luther King, Jr. and the Tradition of Non-Violence*, Record of the Special Session of the Special Committee against Apartheid held in Atlanta, on the (January 16, 1979).

The American Negro Leadership Conference on Africa: Resolutions, Arden House Campus of Columbia University, Harriman, New York, Michigan University. https://kora.matrix.msu.edu/files/50/304/32-130-66-84-african_activist_archive-a0a0l4-a_12419.pdf.

Transcripts of Dr. Martin Luther King, Archives & Special Collections, Amherst College, Amherst, MA. www.amherst.edu/library/archives/holdings/mlk/transcript.

Declarations

Declaration of Conscience: An Appeal to South Africa, Day of Protest, Human Rights Day, December 10, 1957." Human Rights Day, December 2, 1957.

DuBois, W. E. B. and NAACP, *An Appeal to the World: A Statement of Denial of Human Rights to Minorities in the Case of Citizens of Negro Descent in the United States of American and an Appeal to the United Nations for Redress* (1947). www.blackpast.org/global-african-history/primary-documents-global-african-history/1947-w-e-b-dubois-appeal-world-statement-denial-human-rights-minorities-case-citizens-n/.

UNIA *Declaration of Rights of the Negro People of the World*, New York, August 13, 1920. Reprinted in Robert Hill, ed., *The Marcus Garvey and Universal Negro Improvement Papers*, Volume 2 (Berkeley: University of California Press, 1983). www.ucpress.edu/books/the-marcus-garvey-and-universal-negro-improvement-association-papers-vol-ii/hardcover.

Federal Government

Memorandum From Robert W. Komer and Ulric Haynes of the National Security Council Staff to the President's Special Assistant for National Security Affairs (Bundy), March 30, 1965 (on file with the Office of the Historian, Foreign Relations of the United States, [1964–1968], Volume XXIV, Africa).

U.S. Department of State. *Foreign Relations of the United States, 1958–1960, Africa, Volume XIV, Document 97*. Memorandum of conversation between the U.S. Ambassador in Belgium, William A.M. Burden, and Patrice Lumumba at the U.S. Embassy in Brussels, Office of the Historian, February 24, 1960. https://history.state.gov/historicaldocuments/frus1958-60v14/d97.

U.S. Department of State. *Foreign Relations of the United States, 1964–1968, Volume XXIV, Africa*. Document 181: Telegram from the Embassy in the Congo to the Department of State, Office of the Historian, 1964. https://history.state.gov/historicaldocuments/frus1964-68v24/d181.

U.S. Department of State. *Foreign Relations of the United States, 1964–1968, Volume XXIV, Africa*. Memorandum from the President's Special Assistant for National Security Affairs (Bundy) and Ulric Haynes of the National Security Council Staff to President Johnson, Office of the Historian 1965.https://history.state.gov/historicaldocuments/frus1964-68v24/d606.

United States Senate Select Committee to Study Governmental Operations with Respect to Intelligence Activities. *Alleged Assassination Plots Involving Foreign Leaders: An Interim Report*, November 20, 1975. www.intelligence.senate.gov/sites/default/files/94465.pdf.

U.S. Senate Select Committee to Study Governmental Operations with Respect to Intelligence Activities. *Intelligence Activities – The National Security Agency and Fourth Amendment Rights*. Hearings, 94th Cong., 1st sess., October 29 and November 6, 1975. www.intelligence.senate.gov/sites/default/files/94intelligence_activities_V.pdf.

International Organizations

Annan, Kofi, United Nations Secretary-General, Forty Years after Sharpeville Massacre, Fight against Racism Not Yet Won, Says Secretary-General in Message on International Day, March 21, 2003. United Nations Security Council Resolution 134 (1960), adopted by the Security Council at its 856th meeting, of April 1, 1960.

Asian-African Conference. *Final Communiqué of the Asian-African Conference of Bandung.* Luxembourg Centre for Contemporary and Digital History, 1955. www.cvce.eu/en/obj/final_communique_of_the_asian_african_conference_of_bandung_24_april_1955-en-676237bd-72f7-471f-949a-88b6ae513585.html.

Boutros-Ghali, Boutros, UN Department of Public Information, UN Secretary-General. *The United Nations and apartheid, 1948–1994.* New York: United Nations Digital Library, 1994. https://digitallibrary.un.org/record/198101?ln=en&v=pdf.

South West Africa (Eth. v. S. Afr.; Liber. v. S. Afr.), 1962 I.C.J. 319 (Dec. 21). www.worldcourts.com/icj/eng/decisions/1962.12.21_south_west_africa.htm.

United Nations Against Apartheid. *International tribute to Martin Luther King, Jr.: record of the special session of the Special Committee against Apartheid held in Atlanta, on the 16 January 1979, to pay tribute to the late Reverend Dr. Martin Luther King, Jr. on the occasion of his 50th birthday,* United Nations Digital Library, 1979. https://digitallibrary.un.org/record/75907?ln=en&v=pdf.

United Nations. *Charter of the United Nations.* Article 1. San Francisco, 1945.

United Nations. *Charter of the United Nations.* Articles 2 and 3. XV UNCIO 335, 1945.

United Nations. *Preamble, Charter of the United Nations and Stature of the International Court of Justice.* New York: United Nations, Office of Public Information, 1945.

Legal Cases

Brown v. Board of Education of Topeka, 347 U.S. 483 (1954).

International Court of Justice. *South-West Africa Cases (Ethiopia v. South Africa; Liberia v. South Africa), Second Phase,* 1966. www.refworld.org/jurisprudence/caselaw/icj/1966/en/90239.

Plessy v. Ferguson, 163 U.S. 537 (1896).

U.S. Reports: Dred Scott v. Sandford, 60 U.S. (19 How.) 393 (1856). www.loc.gov/item/usrep060393a/.

News

"Africa 'Marshall Plan' asked by Negro leaders," *The Washington Post* (Tuesday, December 18, 1972).

"Dr. King, Other Prominent U.S. Christian Clergymen Urge Support for Israel," *Jewish Telegraphic Agency, New York Times,* May 29, 1967, archived at http://web.archive.org/web/20160109103941/; www.jta.org/1967/05/29/archive/dr-king-other-prominent-u-s-christian-clergymen-urge-support-for-israel.

"Goldberg Says U.S. Will Sign U.N. Pact for Racial Equality." *New York Times,* July 7, 1966. pg. 22. www.nytimes.com/1966/07/07/archives/goldberg-says-us-will-sign-un-pact-for-racial-equality.html.

Handler, M. S. "U.S. Negroes Link Aid to Sub-Saharan African Nations with Rights Struggle." *The New York Times,* November 25, 1962, and April 4, 1963.

Hughes, Emmet J. "The Negro's New Economic Life." *Fortune*, September 1956.
King, Martin Luther, Jr. "Civil Rights Leaders May Go to Nigeria," *New York Amsterdam News*, January 13, 1968.
King, Martin Luther, Jr. "His Influence Speaks to World Conscience," *Hindustan Times*, January 30, 1958. https://kinginstitute.stanford.edu/king-papers/documents/his-influence-speaks-world-conscience.
King, Martin Luther, Jr. "Pilgrimage to Nonviolence," *Christian Century*, April 13, 1960. pg. 439–441. https://kinginstitute.stanford.edu/king-papers/documents/pilgrimage-nonviolence.
King, Martin Luther, Jr. "The Negro Looks at America, People in Inaction," *New York Amsterdam News*, December 8, 1962.
King, Martin Luther, Jr. "The Nightmare of Violence," *New York Amsterdam News*, March 13, 1965.
"New SCLC Head Vows: 'No Force Can Stop His Work' 'Violence Continues in Ghetto'; Special Memorial to Dr. King," *The Chicago Defender*, December 23, 1968.
"The SOUTH: Attack on the Conscience," *Time*, February 18, 1957. https://time.com/archive/6611429/the-south-attack-on-the-conscience/.
Turner, Renee D. "Remembering the Young King." *Ebony* (43), January 1988.

Photos

Bombing of Fred Shuttlesworth's house beside Bethel Baptist Church on 29th Avenue North in Birmingham, Alabama, Birmingham News, December 25, 1956, in the Alabama Department of Archives and History, Alabama Media Group Collection, https://digital.archives.alabama.gov/digital/collection/amg/id/195666.

Sermons, Speeches, Statements

King, Martin Luther, Jr. "*Beyond Vietnam – A Time to Break Silence.*" Riverside Church, New York, April 4, 1967. www.americanrhetoric.com/speeches/mlkatimetobreaksilence.htm.
King, Martin Luther, Jr. "*Beyond Vietnam and Remaining Awake through a Great Revolution.*" 90th Congress, 2nd session, *Congressional Record* 114, April 9, 1968.
King, Martin Luther, Jr. "*The Birth of a New Nation.*" Sermon delivered at Dexter Avenue Baptist Church, Montgomery, AL, April 7, 1957. https://kinginstitute.stanford.edu/king-papers/documents/birth-new-nation-sermon-delivered-dexter-avenue-baptist-church.
King, Martin Luther, Jr. "*Call for an International Boycott of Apartheid South Africa.*" Address delivered at Hunter College, New York City, Human Rights Day, December 10, 1965. https://africanactivist.msu.edu/recordFiles/210-849-20874/mlkspeechopt.pdf.
King, Martin Luther, Jr. "*Challenge to the Nation's Social Scientist.*" Speech delivered at the American Psychological Association Annual Convention, September 1967. www.apa.org/topics/equity-diversity-inclusion/martin-luther-king-jr-challenge.
King, Martin Luther, Jr. "*Dr. Martin Luther King Jr.'s visit to WMU.*" Transcript of speech delivered at Western Michigan University, Kalamazoo, MI, December 18, 1963. https://libguides.wmich.edu/mlkatwmu/speech.
King, Martin Luther, Jr. "*Honoring Dr. Du Bois.*" FREEDOMWAYS Magazine (February 23, 1968). http://pmeaye.tripod.com/kingondubois.pdf.
King, Martin Luther, Jr. "*Israel ... is one of the great outposts of democracy in the world.*" 1967. 0:12. Accessed August 14, 2022. www.youtube.com/watch?v=kvr2Cxuh2Wk.

King, Martin Luther, Jr. "*Let My People Go.*" Speech at Hunter College, New York, December 10, 1965. https://kora.matrix.msu.edu/files/50/304/32-130-1121-84-GMH%20ACOA%2068MLK.pdf.
King, Martin Luther, Jr. "*Nobel Lecture.*" The Nobel Prize, Oslo, Norway, December 11, 1964. www.nobelprize.org/prizes/peace/1964/king/lecture/.
King, Martin Luther Jr., Press Statement regarding "Stand-ins," February 19, 1962 (on file with The King Center Archives).
King, Martin Luther, Jr. "*The Quest for Peace and Justice.*" Nobel Peace Prize, University of Oslo, December 11, 1964. www.nobelprize.org/prizes/peace/1964/king/acceptance-speech/.
King, Martin Luther, Jr., *Recommendations to the SCLC Executive Committee*, September 30, 1959, https://kinginstitute.stanford.edu/king-papers/documents/recommendations-sclc-executive-committee.
King, Martin Luther, Jr. "The Role of the Behavioral Scientist in the Civil Rights Movement," *Journal of Social Issues* 24, no. 1 (1968). https://doi.org/10.1111/j.1540-4560.1968.tb01465.x.
King, Martin Luther, Jr. Speech delivered at an Anti-Vietnam War Demonstration in front of the UN Secretariat Building, New York, April 15, 1967. https://webtv.un.org/en/asset/k1j/k1j81m5gdl.
King, Martin Luther, Jr. Statement delivered at the American Negro Leadership Conference, 1962. https://kinginstitute.stanford.edu/apartheid.
King, Martin Luther, Jr. "*The Three Evils of Society,*" Address delivered at the National Conference on News Politics, August 31, 1967. Transcribed from Internet Recording www.youtube.com/watch?v=6sT9HjhocHM.
Khrushchev, Nikita Sergeevich. *Speech by Mr. Khrushchev, Chairman of the Council of Ministers of the Union of Soviet Socialist Republics, at the 869th Plenary Meeting of the 15th Session of the United Nations General Assembly on September 23*, 1960, Wilson Center Digital Archive. https://digitalarchive.wilsoncenter.org/document/speech-mr-khrushchev-chairman-council-ministers-union-soviet-socialist-republics-869th.
Nyerere, Julius. "*The Dilemma of the Pan-Africanist,*" Address to the Assembled Audience to the Inauguration of Chancellor of the University of Zambia, 1966. www.blackpast.org/global-african-history/1966-julius-kambarage-nyerere-dilemma-pan-africanist/.

Radio

"America's chief moral dilemma." KPFA. Pacifica Radio Archives, American Archive of Public Broadcasting, Boston (1967). https://americanarchive.org/catalog/cpb-aacip-28-fn10p0x51h.
King, Martin Luther, Jr. and Haley, Alex, "*PLAYBOY Interview: Martin Luther King.*" Interviewed by PLAYBOY, January 1965. www.playboy.com/read/playboy-interview-martin-luther-king/?srsltid=AfmBOor-MMNpjjsmgdIxrr4g-CAwOs2ObJEEbhvEsWlhg9aL5gNMgjz5.
King, Martin Luther, Jr. Commented at an event. WSB Television News Video Archive, University of Georgia, May 28, 1960.
King, Martin Luther, Jr. Interviewed by Tom Jerriel and John Casserly. "*Issues and Answers.*" June 18, 1967, on ABC. Transcript of archived at The King Center Archives, http://web.archive.org/web/20150304113151/www.thekingcenter.org/archive/document/abcs-issues-and-answers-mlk-interview.
King, Martin Luther, Jr. "Israel … is one of the great outposts of democracy in the world." www.youtube.com/watch?v=kvr2Cxuh2Wk.
King, Martin Luther, Jr. "*Radio Interview Regarding Nobel Peace Prize.*" Oslo, Norway, December 9, 1964.

SECONDARY SOURCES

Books and Book Chapters

Abdulmumini, Oba (2011). The Future of Customary Law in Africa, in J. Fenrich, P. Galizzi, and T. Higgins (Eds.), *The Future of Customary Law in Africa* (Cambridge: Cambridge University Press, 2011), pp. 58–80.
Abdulqawi, Yusuf A. *Pan-Africanism and International Law*. Boston: Brill (Martinus Nijhoff), 2015.
Akpan, Ntieyoung U. *The Struggle for Secession 1966–1970*. Oxford: Routledge, 1972.
Albert, Peter J. and Hoffman, Ronald. *We Shall Overcome: Martin Luther King, Jr. and the Black Freedom Struggle*. New York: Pantheon Books, 1990.
Alexander, Michelle and West, Cornell. *The New Jim Crow: Mass Incarceration in the Age of Colorblindness*. New York: The New Press, 2012.
Ansbro, John J. *Martin Luther King, Jr: The Making of a Mind*. Maryknoll, NY: Orbis Books, 1984.
Aptheker, Herbert. *American Negro Slave Revolts*. New York: International Publishers, 1974.
Aristotle, *Aristotle's Politics*. Oxford: Clarendon Press, 1905.
Baldwin, Lewis V. *To Make the Wounded Whole: The Cultural Legacy of Martin Luther King Jr*. Minneapolis: Fortress Press, 1992.
Baldwin, Lewis V. *Toward the Beloved Community: Martin Luther King, Jr., and South Africa*. Cleveland, OH: Pilgrim Press, 1995.
Barbour, Floyd B. *The Black Power Revolt; A Collection of Essays*. Boston: P. Sargent, 1968.
Brightman, Edgar S. Religion as Truth, in Vergilius Ferm (Ed.), *Contemporary American Theology*, 1932.
Brownlie, Ian. *Principles of Public International Law*. Oxford: Oxford University Press, 1999.
Carson Clayborne (ed.), A Realistic Look at the Question of Progress in the Area of Race Relations, Address Delivered at St. Louis Freedom Rally (April 10, 1957), in Clayborne Carson, et al. (eds.), *King Papers, Volume IV: Symbol of the Movement*, 175 (January 1957–December 1958) (Berkeley: University of California Press, 2000).
Clayborne, Carson. *The Autobiography of Martin Luther King, Jr*. New York: Warner Books, 2001.
The Civil Rights Congress. *We Charge Genocide: The Historic Petition to the United Nations for Relief from a Crime of the United States Government against the Negro People*. Edited by William L. Patterson. 2nd ed. 1951.
Cone, James H. Martin Luther King, Jr., and the Third World, in Wade Clark Roof (Ed.), *World Order and Religion* 119, 1991.
Crawford, Vicki L. and Baldwin, Lewis V. *Reclaiming the Great World House: The Global Vision of Martin Luther King, Jr*. Athens: The University of Georgia Press, 2019.
Delany, Martin Robison and Delany, Robert Campbell. *Search for a Place: Black Separatism and Africa*. Ann Arbor: University of Michigan Press, 1969.
Dixie, Quinton and Eisenstadt, Peter. *Visions of a Better World: Howard Thurman's Pilgrimage to India and the Origins of African American Nonviolence*. Boston: Beacon Press, 2011.
Duvalier, Dr. François. *A Tribute to the Martyred Leader of Non-Violence Reverend Martin Luther King Jr*. Port-au-Prince: Presses Nationales, 1968.
Eig, Johnathan. *King: A Life*. New York: Farrar, Straus and Giroux, 2023.
Elias, Taslim O. *The Nature of Customary Law*. Manchester: Manchester University Press, 1956.

Faraji, Salim. *Roots of Nubian Christianity Uncovered: The Triumph of the Last Pharaoh*. Trenton, NJ: Africa World Press, 2012.

Felder, Cain H. *Race, Racism, and the Biblical Narratives: On Use and Abuse of Sacred Scripture*. Minneapolis: Fortress Press, 2023.

Galizzi, Paolo, "The Future of African Customary Law." *Fordham Law Legal Studies Research Paper* No. 2779322, The Future of African Customary Law (Jeanmarie Fenrich, Paolo Galizzi & Tracy Higgins eds., Cambridge University Press: 2011), https://ssrn.com/abstract=2779322.

Garrow, David. *Bearing the Cross: Martin Luther King, Jr. and the Southern Christian Leadership Conference*. New York: William Morrow Paperbacks, 2004.

Garrow, David. *Protest at Selma: Martin Luther King, Jr. and the Voting Rights Act of 1965*. New Haven, CT: Yale University Press, 1978.

Goldman, Peter. *The Death and Life of Malcolm*. Champaign, IL: University of Illinois Press, 2013.

Heywood, Linda M. (Linda Marinda), *African Americans in U.S. Foreign Policy: From the Era of Frederick Douglass to the Age of Obama*. 1st ed., University of Illinois Press, 2015. https://librarysearch.adelaide.edu.au/discovery/fulldisplay/alma9928219855501811/61ADELAIDE_INST:UOFA.

Houser, George M. Freedom's Struggle Crosses Oceans and Mountains: Martin Luther King, Jr., and the Liberation Struggles in Africa and America, in Peter J. Albert and Ronald Hoffman (Eds.), *We Shall Overcome: Martin Luther King, Jr., and the Black Freedom Struggle*, 1993, pp. 170–196.

Houser, George, Martin Luther King, Jr., and International Movements of Liberation, in Peter J. Albert and Ronald Hoffman (Eds.), *We Shall Overcome: Martin Luther King, Jr., and the Black Freedom Struggle* (Panthron Books and United States Capitol Historical Society, 1941).

Kapur, Sudarshan. *Raising Up a Prophet: The African-American Encounter with Gandhi*. Boston: Beacon Press, 1992.

Kramer, Martin. *In the Words of Martin Luther King: The War on Error: Israel, Islam, and the Middle East*. New Brunswick, NJ: Transaction, 2016.

Kilson, Martin and Hill, Adelaide Cromwell. *Apropos of Africa: Sentiments of Negro American Leaders on Africa from the 1800s to the 1950s*. London: Routledge, 1969.

King, Coretta Scott. *My Life with Martin Luther King, Jr.* New York: Henry Holy & Company, 1992.

King, Martin Luther, Jr. *The Autobiography of Martin Luther King JR.* (Clayborne Carson ed., 1998).

King, Martin Luther, Jr. Honoring DuBois, Published speech in *Freedomways* 8 (1968), p. 6.

King, Martin Luther, Jr. Let My People Go, in Cornel West (Ed.), *The Radical King* (Boston: Beacon Press, 2015).

King, Martin Luther, Jr. *Letter from Birmingham Jail*. London, UK: Penguin Classics, 2018.

King, Martin Luther, Jr. *A Speech Regarding the Influence of African Movements on U.S. Students*, The King Center Archives, May 1962, p. 3.

King, Martin Luther, Jr. *Stride towards Freedom*. New York: Harper and Row, 1958.

King, Martin Luther, Jr. *Stride toward Freedom: The Montgomery Story*. Boston: Beacon Press, 1958, p. xv.

King, Martin Luther, Jr. *Where Do We Go from Here: Chaos or Community?* New York: Beacon Press, 1967.

King, Martin Luther, Jr. *Where Do We Go from Here: Chaos or Community?* Boston: Beacon Press, 1968, pp. 169–170.

King, Martin Luther, Jr. *Why We Can't Wait*. New York: Signet Classics, 2000.
King, Martin Luther, Sr. *Daddy King: An Autobiography*. Kansas City, MO: Beacon Press, 2017.
King, Martin Luther, Sr. *Daddy King: An Autobiography*. Boston: Beacon Press, 2017, p. 89.
King James Bible, Bible Gateway. www.biblegateway.com/verse/en/Ephesians%206%3A12.
Laqueur, Walter. *A History of Zionism: From the French Revolution to the Establishment of the State of Israel*. New York: Knopf Doubleday Publishing Group, 2003.
Levitt, Jeremy I. Beloved Pan-Africanism: Martin Luther King's Stride toward Africa, International Human Rights, and the Black International Tradition, in Z. Yihdego, M. G. Desta and M. B. Hailu (Eds.), *Ethiopian Yearbook of International Law 2019. Ethiopian Yearbook of International Law* (Cham: Springer, 2019). https://doi.org/10.1007/978-3-030-55912-0_8.
Levitt, Jeremy I. *The Evolution of Deadly Conflict in Liberia: From "Paternaltarianism" to State Collapse*. Durham, NC: Carolina Academic Press, 2005.
Levitt, Jeremy I. Pan-Africanism, in *Encyclopedia of Globalization, Volume Three, N to T* (London: Routledge, 2007). https://papers.ssrn.com/sol3/papers.cfm?abstract_id=2221627.
Lewis, David Levering. *W.E.B DuBois: Biography of a Race, 1868–1919*. New York: Henry Holy & Co, 1994.
Lincoln, C. Eric. *The Black Muslims in America*. 3rd ed. New York: William B. Eerdmans, 1994.
Long, Micheal G. *Against Us, but for Us: Martin Luther King, Jr. and the State*. Macon, GA: Mercer University Press, 2002.
Madiebo, Alexander A. *The Nigerian Revolution and the Biafran War*. Oxford: Fourth Dimension Publishing Company, 2000.
Malcolm, X. *Malcolm X on Afro-American History*. New York: Pathfinder Press, 1990.
Malcolm, X. *Malcolm X Speaks: Selected Speeches and Statements*. Edited by George Breitman. New York: Grove Press, 1965.
McCray, Walter A. *The Black Presence in the Bible: Discovering the Black and African Identity of Biblical Persons and Nations/Teacher's Edition*. Chicago: Black Light Fellowship, 1995.
McCray, Walter A. *The Black Presence in the Bible and the Table of Nations: Genesis 10: 1–32*. Chicago: Black Light Fellowship, 1995.
Meriweather, James H. *Proudly We Can Be Africans: Black Americans and Africa, 1935–1961*. Chapell Hill: The University of North Carolina Press, 2002.
Meriwether, James H. *Tears, Fire, and Blood: The United States and the Decolonialization of Africa*. Chapel Hill: University of North Carolina Press, 2021.
Nyerere, J. K. The Dilemma of the Pan-Africanist, in J. K. Nyerere (Ed.), *Freedom and Socialism*. Oxford: Oxford University Press, 1968, p. 208.
O'Reily, Kenneth. *Racial Matters: The FBI's Secret File on Black America, 1960–1972*. London; Free Press, 1991.
Richardson, Henry III. *The Origins of African-American Interests in International Law*. Durham, NC: Carolina Academic Press, 2008.
Roark, James L. "American Black Leaders: The Response to Colonialism and the Cold War, 1943–1953." *The African American Voice in U.S. Foreign Policy since World War II*. New York: Routledge, 1999.
Robinson, Cedric J., *Black Marxism: The Making of the Black Radical Tradition*. Chapel Hill: University of North Carolina Press, 1983.
Robinson, Cedric J. and Kelley, Robin D. G. *Black Marxism: The Making of the Black Radical Tradition*. Chapel Hill: The University of North Carolina Press, 2000.

Sadler, Rodney S. *Can a Cushite Change His Skin? An Examination of Race, Ethnicity, and Othering in the Hebrew Bible*. New York: T&T Clark International, 2009.

Shelby, Tommie and Terry, Brandon M. *To Shape a New World: Essays on the Political Philosophy of Martin Luther King, Jr.* Cambridge, MA: Belknap Press, An Imprint of Harvard University Press, 2018.

Skinner, Elliott P. *African Americans and U.S. Policy Toward Africa 1850=1924: In Defense of Black Nationality*. Washington, DC, Howard University Press, 1992.

Terry, Brandon M. "Requiem for a Dream: The Problem-Space of Black Power." from the book *To Shape a New World*. Cambridge, MA: Harvard University Press, 2018.

Thoreau, Henry D. *Civil Disobedience*. Lexington, KY: Empire Books, 2011.

Viorst, Milton. *Zionism: The Birth and Transformation of an Ideal*. New York: Thomas Dunne Books, 2016.

Walters, Ronald W. *Pan Africanism in the African Diaspora: An Analysis of Modern Afrocentric Political Movements*, Detroit, MI: Wayne State University Press, 1993.

Wilson, John A. *Authority and Law in the Ancient Egypt*. American Oriental Society, 1954.

Periodicals

Abrahamsen, Rita. "Internationalist, Sovereigntists, Nativists: Contending Visions of World Worder in Pan-Africanism." *Cambridge University Press* 45, no. 1 (2020). www.cambridge.org/core/journals/review-of-international-studies/article/abs/internationalists-sovereigntists-nativists-contending-visions-of-world-order-in-panafricanism/85ED07FAA4CCB08F6CDB2A532437B3E2.

Adams, Alvin, Malcolm X "Seemed Sincere" about Helping Cause: Mrs. King, *Jet Magazine*, March 11, 1965.

Alford, Roger. "The Impact of Martin Luther King on International Law." OpinioJuris, January 21, 2008. https://opiniojuris.org/2008/01/21/the-impact-of-martin-luther-king-on-international-law/.

Baldwin, Lewis V. "Malcolm X and Martin Luther King, Jr." What They Thought about Each Other." *Islamic Studies* 25, no. 4 (1986): 395–416. www.jstor.org/stable/20839793.

Baldwin, Lewis V. "A Reassessment of the Relationship between Malcom X and Martin Luther King, Jr." *The Western Journal of Black Studies* 103 (1989).

Brown, DeNeen L. "The Sermon Where MLK Spoke Candidly on the Arab-Israeli Conflict." *The Washington Post*, January 15, 2024.

Bryson, Dobson. "Tallahassee Civil Rights Icon Rev. C.K. Steele Gets Section of Orange Avenue Remained in His Honor." *Tallahassee Democrat*, January 18, 2019. www.tallahassee.com/story/news/2019/01/18/late-civil-rights-hero-rev-c-k-steele-gets-roadway-named-his-honor/2600413002/.

Campus, Leonardo "Martin Luther King's Reaction to the Cuban Missile Crisis." *European Journal of American Studies* 12–2, no. 2017 (October 20, 2017). http://journals.openedition.org/ejas/12186; https://doi.org/10.4000/ejas.12186.

Clarke, John H. "Pan-Africanism: A Brief History of An Idea in the African World." *Présence Africaine*, Nouvelle Série, No, 145 (1988).

Cone, James H. "Martin Luther King, Jr., Black Theology–Black Church." *Theology Today* 40, no. 4 (January 1, 1984).

Cone, James H. "Martin Luther King, Jr., and the Third World." *The Journal of American History* 74, no. 2 (1987): 455–467. https://doi.org/10.2307/1900033.

Desrosiers, Kyle. "Beacons of Hope: Our Interreligious S/Heroes-Rev. Howard Thurman." June 7, 2023. https://hebrewcollege.edu/blog/beacons-of-hope-our-interreligious-s-heroes-rev-howard-thurman/.
Dyer, Edgar. "A 'triumph of justice' in Alabama: The 1960 Perjury Trial of Martin Luther King, Jr." *The Journal of African American History* 88, no. 3 (2003). https://go.gale.com/ps/i.do?id=GALE%7CA108788089&sid=googleScholar&v=2.1&it=r&linkaccess=abs&issn=15481867&p=LitRC&sw=w&userGroupName=anon%7Eba33e297&aty=open-web-entry. Accessed August 11, 2022.
Edwards, Phil. "This Is the Telegram MLK Sent Malcolm X's Wife after Her Husband's Assassination." *Vox*, January 18, 2019. www.vox.com/2015/2/21/8078739/mlk-malcolm-x-telegrams.
Elias, T. Olawale. "Insult as an Offence in African Customary Law." *African Affairs* 53, no. 210 (1954): 66.
Evan, Tony. "Black Heritage throughout Bibilical History." *BibleToLife*, March 8, 2022. https://bibletolife.com/resources/articles/black-heritage-throughout-biblical-history/.
Farmer, Ashley. "Reframing African American Women's Grassroots Organizing: Audley Moore and the Universal Association of Ethiopian Farmer Women 1957–1963." *The Journal of African American History* 101, no. 1–2 (2016). www.journals.uchicago.edu/doi/abs/10.5323/jafriamerhist.101.1-2.0069?mobileUi=0/.
Farquharson, J. A. "To the Benefit of Africa, the World and Ourselves: The American Negro Leadership Conference on Africa (ANLCA) Mission to Nigeria, 1966–1968." *The Journal of Global History* (2022). https://ideas.repec.org/a/cup/jglhis/v17y2022i3p457-476_6.html#:~:text='To%20the%20benefit%20of%20Africa%2C%20the%20world%2C,on%20Africa%20(ANLCA)%20Mission%20to%20Nigeria%2C%201966%E2%80%931968.
Felder, Cain Hope. "Blacks in Biblical Antiquity." *American Bible Society*. https://biblere sources.americanbible.org/resource/blacks-in-biblical-antiquity.
Gandhi, Mahatma. "Gandhi's Philosophy of Nonviolence." www.mkgandhi.org/africaneeds gandhi/gandhis_philosophy_of_nonviolence.php.
"Germany official recognizes colonial-era Namibia genocide." *BBC News*. May 28, 2021. www.bbc.com/news/world-europe-57279008.
Heerten, Lasse and Moses, A. Dirk. "The Nigeria–Biafra War: Postcolonial Conflict and the Question of Genocide." *Journal of Genocide Research* 16, no. 2–3 (2014): 169–203. https://doi.org/10.1080/14623528.2014.936700.
King, Martin Luther, Jr. "King's Challenge to the Nations's Social Scientists." *American Psychological Association, Journal of Social Issues* 24, no. 1 (1968).
King, Martin Luther, Jr. "Nonviolence and Racial Justice." *Christian Century* 74 (February 6, 1957): 165–167.
Kramer, Martin. "Where MLK Really Stood on Israel and Palestinians." *Mosiaac*. March 13, 2019. https://mosaicmagazine.com/observation/israel-zionism/2019/03/where-mlk-really-stood-on-israel-and-the-palestinians/.
Levitt, Jeremy I. "The African Origins of International Law: Myth or Reality?" *UCLA Journal of International Law and Foreign Affairs* 19, no. 113 (2015). https://papers.ssrn.com/sol3/papers.cfm?abstract_id=2645865.
Levitt, Jeremy I. "Beyond Borders: Martin Luther King, Jr., Africa and Pan-Africanism." *Temple Journal of International and Comparative Law* 31, no. 1 (Spring 2017): 315.
Levitt, Jeremy I. "Was Martin Luther King Jr. a Pan-Africanist?" (unpublished) (April 2006).
Livingston, Samuel T. "An Unbroken Bond: The Role of Africa in Martin Luther King Jr.'s Liberation Thought and Praxis." *The Compass: Journal of the Association for the Study of Classical African Civilizations* (unpublished) (2016).

Lovelace, H. Timothy Jr. "Martin, Ghana, and Global Legal Studies," *Indiana Journal of Global Legal Studies* 25, no. 2 (2018): Article 5. www.repository.law.indiana.edu/ijgls/vol25/iss2/5.

Mays, Benjamin E. "The Color Line around the World." *Journal of Negro Education* 6, no. 2 (April 6, 1937): 141.

Mays, Benjamin E. "The Color Line around the World in The Complete Bibliography of 'The Journal of Negro Education,' 1932–2006," *The Journal of Negro Education* 75, no. 2 (2006): 73–318. www.jstor.org/stable/40037237.

Miller, Jason. "Langston Hughes and Martin Luther King, Jr.: Together in Nigeria." *South Atlantic Review* 83, no. 1 (2018): 22–41. www.jstor.org/stable/90019867.

Ndulo, Muna. "African Customary Law, Customs, and Women's Rights." *Indiana Journal of Global Legal Studies* 87 (2011). www.repository.law.indiana.edu/ijgls/vol18/iss1/5/.

Ogwurike, C. "The Source and Authority of African Customary Law." *University of Ghana Law Journal* 3, no. 1 (1966).

Rediker, Marcus. "Atonement." *The Los Angeles Times*. January 21, 2008. www.latimes.com/archives/la-xpm-2008-jan-21-oe-rediker21-story.html.

Richardson, Henry J. III. "Dr. Martin Luther King, Jr. as an International Human Rights Leader." *Villanova Law Review* 52, no. 3 (2007): 471–486. https://digitalcommons.law.villanova.edu/vlr/vol52/iss3/2/.

Richardson, Henry J. III. "From Birmingham's Jail to beyond the Riverside Church: Martin Luther King's Global Authority." *Temple University Legal Studies Research Paper* No. 2015–08 (2015). https://ssrn.com/abstract=2554549.

Richardson, Henry J. III. "The Origins of African American Interests in International Law." *Buffalo Human Rights Law Review* 17 (2011): 1–22.

Scott, William R. "Black Nationalism and the Italo-Ethiopia Conflict 1934–1936." *The Journal of Negro History* 63, no. 2 (1978).

Shepperson, George. "Notes on Negro American Influences on the Emergence of African Nationalism." *The Journal of African History* 1, no. 2 (1960): 299–312. https://doi.org/10.1017/S0021853700001869.

Shivji, Issa G. "Interventions Issue 1: What Is Pan-Africanism." *TriContinental Pan Africa* (2023). https://thetricontinental.org/pan-africa/shivji-interventions-1/.

Tadias Magazine. "MLK's Invitation from Haile Selassie in 1964." January 18, 2016. www.tadias.com/01/18/2016/mlks-invitation-from-haile-selassie-in-1964/.

Thomas, Dr. Dominique and National Center for Institutional Diversity. "The Black Radical Tradition of Resistance: A Series on Black Social Movements." *Medium*. (2019). https://medium.com/national-center-for-institutional-diversity/the-black-radical-tradition-of-resistance-7277f09ef396.

Udom-Essein, E. U. "The Relationship of Afro-Americans to African Nationalism." *Freedomways* II, no. 4 (Fall 1962).

Whitaker, Matthew C. "African on My Mind: The Making of Martin Luther King, Jr.'s Transnational Consciousness." *The Annual Meeting of the Organization of American Historians, Washington, D.C.* (unpublished), 2006.

Yabuka, Mina. "The Interconnectedness of Black Liberation: The Cross-Political Relationship of African American Leaders in the Struggle for Independence and the Civil Rights (1950–60)." *Carolina Digital Repository* (2022). https://cdr.lib.unc.edu/downloads/xd07h309d?locale=en.

Index

Abernathy, Ralph, 35
Abrahamsen, Rita, 116
Abubakar, Dara, 114
accommodationism, 46, 158
ACOA. See American Committee on Africa
Africa, African people and. See also African natural law; anti-Black violence; Black agency; foreign policy; Pan-Africanism; specific countries
   African American emigration to
      to Liberia, 117–118
      to Sierra Leone, 117–118
      Universal Negro Improvement Association programs, 118
   American Committee on Africa and
      Americans for South African Resistance Movement and, 67
      in anti-Apartheid movement, 67, 68–69, 100
      anticolonialism and, 67, 68
      establishment of, 67
      King, M. L., Jr., and, 4–5, 47, 67–70
      support for political parties in Africa, 67–68
   American Negro Leadership Conference on Africa, 5, 76–77
   ancestral legacy of, 161–162
   Black liberation movement in, 60–67
      commonality with African Americans in, 61–62
   customary law tradition in, 111
      African natural law and, 111–114
   decolonization movement in, Nigeria role in, 72
   global kinship with, 37–38
   King, M. L., Jr., and
      American Committee on Africa and, 4–5, 47, 67–70
      international influence of, 75–87, 151–160
      return to, 70–74
   Malcolm X in, 40–41
   Marshall Plan for Africa, 90–91
   nationalist movements in, 98–99
   Organization of African Unity and, 109–110, 130
   Thurman in, 27
The Africa League, 95
African Americans. See also anti-Black violence; Black agency; specific topics
   American Negro Leadership Conference on Africa, 5, 76–77, 80
   Black liberation movement for, 60–67
      commonality with Africans in, 61–62
   Black nativism and, 38
   Black Power Movement and, 115
   citizenship rights for, 46
   Dred Scott v. Sandford and, 45–46, 74, 112
   emigration to Africa
      to Liberia, 117–118
      to Sierra Leone, 117–118
      Universal Negro Improvement Association programs, 118
   human rights organizations and, 30–31
   Jewish experience and, 139
   on new African leadership class, 82
   student movements support of African freedom, 82
   UN Charter for Black Americans, 30
   US Agency for International Development and, 62
African National Congress (ANC), 52–53, 59–60, 68, 152–154
   King, M. L., Jr., support of, 76, 100
African natural law, 111–114
   MA'AT as justice tradition, 113, 143
   self-determining identity principle in, 114
African Woman's League, 52–53
Africanness, 150
Airlift Africa scholarship program, 86
Akoa, F., 70–71

175

Algeria, 67–68, 80–82, 98. *See also* Ben Bella, Ahmad
Almeida, Deolinda Rodriques Francisco de, 79
American Committee on Africa (ACOA), 152, 156
  Americans for South African Resistance Movement and, 67
  Angola and, 79–80
  in anti-Apartheid movement, 67, 68–69, 100, 101–102
  anticolonialism and, 67, 68
  establishment of, 67
  King, M. L., Jr., and, 4–5, 47, 67–70, 87–99
  Southern Christian Leadership Conference and, 94
  support for political parties in Africa, 67–68
  US foreign policy on African influenced by, 87–99
American Nazi Party, 43
American Negro Leadership Conference on Africa (ANLCA), 5, 76–77, 152, 156
  in anti-Apartheid movement, 101–102
  Black International Tradition and, 93
  establishment and origins of, 88
  financial support for, 90
  by US foundations, 92
  Johnson, L. B., and, 89–90
  Kennedy, J. F., and, 89
  Marshall Plan for Africa and, 90–91
  Nigerian Civil War and, 96–98
  Pan-Africanism and, 91–92, 93
  political support for, 90
  religious missions and, 94
American Psychological Association (APA), 15, 137
Americans for South African Resistance Movement, 67
ANC. *See* African National Congress
Anekwe, Simon Obi, 96–97
Angola
  American Committee on Africa and, 79–80
  American Negro Leadership Conference on Africa and, 76–77
  nationalist movement in, 98
  Portuguese genocidal activities in, 79–80, 89
Ankrah, Joseph A., 96–97
ANLCA. *See* American Negro Leadership Conference
anti-Apartheid movement
  American Committee on Africa and, 67, 68–69, 100, 101–102
  American Negro Leadership Conference on Africa and, 101–102
  Black International Tradition and, 101–102

Declaration of Conscience Against Apartheid, 68–69, 101–102
King, M. L., Jr., and, 23, 47, 52–54, 99–103
  Baldwin, L., on, 99
  "Beloved Pan-Africanism" and, 103
  "Let My People Go" speech and, 63, 99–100, 102
anti-Black violence, 13–14, 56–60
  Black civil rights movement as cause of, 57–58
  Black International Tradition as response to, 112–113
  federal interventions against, 57
  against King, M. L., Jr., 56
anticapitalism, for King, M. L., Jr., 11
anti-colonialism
  American Committee on Africa and, 67, 68
  Pan-Africanism and, 98–99
  under Universal Declaration of Human Rights, 31–32
APA. *See* American Psychological Association
Apartheid policy, in South Africa
  League of Nations mandates and, 69
  US foreign policy and, 59, 103
Appeal to the Colored Citizens of the World (Walker), 21, 114–115
Arab-Israeli War, 124, 136–137
Aristotle, 18–19
armed revolt. *See also* nonviolence
  to counter racial segregation, 23
Armitage, Sir Robert, 98–99
Atlanta, Georgia, 11–12, 95. *See also* Sweet Auburn community
Atlanta Constitution, 16–17
Azikiwe, Nnamdi, 4–5, 52, 66, 71, 72, 80, 140–141

Baker, Ella, 57
Baldwin, Lewis, 1, 5, 41, 51–52, 75, 76, 87
Ballou, Maude, 42
Baltimore Afro-American, 89
Banda, Hastings, 82
Bandung Conference, in Indonesia, 118–119, 120
Barbour, J. Pius, 27
Belafonte, Harry, 77, 83
"Beloved Pan-Africanism," 2, 149
  anti-Apartheid movement and, 103
  Black International Tradition and, 141–143
  Black liberation movement and, 60
  five pillars of, 2, 143
  scope of, 65
Ben Bella, Ahmed, 80–82
Ben Soloman, Job, 117–118
Bentham, Jeremy, 18–19
Biafran War of 1967. *See* Nigerian Civil War

"The Birth of a New Nation" (King, M. L., Jr.), 60–62, 63, 64, 65, 104, 141–142
  Pan-Africanism in, 157
BIT. *See* Black International Tradition
Black agency, 111
Black churches, Black church tradition
  bombing of Sixteenth Street Baptist Church, 79
  Dexter Avenue Baptist Church, 33, 59–60
  Ebenezer Baptist Church, 11–12
  racial justice through, 11
  radical consciousness for King, M. L., Jr., 11–12
Black codes, 30–31
Black International Tradition (BIT), 1, 74
  African natural law and, 111–114
  American Negro Leadership Conference on Africa and, 93
  anti-Apartheid movement and, 101–102
  Bella and, 81
  "Beloved Pan-Africanism" and, 141–143
  Black radical tradition and, 121
  Critical Race Feminism and, 114
  Critical Race Theory and, 114
  Dred Scott v. Sandford and, 112
  historiography of, 111
  international law and, 111–114
  Pan-Africanism and, 74, 105, 108–114
  as response to anti-Black violence, 112–113
  Third World Approaches to International Law and, 114
  white supremacy and, 148
Black liberation movement, 60–67
  African American students' role in, 82
  "Beloved Pan-Africanism" and, 60
  "The Birth of a New Nation" and, 60–62
  in Caribbean region, 82–83
Black Marxism, 115–116
Black nationalism, 52, 115, 116, 122–141, 158
Black nativism, 38
Black Power Movement, 115
Black radical tradition, 10, 115, 121
Black Zionism, 122–127, 133–141
  ancient religious traditions as influence on, 138, 139
  "Back to Africa" movement and, 134–135
  Christianity and, 139
  rejection of, 139–140
Borders, William Holmes, 27
Brightman, Edgar S., 25–26
Brotherhood of Sleeping Car Porters, 51
Browder, Aurelia S., 29
Browder v. Gayle, 29–30, 33–34
Brown, Theodore E., 88, 96–98, 122–123
Brown v. Board of Education, 33, 45, 57–58, 83–84
Bunche, Ralph, 51

Cameroon, 70–71
Campbell, Robert, 150–151
capitalism, as economic theory, King, M. L., Jr., on, 21–22
Caribbean region. *See also specific countries*
  Black liberation movement in, 82–83
  King, M. L., Jr., legacy in, 82–83, 87
Carmichael, Stokely, 83
Carson, Clayborn, 27
Carter, Robert L., 29
Cartwright, Marguerite, 71
CERD. *See* United Nations
Chalmers, Allen Knight, 25
Chiume, Kanyama, 95
Christian Century, 45
Christianity, Black Zionism and, 139
Civil Rights Act of 1964, US, 42
Civil Rights Congress (CRC), 30–31
civil rights movement, in US. *See also* Black Power Movement
  anti-Black violence as response to, 57–58
  Black students' role in, 85–86
  non-separatist approach, 115
Clarke, John Henry, 62
CMMLK. *See* Dr. Martin Luther King Jr. Memorial Center
COINTELPRO. *See* Counterintelligence Program
colonialism, in Ghana, 51–52
Colvin, Claudette, 29, 33–34. *See also Browder v. Gayle*; Montgomery Bus Boycott
communism, King, M. L., Jr., on, 21–22
Cone, James H., 1, 39, 106, 143
Congress of Racial Equality (CORE), 4–5
Counterintelligence Program (COINTELPRO), FBI, 44–45
CRC. *See* Civil Rights Congress
Critical Race Feminism, 114
Critical Race Theory, 114
Crozer Theological Seminary, 18–24
  access to African American literary works, 21
  ancient Egyptian sources for, 18–19, 20–21
  approach to American racism, 22–23
  early Afro-centric thinking, 20–21
  global economic theories and systems, 21–22
  human rights sensibility developed at, 19
  philosophical influences at, 18–19
Cuba, 87
Cuffe, Paul, 117–118
customary law tradition, in Africa, 111
  African natural law and, 111–114
  MA'AT as justice tradition, 113, 143

Daddy King (Young), 12
Danquah, Mabel Dove, 55
Davis, George W., 25
Declaration of Conscience Against Apartheid, 68–69
decolonization movement, in Africa, 72, 144
Delaney, Martin, 114–115, 150–151
Democratic Republic of the Congo, 128–131. *See also* Lumumba, Patrice
desegregation, racial
  after *Brown v. Board of Education*, 33, 45, 57–58, 83–84
  as national movement, 34
  Plessy v. Ferguson and, 33, 46
DeWolf, Lotan Harold, 25
Dexter Avenue Baptist Church, 33, 59–60
Diop, Cheikh Anta, 114
Dominican Republic, US involvement in, 100
Dr. Martin Luther King Jr. Memorial Center (CMMLK), in Havana, Cuba, 87
Dred Scott v. Sandford, 45–46, 74, 112
Du Bois, W. E. B., 5, 31, 114, 144
  in Ghana, 62–63
    immigration to, 66
  as human rights leader, 106
  King, M. L., Jr. relationship with, 103–107, 116–117, 148–149
    "Honoring Du Bois," 63, 104–105
  Pan-Africanism and, 37, 63, 103–107, 149–150, 151
  "Talented Tenth," 158
Duckett, Alfred, 54
Dulles, Allen, 128–129
Durr, Clifford, 29
Duvalier, Francois (Papa Doc), 83

Ebenezer Baptist Church, 11–12, 95
Economic Recovery Act of 1948, US, 90–91
Eig, Jonathan, 22
Eisenhower, Dwight, 38–39, 47, 57, 103
Eisenman, Abram, 42
Ellison, Ralph, 21
Ethiopia, 95–96, 105. *See also* Selassie, Haile

Farmer, James, 88
Federal Bureau of Investigation (FBI), US
  COINTELPRO program, 44–45, 48
  investigation of Black nationalism, 52
feminism. *See* Critical Race Feminism
Folsom, James E., 35
foreign policy, US, for Africa
  American Committee on Africa as influence on, 87–99
  for Apartheid policy, 59, 103
  Black International Tradition and, 1
  under Johnson, L. B., 58–59
  King, M. L., Jr., challenges to, 77
  Lumumba assassination and, 128–131
Fortune magazine, 8
Friedman, Nathan, 133–136

Gandhi, Mahatma (Mohandas K. Gandhi), 3–4, 18, 21, 23–24, 26–27, 40
Garvey, Marcus, 17, 63, 82–83, 118, 125–126, 158
  "Back to Africa" movement, 127–133, 134–135
  Universal Negro Improvement Association programs, 118, 134–135
Gayle, William A., 29–30. *See also Browder v. Gayle*
Gbedemah, K. A., 40, 120–121
Geneva Conventional Law, 32–33
genocide, in Angola, 79–80
Georgia, 8–9. *See also* Atlanta, Georgia
Ghana
  African American visitors to, 62–63
  colonialism in, 51–52
  King, C. S., in, 51
  King, M. L., Jr., in, 2, 50–54, 66–67
    criticisms of, 51–52
  national independence for, 52, 60, 83–84
Ghana (Nkrumah), 21
global Blackness, 141–145
Global South, 12
Golden As Our Land (Danquah), 55
Gowon, Yakubu, 96–97
Grange, Lester B., 51
Gray, Fred D., 29–30
"Great World House" concept, 120–121
Gunther, John, 67

Hailey, Alex, 160, 161
Haiti, 83
Haitian Revolution, 143
Harlem Race Riot of 1935, 31
Harlem Renaissance, 31
Hawkins, Edler (Reverend), 70
Haynes, Ulric, 59
HBCUs. *See* Historically Black Colleges and Universities
Heffner, Richard, 57–58
Height, Dorothy, 88
Herzel, Theodor, 123
Historically Black Colleges and Universities (HBCUs), 16, 18. *See also* Morehouse College
  African Studies programs at, 92
  student movements at, 86
Hobbes, Thomas, 18–19

"Honoring Du Bois" (King, M. L., Jr.), 63, 104–105
Hoover, J. Edgar, 48. *See also* Federal Bureau of Investigation
Houser, George, 4–5, 67, 94, 117–118, 149–150
  in Americans for South African Resistance Movement, 67
  letters to King, M. L., Jr., 79
  on Pan-Africanism and, 150–151
Hughes, Langston, 52, 72
human rights. *See also* civil rights movement
  under Civil Rights Act of 1964 (US), 42
  Du Bois as human rights leader, 106
  under Geneva Conventional Law, 32–33
  as philosophy for King, M. L., Jr.
    Crozer Theological Seminary as influence on, 19
    under United Nations Charter, 25–26
    under Universal Declaration on Human Rights, 25–26
  in UN Charter, 25–26, 93
  Universal Declaration on Human Rights, 25–26, 31–32
  South Africa's violation of, 52–53
humanitarian law, Geneva Conventional Law and, 32–33
Hungary, 39

"I Have a Dream" (King, M. L., Jr.), 106, 107
ICJ. *See* International Court of Justice
India, 66. *See also* Gandhi, Mahatma (Mohandas K. Gandhi); Nehru, Jawaharlal
International Convention on the Elimination of All Forms of Racial Discrimination (CERD). *See* United Nations
International Court of Justice (ICJ), 95–96
international law, 111–112
  Black International Tradition and, 111–114
  Third World Approaches to International Law, 114
Israel, 124. *See also* Zionism
  Arab-Israeli War, 124, 136–137
  Israel–Palestine conflict, 123–125

Jack, Homer, 118
Jamaica, 83
James, C. L. R., 37, 39–40, 83, 114. *See also* Pan-Africanism
Jemison, T. J., 57
Jesus and the Disinherited (Thurman), 21, 27
Jewish identity, 138–139
Jewish Zionism, 123–125
  Arab-Israeli War and, 124, 136–137
  Israel–Palestine conflict, 123–125

Jewish identity and, 138–139
World Zionist Organization, 123, 125
Jim Crow law, 33
  in Georgia, 8–9
  King, M. L., Jr., on, 46–47, 48
  in Montgomery, Alabama, 33–34
  Montgomery Bus Boycott as influence on, 34
Johnson, Leslie G., 127, 128, 131–133
Johnson, Lyndon B., 47, 58–59, 100
Johnson, Mordecai, 3–4, 23
Jones, David Dallas, 62–63, 142
Julian, Hubert Fauntleroy, 106

Kaunda, Kenneth, 95
Kelsey, George, 17, 27
Kennedy, John F., 47, 62, 89, 140–141
Kennedy, Robert F., 48
Kenya, 52, 83. *See also* Mboya, Tom
  Airlift Africa scholarship program, 86
  national independence for, 79
Khrushchev, Nikita, 31–32, 73–74
King, Alberta Williams (Mother King), 10, 12
King, Coretta Scott, 35, 43–44
  in Ghana, 51
  in Israel, 124
  in Nigeria, 72–73
King, James Albert, 12
King, Martin Luther, Jr., 51. *See also* American Committee on Africa; American Negro Leadership Conference on Africa; Crozer Theological Seminary; *specific topics*
  as accommodationist, 46, 158
  African National Congress and, 76, 100
  American Committee on Africa and, 4–5, 47, 67–70, 87–99
  anti-Apartheid advocacy by, 23, 47, 52–54, 99–103
  anticapitalism for, 11
  on armed revolt, 23
  assassination of, 79
  awards and honorifics for, 151–160
    honorary degrees, 155
  Bella and, 80–82
  "The Birth of a New Nation," 60–62, 63, 64, 65, 104, 141–142
    Pan-Africanism in, 157
  as Black Africanist, 77
  Black liberation movement and, 60–67
  at Boston University School of Theology, 25–27
  Cameroon and, 70–71
  on capitalism, 21–22
  Caribbean legacy of, 82–83, 87
  childhood for, 7
  on communism, 21–22

King, Martin Luther, Jr., (cont.)
  criminal and legal persecution of, 29–30, 140–141
  Cuba and, 87
  Dexter Avenue Baptist Church and, 33, 59–60
  Du Bois and, 63, 103–107, 116–117, 148–149
  early influences on, 8–16
    Mays as, 18
    parents as, 8, 10–11
    in Sweet Auburn community, 8–9
  Gandhi, Mahatma, as influence on, 18
  in Ghana, 2, 50–54, 66–67
    criticisms of, 51–52
  global popularity and legacy of, 50–56, 75–76, 111, 143, 146–160
  global progressivism influenced by, 39–40
    newspapers and journals as influence on, 66–67
  global travels for, 66
  "Great World House" concept, 120–121
  "Honoring Du Bois," 63, 104–105
  "I Have a Dream," 106, 107
  Johnson and, 23
  "Let My People Go," 63, 99–100, 102
  "Letter from a Birmingham Jail," 56
  Mboya and, 77–79, 80
  at Morehouse College, 16–18
    intellectual and physical safety of, 16
    social consciousness developed at, 16–17
    Thoreau as influence, 16
  at multiracial church, 15
  in Nigeria, 72
    response to Nigerian Civil War, 96–98, 103
  Nkrumah and, 40, 50–54, 63, 77, 120–121
  Nobel Peace Prize for, 110–111
  nonviolent resistance philosophy for, Gandhi, Mahatma, as influence on, 23–24
  as Pan-Africanist, 1–6
    "Beloved Pan-Africanism," 2
  Personalistic philosophy for, 25–26
  racial segregation experienced by, 14
  radical consciousness for, 10
    Black church tradition and, 11–12
  relationship with Malcolm X, 41–44
    conflicts within, 41, 44
    correspondence and meetings, 41–44
  return to Africa, 70–74
  Southern Christian Leadership Conference and, 58
  Stride Toward Freedom, 26, 36, 59–60, 78, 117
  Thurman as influence on, 27
  Vietnam War opposed by, 144
King, Martin Luther, Sr. (Daddy King), 8, 9–11
  autobiography of, 12
  Ebenezer Baptist Church and, 11–12
  global influences on, 11–12
  in Global South, 12
  racism against, 13–14
    anti-white sentiments as result of, 13–14
    contestation of, 14
King, Yolanda, 35
Komer, Robert, 59
Korngold, Ralph, 21
Ku Klux Klan, 10, 42

Langford, Charles D., 29
League of Nations, 69, 105
Lee, Robert, 62–63
Lee, Sara, 62–63
legal traditions. *See* African natural law; customary law tradition; international law; Jim Crow law
"Let My People Go" (King, M. L., Jr.), 63, 99–100, 102
"Letter from a Birmingham Jail" (King, M. L., Jr.), 56
Levison, Stanley, 57
Liberia
  African American emigration to, 117–118
  International Court of Justice and, 95–96
  South Africa and, 96
Livingston, Samuel, 9
Locke, John, 18–19
Lomax, Louis E., 21
Lumumba, Patrice, 82, 128–131
  assassination of
    US public response to, 129
    US role in, 128–131
Luthuli, Albert, 59–60, 100–101

MA'AT (Egyptian goddess), 19
MA'AT, as justice tradition, 113, 143
Malawi (formerly Nyasaland), 82, 83, 98–99
Malcolm X. *See also* Nation of Islam
  in Africa, 40–41
  assassination of, 44
  King, C. S., and, 43–44
  in Middle East, 42
  Nkrumah and, 40–41
  Pan-Africanism and, 46–47
  relationship with King, M. L., Jr., 41–44
    conflicts within, 41, 44
    correspondence and meetings, 41–44
  Student Nonviolent Coordinating Committee and, 43
Mandela, Nelson, 68, 151–154
Manley, Norman, 51, 83
March on Washington for Jobs and Freedom, 79

Marshall, George, 90–91
Marshall, Thurgood, 29
Marshall Plan, 90–91
Mays, Benjamin, 3–4, 18, 21
Mboya, Tom, 52
   African American's public support for, 82
   Airlift Africa scholarship program, 86
   assassination of, 79
   King, M. L., Jr., and, 77–79, 80
   Southern Christian Leadership Conference and, 77–78
   in US, 95
   Youth March for Integrated Schools organizers and, 77
McDonald, Susie, 29.
   See also Browder v. Gayle
Meriwether, James, 89
MIA. *See* Montgomery Improvement Association
Middle East region, Malcolm X trip to, 42
Mill, John Stuart, 18–19
Montgomery, Alabama, Jim Crow law in, 33–34
Montgomery Bus Boycott, 2
   Browder v. Gayle and, 29–30, 33–34
   global donations for, 35
   global impact of, 29–35
   inciting factors for, 33–34
   James on global impact of, 40
   Jim Crow legal structure weakened by, 34
   King, M. L., Jr., arrest during, 29
   as racial justice pilgrimage, 34–35
   US presidential reaction to, 47
Montgomery Improvement Association (MIA), 29, 33–34
Moore, Audely, 114
Morehouse College
   King, M. L., Jr., at, 16–18
      intellectual and physical safety of, 16
      social consciousness of, 16–17
      Thoreau as influence on, 16
   Mays at, 3–4, 18
Mozambique
   nationalist movement in, 98
   white supremacy policies in, 89
Muelder, Walter, 25
Muhammad, Elijah, 42
Mussolini, Benito, 105
Muste, A. J., 22, 24
My Life with Martin Luther King, Jr. (King, C. S.), 72–73

NAACP. *See* National Association for the Advancement of Colored People
Namibia, 96
Namwambe, Ouma, 87

Nation of Islam, 41, 44
National Association for the Advancement of Colored People (NAACP), 8, 10, 30–31, 51
National Liberation Front of Algeria, 67–68
National Negro Congress (NNC), 30–31
National Urban League, 51
nationalism. *See* Black nationalism
Nehru, Jawaharlal, 40, 66
New York Amsterdam News, 88, 129
New York Times, 91–92, 129
Niebuhr, Karl Paul Reinhold, 24
Nigeria, 60, 66, 71–73. *See also* Azikiwe, Nnamdi
   civil war in, 96–98, 103, 125
   decolonization movement influenced by, 72
Nigerian Civil War (Biafran War of 1967), 96–98, 103, 125
Nixon, E. D., 33–34
Nixon, Richard, 39
Nkomo, Joshua, 95
Nkrumah, Kwame, 4–5, 21, 72, 95
   African American's public support for, 82
   King, M. L., Jr., and, 40, 50–54, 63, 77, 120–121
   Malcolm X and, 40–41
   Pan-Africanism for, 52, 151
NNC. *See* National Negro Congress
Nobel Peace Prize, 110–111
non-separatist civil rights approach, to Pan-Africanism, 115
nonviolence, as social philosophy
   Gandhi and, 18, 23–24
   for King, M. L., Jr., 23–24
      Rustin as influence on, 35
   Satyagraha philosophy as foundation for, 23–24
nuclear weapons, testing of, King, M. L., Jr., opposition to, 53
Nyasaland. *See* Malawi
Nyerere, Julius, 63–64, 108–109, 151

OAU. *See* Organization of African Unity
Obama, Barack, 61
Ojukwu, Chukwuemeka Odumegwa, 96–97
"On Civil Disobedience" (Thoreau), 16
Organization of African Unity (OAU), 109–110, 130
The Origins of African-American Interests in International Law (Richardson), 111–112

Padmore, George, 21, 83, 114
Pan-African Congress, 62
Pan-Africanism. *See also* "Beloved Pan-Africanism"; Black liberation movement; Black Zionism
   Africanness and, 150

Pan-Africanism (cont.)
  anti-colonialism and, 98–99
  "Back to Africa" movement, 127–133, 134–135
  at Bandung Conference, 118–119, 120
  Black International Tradition and, 74, 105, 108–114
  Black Marxist approach, 115–116
  Black nationalist approach, 115, 116, 122–141
  Black Power Movement and, 115
  black radical tradition and, 10, 115, 121
  conceptual approach to, 1–3, 108–114
  core principles of, 104
  decolonization movement and, 144
  definition of, 1, 115–116, 149
  Du Bois and, 37, 63, 103–107, 149–150, 151
  global Blackness and, 141–145
  "Great World House" concept, 120–121
  historiography of, 2–6
  Houser and, 150–151
  international approach, 36–49
  King, M. L., Jr., and, 1–6
    "Beloved Pan-Africanism," 2
    internationalization of movement by, 36–49
    radicalization of, 36–49
  Malcolm X and, 46–47
  methodological approach to, 2–6
  Nkrumah and, 52
  non-separatist civil rights approach, 115
  racial ancestry thesis and, 121–122
  as radical movement
    as anti-colonialist, 37–38
    during Cold War era, 36
    for King, M. L., Jr., 36–49
  roots of, 62
  scope of, 1–3, 62, 114–122
  Selassie and, 110
  universalism as distinct from, 106, 118
Parks, Rosa, 29, 33–34. *See also* Montgomery Bus Boycott
Patterson, William L., 31
personalism, 25–26, 161
Plato, 18–19
Plessy v. Ferguson, 33, 46, 74
Potier, Sidney, 83
Portugal, 79–80, 89
Powell, Adam Clayton, 51, 118
Pritchard, James Bennett, 20
progressive reformism, 158

Quakers, 110–111

race riots, in US, 84–85
racial ancestry thesis, 121–122

racial justice
  Black church and, 11
  Black International Tradition and, 74
  Montgomery Bus Boycott as, 34–35
racism. *See also* civil rights movement; desegregation; segregation; white supremacy
  Dred Scott v. Sandford, 45–46, 74, 112
  experienced by King, M. L., Jr., 13–16
  experienced by King, M. L., Sr., 13–14
  Plessy v. Ferguson, 33, 46, 74
Randolph, A. Philip, 51, 77, 88, 96. *See also* American Negro Leadership Conference on Africa
Rauschenbusch, Walter, 18–19
Reddy, E. S., 101–102
Republic of Zambia (formerly Rhodesia), 95
Rhodesia. *See* Republic of Zambia; Zimbabwe
Richardson, Henry J., III, 1, 111–112
Robeson, Paul, 31
Robinson, Cedric, 10, 114–115
Robinson, Jo Anne, 33
Robinson, John C., 106
Rockwell, George Lincoln, 43
Rousseau, Jean-Jacques, 18–19
Rustin, Bayard, 4–5, 35, 40, 57
  in Americans for South African Resistance Movement, 67
  Southern Christian Leadership Conference and, 58
  Youth March for Integrated Schools, 77

Satyagraha philosophy, nonviolence and, 23–24
SCLC. *See* Southern Christian Leadership Conference
segregation, racial, in US
  armed revolt as answer to, 23
  Khrushchev on, 73–74
  King, M. L., Jr., experiences of, 14, 15–16
  Plessy v. Ferguson, 33, 46, 74
  as UN issue, 84–85
Selassie, Haile, 97–98, 105, 110
Selma, Alabama, 43–44
Senegal, 117–118
Senghor, Léopold Sédar, 114
Sepia Magazine, 54
Sharpeville Massacre, 152–154
Shelby, Tommie, 117
Shuttlesworth, Fred L., 56, 57
Sierra Leone, 117–118
Sixteenth Street Baptist Church, bombing of, 79
Smiley, Glen, 35
Smith, Mary Louise, 29. *See also Browder v. Gayle*

SNCC. *See* Student Nonviolent Coordinating Committee
South Africa
  African National Congress in, 52–53, 59–60, 68
    King, M. L., Jr., support of, 76
  Americans for South African Resistance Movement, 67
  Apartheid policy in
    League of Nations mandates and, 69
    US foreign policy and, 59, 103
  Ethiopia and, 96
  Liberia and, 96
  Namibia and, 96
  Satyagraha philosophy in, 23–24
  Sharpeville Massacre, 152–154
  violation of Universal Declaration on Human Rights, 52–53
South West Africa. *See* Namibia
Southern Christian Leadership Conference (SCLC), 57, 132–133, 152, 156
  American Committee on Africa and, 94
  Mboya and, 77–78
  Rustin role in, 58
  scholarship programs, 86
Southern Negro Leaders Conference on Transportation and Non-Violent Integration, 56–57
Steele, C. K., 56, 57
Steere, Dorothy M., 40
Stono Rebellion, 150
Stride Toward Freedom (King, M. L., Jr.), 26, 36, 59–60, 78, 117
student movements
  Black students participation in
    in civil rights movement, 85–86
    support of African freedom, 82
  at HBCUs, 86
Student Nonviolent Coordinating Committee (SNCC), 43
Suárez Ramos, Raúl, 87
Sutherland, Bill, 4–5, 40, 63–64, 67
Sweet Auburn community, in Atlanta, 8–9
  African American identity influenced by, 9
  African American organizations in, 8–9
  as cultural center for African American life, 8, 9
  cultural memory influenced by, 9
  NAACP in, 8

"Talented Tenth," 158
Tambo, Adelaide, 52–53
Tambo, Oliver, 52–53, 100
Taney, Roger (Chief Justice), 45, 112. *See also* Dred Scott v. Sandford
Tanzania, 63–64, 108–109
Terry, Brandon, 117, 121–122
Third World Approaches to International Law (TWAIL), 114
Thomas, John Jacob, 114
Thoreau, Henry David, 16
Thurman, Howard, 21, 26, 27
  Gandhi, Mahatma, and, 26–27
  King, M. L., Jr., and, 27
  teaching in Africa, 27
Time Magazine, 34, 48
To Make the Wounded Whole, 75
Toward the Beloved Community (Baldwin, L.), 1, 5
Truman, Harry S., 31, 90–91
Tubman, William, 97
TWAIL. *See* Third World Approaches to International Law
Twain, Mark, 46

UDHR. *See* Universal Declaration on Human Rights
Uganda, 87
UN. *See* United Nations
UNIA programs. *See* Universal Negro Improvement Association
United Nations (UN)
  Charter for Black Americans, 30
  establishment of, 31
  International Convention on the Elimination of All Forms of Racial Discrimination, 145
  racial segregation in US as grievance at, 84–85
  UN Charter, 25–26, 93
United States (US). *See also* foreign policy; *specific topics*
  Black liberation movement in, 60–67
  Black Power Movement in, 115
  Civil Rights Act of 1964, 42
  Economic Recovery Act of 1948, 90–91
  Federal Bureau of Investigation, 44–45, 48, 52
  policy towards Hungary, 39
  race riots in, 84–85
  US Agency for International Development and, 62
Universal Declaration on Human Rights (UDHR), 25–26, 31–32
Universal Negro Improvement Association (UNIA) programs, 118, 134–135
universalism, Pan-Africanism as distinct from, 106, 118
US. *See* United States
US Agency for International Development (USAID), 62

Vietnam War, opposition to, 144
violence. *See* anti-Black violence

Walker, David, 21, 114–115
Walters, Ron, 115–116
Washington, Booker T., 158
white supremacy. *See also* Apartheid policy; Jim Crow law; segregation
   Black International Tradition and, 148
   in Portuguese colonial policy, 79–80, 89
Wilkins, Roy, 51, 77, 88, 95, 96, 107. *See also* American Negro Leadership Conference on Africa
Williams, A. D. (Reverend), 10, 12
Williams, George Washington, 114
Williams, Henry Sylvester, 62
Wood, James R., 132
World Zionist Organization, 123, 125
Wright, Richard, 118

Young, Andrew, 12, 154
Young, Whitney M., Jr., 88, 96
Youth March for Integrated Schools, 77

Zimbabwe (formerly Rhodesia), 95
Zionism
   Black, 122–127, 133–141
      ancient religious traditions as influence on, 138, 139
      "Back to Africa" movement and, 134–135
      Christianity and, 139
      rejection of, 139–140
   Jewish, 123–125
      Arab-Israeli War and, 124, 136–137
      Israel–Palestine conflict, 123–125
      Jewish identity and, 138–139
      World Zionist Organization, 123, 125
   origins of, 123

For EU product safety concerns, contact us at Calle de José Abascal, 56–1°,
28003 Madrid, Spain or eugpsr@cambridge.org.